The Anatomy of an Egyptian Intellectual

YAHYA HAQQI

The
Anatomy
of an
Egyptian
Intellectual
YAHYA HAQQI

by Miriam Cooke

3CP

An Original by Three Continents

For Edit and Hedley

TABLE OF CONTENTS

ABBREVIATIONS USED

For convenience I shall use the following abbreviations when referring to each of Yahya Haqqi's works (the dates refer to the edition used):

Antar: *Antar wa Juliat* (Cairo, 1960) (*Antar and Juliet*)

Dama: *Dama fa ibtisama* (Cairo, 1965) (*A Tear Then a Smile*)

Dima: *Dima wa tin* (Cairo, 1955) (*Mud and Blood*)

Fajr: *Fajr al-qissa al-misriya* (Cairo, 1975) (*Dawn of the Egyptian Story*)

Fikra: *Fikra fa ibtisama* (Cairo, 1962) (*A Thought Then a Smile*)

Haqiba: *Haqiba fi yad musafir* (Cairo, 1969) (*Suitcase in the Hand of a Traveller*)

Itr: *Itr al-ahbab* (Cairo, 1971) (*The Perfume of Loved Ones*)

Khalliha: *Khalliha ala Allah* (Cairo, n.d.: Dar al-Katib al-Arabi li at-tibaa wa an-nashr, Cairo) (*Leave it to God*)

Khutuwat: *Khutuwat fi an-naqd* (Cairo, n.d.: Maktabat Dar al-Uruba, Cairo) (*Steps in Literary Criticism*)

Nas: *Nas fi az-zill* (Cairo, 1971) (*People in the Shade*)

Qindil: *Qindil Umm Hashim* (Cairo, 1975) (*The Saint's Lamp*)

Sahh: *Sahh an-naum* (Cairo, 1976) (*Good Morning!*)

Taala: *Taala mai ila al-kunsir* (Cairo, n.d.: Dar al-Katib al-Arabi li at-tiba wa an-nashr, Cairo) (*Come to the Concert*)

Umm: *Umm al-Awajiz* (Cairo, 1955) (*Mother of Miracles*)

Unshuda: *Unshuda li al-basata* (Cairo, 1972) (*An Anthem to Simplicity*)

Ya Lail: *Ya Lail ya Ain* (Cairo, 1972) (*O Lail O Ain*)

I have retained the original and complete form for all other works cited less frequently.

PREFACE

This is a study of Yahya Haqqi, a twentieth century Egyptian writer. The outline sketch of his life precedes an enquiry into Haqqi's attitude to religion and mysticism (Chapter 1). He stresses the importance of the spiritual quest to artistic endeavor, and also moralizes about the corrupting effects of social intercourse on the individual, especially the prototypical oppressed, the *fellah* (Chapter 2). His integrative views of art, religion, and conscience extend to Haqqi's analysis of Egypt before and after the Revolution (Chapter 3). It is the discussion of how ancient and modern Egypt cohere which informs Haqqi's recurrent problem of identity, and illumines his paradoxical stance vis-à-vis the West (Chapter 4). Haqqi's attitude toward women exemplifies the multiple issues with which he never ceases to wrestle (Chapter 5).

His outstanding role in contemporary Egyptian letters derives, in part, from his insight into the aesthetic as well as the didactic function of literary criticism (Chapter 6). Humor is one of Haqqi's most skillful literary devices, illustrating without exhausting the several layers of paradox he perceives in present day Egyptian society (Chapter 7). Other aspects of Haqqi's style, e.g. his imagery, narrative technique, literary application of the colloquial, and function of plot, also merit detailed attention (Chapters 8 and 9). Finally, it is Haqqi's relationship to the political, communal tone of modern Egypt and to the underlying resilience of the Egyptian national character which distinguishes him as the *adib* (*littérateur*) *par excellence* of his country and his people.

While acknowledgments for the inspiration, continuation, and completion of this work are numerous, including friends and teachers at St. Antony's College, Oxford, it is to Mustafa Badawi that I owe a special debt of gratitude, for his scholarly insight but also for his enduring friendship.

INTRODUCTION

This work is difficult to characterize. It is biography, literary criticism, and history. It assembles facts that will enable you to see a man in his place in time. The material which follows, while dealing with the substance of one man's life, does not pretend to be an exhaustive biographical study; Sartre's awesome trilogy on Flaubert should discourage any but the bravest from such an undertaking. Nor is this a critical work, although there certainly are passages of what might be termed literary criticism. In these pages you will meet a diplomat, a journalist, a patriot, an intellectual, a man who was born into a generation of political activists but who was always on the edge, watching, caring, noting, but not participating. He was not the greatest novelist of the 20th century, nor was he its greatest philosopher, but his concern for his fellow man—a concern crafted in inimitable prose—raised him above his compatriots and contemporaries.

When I embarked on this work, I was interested to discover what I could learn about this man, Yahya Haqqi, through his discourse. I wanted to see how an *oeuvre* as a whole, and each statement as an atom, present to the reader a certain vision of the world.

For an organizing principle, I could have used chronology. At the level of artistry, for example, chronology delineates and clarifies his maturity as a writer; at the level of criticism it informs of his growth in literary stature; at the level of ideas it traces the development of his *Weltanschauung.*

But chronology is merely one possible perspective. Any modification that time may have wrought, any contradiction that may have arisen can be a new perspective on the same problem connecting it with another structure from which it had previously been independent. To take a concrete example, we see that Haqqi's spiritual quest seems to lead him to reject an established religion that does not accommodate the individual. Still in search of spiritual fulfillment, Haqqi can be seen to pass through an ascetic as well as an intellectual mystical stage, with all the retractions, confusions, and contradictions involved.

And yet at any one point along this line of religious growth, it is possible to detect the burgeoning of new series: the line bifurcates to connect with other lines—in this case the line that interested me was a line of artistic creation.[1] In turn this new series formed by the connection between the lines of religion and art helps to bypass the contradictions inherent in the independent line of artistic creation (i.e., the artist *qua* communicator) by identifying communication with experience. The mystical experience merges with a humanism, so that the moment of understanding is the means to lose the individuality, not in the truth, the godhead, the collective unconscious, but in man and more particularly Egyptian man, his brother, himself. If the analysis remains imprisoned within linear series, constantly drawing upon ultimate references, then tangential connections will not be seen. The statement is not merely the fulfillment, disappointment, or contradiction of an anticipation created by a preceding statement; it is a totality which can connect with other statements (e.g., a phrase in an essay on Ghalib can connect with a fictive conversation from other series—political events, emotions, a night at the opera).[2]

But why adopt such an approach? Why refuse development, evolution, continuity, and influences which constantly draw on a referential absolute? This approach is the expression of a refusal to perceive Haqqi and his *oeuvre* within hierarchical structures, be they comparative structures or internal structures, or a selection of important statements and a rejection of less important or "irrelevant" statements. Is some detail from an autobiography or an interview more significant than statements put into the mouth of a protagonist of a short story? Is something written in 1977 more relevant to our view of the man today than what he said as a young man? I was not interested in identifying hierarchical relationships between various statements and various series. What did interest me was to see how all the kaleidoscopic statements of an *oeuvre* freed into a wide discursive field impress upon the reader an image of the man.

More particularly, the issues that interested me were not Haqqi's voluntary projections of individual concerns through any one particular work, but rather undefined, unavowed problems that each work and statement might help to clarify or define. In creating, the writer engages himself beyond the particular work (short story, literary criticism, essay) with his conception of the world. No work is free of this fundamental relationship: the word binds the writer to his world.

This proposition may be schematically presented as a spoked wheel. In the center is the concept, the metaphysical concern, and from this center radiate the numerous spokes to the numerous Haqqis standing on the periphery. The spokes ("The Saint's Lamp," *Good Morning!*, Mahmud Tahir Lashin, an autobiographical account, an editorial in *Al-Majalla*) are perspectives on the world, casting a light that should not be obscured because of externally imposed criteria of categorization, such as genres. Genres are barriers drawn between one kind of writing and another, barriers that are seen as defining not only the mold of the thought, but the thought itself. Is non-fiction quite simply the clear formulation of what the author really thinks, while fiction remains a world apart, subject to its own rules of imagination and intrigue, without any real basis in an explicitly stated philosophy? Or is each genre merely an alternative optic? Indeed, categorization according to genre is not in any way absolute and seems to accord with usage: "The Saint's Lamp" may be used as an autobiography;[3] it may be treated as a long short story; as a historical document; as *Bildungsroman;* as a proposed resolution of the east/west dilemma.[4] A glance at critical works on Haqqi reveals that others have not found his *oeuvre* easy to compartmentalize; for Muhammad Abdallah ash-Shafaqi, Haqqi is an essayist pure and simple;[5] for Sharuni all of Haqqi's works of fiction after "Death and Contemplation" are a mixture of literary essay and short story;[6] for Abbas Khidr, "Death and Contemplation" and "Irony, or the Man with the Black Face" are not fiction ("had they not been published as *Egyptian Stories* we would not have realized they were fiction"[7]), and yet Haqqi's critical essay on Lashin's *Irony of the Flute (Sukhriyat an-nay),* in his view, had a "fictional quality."[8] Mustafa Ibrahim Husain refers to *Good Morning!* as a novel because of its symbolic dimension, but also avers that many critics regard it as a collection of sketches.[9]

Ignoring genres, I have used themes as my criteria of categorization. I wanted to see how Haqqi dealt with being a believer, an artist, an individual, a man and an Egyptian, and by liberating each statement from its obvious network—linear progression in time, or voluntary structure imposed by the writer—I could then make it connect with other, totally different statements. And these new connections helped to identify conscious and unconscious undercurrents that cut across and include the avowed intentions of Haqqi the *adib (littérateur).*

In every work the problem of language and its relationship to life and to the writer's vision of the world is faced anew, so that beyond the stated subject of discourse certain concepts are being dealt with again and again.[10] What I have done, therefore, is to pinpoint certain themes, overlapping centers for the same spoked wheel to which I referred earlier, and by placing myself on the periphery of the circle drawn by the numerous Haqqis, I have tried to create a synthesis which goes beyond and encompasses the vast eclecticism of this *oeuvre.* The centers on which I have focused—religion, art, man, woman, Egypt, the west—are my projections on the *oeuvre.* I accept that what I have done is construction, but I would add that all criticism is construction.[11]

Biographical Note

Born on January 7, 1905 in a Waqf apartment in Harat Mida, Yahya Haqqi was brought up in the heart of popular Cairo—the area surrounding the shrine of Sayyida Zainab, one of the granddaughters of the Prophet Muhammad. Until today Harat Mida is a protected inner world, cut off from the teeming masses outside by a large wooden gate. Yahya's father, as a civil servant in the Waqf Ministry, had been given the apartment, and although his parents moved to Hilmiya, Yahya and his four brothers, Ibrahim, Ismail, Zakariya and Musa, and their sister Fatima, were sent to school in the Zainab area: The Zainab quranic school (*kuttab*); and then the Walidat Abbas al-Awwal school for the children of the Zainab district.[12]

Yahya's Turkish grandfather, Ibrahim, had immigrated into Egypt from the Peleponnesus in the 1860s; and whereas most Turkish families at the turn of the twentieth century jealously guarded a physical and cultural distance from their Egyptian neighbors, often forming separate communities, the Haqqis eschewed such elitism, preferring a purely Egyptian milieu: "The (Zainab) area was a graphic and genuine repository of Egyptian traditions and ways of behavior that dig deep into the past."[13] Yahya tells us that his father, Muhammad (of whom he scarcely writes), had been educated in al-Azhar and was very well-read. One Friday he was in a mosque and since the *imam* was absent, he was called upon to deliver the Friday sermon (*khutba*). Much to everyone's satisfaction and incomprehension he recited a *maqama* by Hariri.[14] And at a time when most women were illiterate Yahya's mother could not only read and write, but her love and understanding of religious literature were an inspiration to her son. It was she who encouraged the pensive Yahya to go to the saints' feasts (*maulids*) that he was to recall with sad nostalgia years later.

After attending secondary schools in Hilmiya Jadida and Giza, Yahya was admitted into the Sultaniya Law School where he studied with Taufiq al-Hakim, for whom he had a low regard at the time.[15] On his graduation in 1925 Haqqi entered government service, working in local (*ahli*) courts.[16] He chose the Nur az-Zalam Sharia Court in the Khalifa Parquet because it was near home, he tells us.[17] Shortly thereafter he moved to Alexandria and into the employ of a Jewish lawyer, who introduced Yahya to the wonders of western culture but did not pay his salary. Yahya had to move on to a more secure, if less culturally stimulating, establishment in Damanhur.

His parents meanwhile were busily organizing his life along lines more suitable for a member of the Haqqi family,[18] and they eventually arranged for him to work with the department of public prosecution as administrative assistant (*muawin idara*). His task was to apply agricultural laws, conduct investigations in cases of minor misdemeanors and in cases of criminal infringement merely to collect information pending the arrival of the prosecutor who alone could administer the oath taking.

In 1927 Haqqi was sent to Manfalut, one of the many sand-colored, dusty settlements that flank the Cairo-Aswan railway line and blend into the unchanging landscape of the Nile Valley. Having cherished the memory of the two years spent there and encapsulated them in an irretrievable though vivid past, Haqqi refuses to return lest he find it changed. But Manfalut cannot have changed much over the last fifty years. Haqqi's old home is still there in Bustan Street, as is the Pasha's house. The two sons and daughter of his old friend Simon Maximus continue to live there. Most of the streets are unpaved, and the principal means of transport is still the donkey, while the rich have the use of two ancient horse-drawn carriages. The town bustles with activity from five in the morning until ten at night when calm returns: the small, rusty workshops close up, the tea-shops collect in the glasses and boxes of backgammon and pull down the clattering metal shutters, and gradually the streets empty of all but the stray dogs and occasional figures hurrying home.

It is clear that although these were two highly influential years for Haqqi, they were far from easy. As a government official he was cut off entirely from the people he longed to help, compelled to execute unjust laws. During a cotton glut, for example, the government issued an order that only one third of the cultivatable land should be sown. The law, however, was promulgated only when the seeds had already sprouted. Haqqi had to go round with the police uprooting all plants in excess of the stipulated quota, and at night he had to burn these plants with gasoline for which the peasants had to pay.[19] He repeatedly deplores the cruelty and greed of other government officials whose only concern is gain, whatever the cost. His experiences in Manfalut were doubtless vital to the development of Haqqi's deep sympathy for the poor and downtrodden.[20]

Although he was cut off physically from his family during this period, he did maintain written contact, particularly with his older brother, Ibrahim, a nationalist and man of letters who had helped edit the controversial journal *As-Sufur (The Unveiling)*. Before leaving Cairo and home, Yahya had spent many hours pouring over Ibrahim's Arabic and foreign books. His love for literature was so great that Ibrahim introduced his brother to a committed literary circle, the Modern School, whose members were fighting for political rights and social justice.[21] Yahya contributed to their magazine, *Al-Fajr* (1925-1926), after first publishing in an Alexandrian paper, *Wadi an-Nil,* some anonymous articles about Egyptian and European lawyers, and in *As-Siyasa al-Usbuiya* a short story (Jan. 19, 1926), "The First Lesson," which is remarkable not only as the first attempt of a young writer but also as a powerful and mature work.[22] In contrast, the stories that he published later that year lack the vividness and imagination of this earlier piece.[23] Indeed, most of the stories that he produced before leaving Egypt in 1929 for Jeddah seem to be sketches for later elaboration: existential issues were merely touched on, as the young writer retired from the challenge, refusing to go beyond description to structure a plot. In 1927 his first article of literary criticism was published: a discussion of Lashin's first collection of short stories, *The Irony of* the Flute (1927). What was significant, Haqqi tells us, is that this was an unknown critic writing about an unknown writer, and yet the article was published in the daily Kaukab ash-Sharq.[24]

In 1929 Haqqi was posted to Jeddah as archivist in the Egyptian consulate—the worst job, since he had come last in the list of candidates accepted. Haqqi talks cynically about Egyptian foreign policy during the first half of the twentieth century: the diplomatic service was lodgings overseas; he once observed that he was never given instructions before leaving on an assignment, but was merely asked by seniors to convey regards to colleagues.[25] During this period he devoted more time to literature than to diplomacy, spending much of his time in the consulate library. Although he was not very prolific, he did contribute some articles to Jaridat al-Balagh using as a pseudonym Abd al-Rahman b. Hasan al-Jabarti, thereby maintaining a strong link with Egypt through its great 19th century chronicler. In 1931 he was transferred to Istanbul where he stayed for three years, living with his family, learning Turkish and observing the Ataturk revolution at close-hand. It was during this period that Haqqi synthesized his impressions of Upper Egypt in fiction. Between 1931 and 1933 he wrote what he now refers to as his saidiyat: five stories which take place in Upper Egypt (Said). These stories were eventually collected and published in 1955. The Blood and Mud collection contains: "The Postman"—the tragic love of a young couple; "A Story from Prison"—the love of a fellah for a gypsy girl; and "Abu Fuda"—the crime committed by an ex-convict because of a woman. The other two saidiyat were published in the Mother of Miracles collection and are: "The Mosque Mat"—an illustration of the gap between official and fellah in the pre-Revolution era; and "The Perfume Bottle"—the infatuation of a young man for a barmaid (although this story is referred to as a saidiya, the plot does take place in Cairo: it is the description of what could happen to a Cairene on his return to the capital after some time spent in Upper Egypt).

In 1934 Haqqi was transferred from Istanbul to Rome as Vice-Consul for two years. With the arrival of Hitler on March 15, 1939 Haqqi was recalled to Egypt where he was appointed Third, and then Second Secretary in the Ministry of Foreign Affairs. Soon after his return Haqqi met the Mutanabbi scholar, Mahmud Shakir, who encouraged the diplomat to start publishing his short stories in book form. Haqqi agreed and in 1944 The Saint's Lamp was published.[26] The title story tells of a young man, Ismail, who returns to Egypt after seven years' opthalmic training in Britain. He is deeply shocked at the poverty and ignorance surrounding him: his cousin, and fiancée, is having her almost blind eyes treated with filthy, but consecrated, oil and her sight is steadily degenerating. Ismail rushes to the Zainab Mosque where the oil is dispensed, and in a fury he smashes the lamp. With his training he is determined to cure the girl himself. But it soon becomes evident that western science cannot cope with the problem. The girl becomes blind, and Ismail leaves home. Time passes and Ramadan comes. Ismail wanders to the square in front of the Zainab Mosque and suddenly, almost mystically, he is filled with love and understanding, a reflection of the light that has suddenly suffused the square. He returns to his parents' home carrying some of the saint's oil. His fiancée is to be treated in the traditional manner but by a western-trained doctor. Emotionally the story is divided into three stages: security, through loathing and disgust, to a rational perception of the need to moderate western science with an understanding of inalienable local beliefs and superstitions. Although the idea of assimilating western science to eastern philosophy is now widely accepted, at the time of its appearance in Egypt "The Saint's Lamp" caused a great stir.

It is interesting that already in 1946 Sayyid Qutb included a chapter on "The Saint's Lamp" in his *Books and Personalities* (*Kutub wa shakhsiyat*). As a Muslim Brother he acclaimed Ismail's return to Islam. Sayyid Qutb's criticism was only the first of many that were later to be written on "The Saint's Lamp," and Haqqi has bemoaned the fact that people seem to think that he has not written anything else.

In 1949, after ten years in Egypt, Haqqi was sent abroad again, this time to Paris as First Secretary to the Egyptian Embassy. In 1951 he was Counsellor to the Egyptian Embassy in Ankara, and the high point in his diplomatic career came with his posting to Libya as ambassador for one year, 1953.[27] While in Paris he had met Jeanne Guihot, a Breton painter and herself a short story writer, and on September 22, 1955 Haqqi married for the second time. His first marriage in 1944 had been to an Egyptian girl, Karima Abd al-Latif Suudi, the daughter of a lawyer and parliamentary representative from Fayyum. The story of their encounter has been variously told, but the following version is one recounted to me by Haqqi's daughter, Noha. A friend had encouraged her father to go to the Maadi train to admire one of two pretty sisters who traveled daily into Cairo. Haqqi went as directed but, unwittingly, admired the wrong sister. He was most impressed: he asked for her hand, and got it! The marriage, however, was short-lived, ending in tragedy when Karima died a few months later in childbed leaving behind a little girl who was then brought up by her maternal grandmother and aunt.[28]

With his second marriage to a non-Egyptian Haqqi left the foreign service to work as general manager for the Internal Trade Administration. This was a year of professional lull that allowed Haqqi finally to concentrate on his writings: in the same year that *Blood and Mud* and *Mother of Miracles* appeared, 1955, Haqqi also published, at his own expense, *Good Morning!*, his only novel. Although he has claimed not to be concerned with politics, this work was voicing, only three years after the Revolution, a dissatisfaction with the dictatorial aspects of a regime others were praising. In an almost schematic fashion Haqqi presents a village before and after the arrival of one of the villagers from the capital where he had been studying. Although superficially the benefits of modernization are impressive—the train being the most obvious example—it is clear that the village has lost its gaiety and solidarity. Each villager is alienated from his neighbor as he pursues his own goal; and in the general growth of self-centeredness the gradual appropriation of authoritarian control by the city-trained villager is disregarded until it is too late—he knows all, sees all, and thus controls all.

Haqqi decided to finance publication of this novel himself so that he could dictate the format in which it was to appear. The presentation was to be sober: the cover title was to be printed and not written in fancy calligraphics; there should be no women on the cover (as was the case with *Antar and Juliet,* despite the fact that the picture had nothing to do with the contents). Five thousand copies were distributed to Cairo's newspaper stands, where they remained on sale for two weeks at a price of ten piasters. Then the volumes were withdrawn and Haqqi made his way to the printer (*Al-Akhbar*) to see how the enterprise had fared—his precautions against the casual reader had worked only too well: 125 copies had sold. The remaining 4,875 were bundled into a taxi and hurried off to the Ezbekiya book stalls, where they sold for half a piaster each.

In 1956 Haqqi was moved to more congenial surroundings as director of the Department of Fine Arts, a new sub-division of the Ministry of National Guidance. This was the first real attempt by the Egyptian government to organize cultural information, by bringing all the arts under the control of one body. Here Haqqi could devote more time to literary endeavors. His autobiography detailing the time spent in Manfalut was serialized in the paper *Al-Jumhuriya,* and appeared in book form under the title *Leave it to God,* in 1959. The following year he published his first collection of literary criticism, *Dawn of the Egyptian Story,* which is an analytical account of the development of the short story and novel in Egypt between 1914 and 1934 (Haikal's *Zainab* until Hakim's *Return of the Spirit*). The collection includes detailed criticism of the lives and works of Haikal, Muhammad Taimur, Mahmud Tahir Lashin and the Modern School, Isa Ubaid and Taufiq al-Hakim, the latter marking the end of the dawn of prose fiction. But the four years that saw Haqqi as director of the Department of Fine Arts were not only productive at a personal level; they were also professionally significant. Haqqi's role in the development of all the arts, but particularly of the popular arts, has often been praised.[29]

One day in 1956 Haqqi was contacted by Fathi Radwan, the Minister of Culture, who informed him that Tito was coming and that an entertainment should be organized. Radwan suggested that Haqqi go to Shari al-Ahram to collect some Spanish and Hungarian dancers from the night-clubs that line this street. Haqqi expressed his dismay at this situation in his book, *O Lail, O Ain.* Are we so poor, he asks, that we have no culture of our own but have to get what we can from cabarets? After all these years had he become nothing more than an impressario?[30] No. Haqqi decided that Tito's visit should be the occasion for the first formal presentation of a truly Egyptian show. After much research the program was ready: first, an orchestra playing pieces from Egyptian folklore, then fifty girls on the *ud,* and finally a *tabla baladi* (drum) recitation—this was the first time that the *tabla* had been heard anywhere other than coffeehouses and popular concerts.[31] The show was put on in the Opera House and was a great success.

Another opportunity for delving into the national heritage, or folklore, arose out of the cultural exchange with China. A troupe of Chinese dancers were sent to Egypt, and Haqqi was then charged with the responsibility of returning the compliment in 1957. The question now was did the Egyptians have a national dance? After searching around it seemed that two and a half dances emerged: the Nubian dance, the *hujjala* (a belly dance from the northwestern desert), and a half-dance, the *tahtib* from Upper Egypt.[32] There were few national dances and no national circus, complained Haqqi, although the streets were full of potential performers: nineteenth century Cairo had been an exciting city full of performing animals, talking birds, clowns and acrobats; today, however, the only street entertainers are record players and radios.[33] An important outcome of Haqqi's interest in, and institutionalization of, popular arts was the establishment of the Mahmud Rida dance troupe which was made up of ballet dancers and also dancers from cabarets and "houses of ill repute."[34] Their first performance was the operetta "Ya Lail Ya Ain," telling the haunting story of the love between the beautiful sea princess, Ain, and Lail, an Upper Egyptian fisherman.

But it was not only in the popular arts that Haqqi's interests lay. Academies and theaters and cinema clubs, showing imported and Egyptian films, were established while he was director of the Department of Fine Arts.[35] He also encouraged the formation of the Cairo symphonic orchestra and operatic groups. In 1959 the Ministry of Culture financed a survey of Upper Egyptian and Nubian music; the results encouraged authorities to sponsor painters, composers, sculptors, poets and film makers from these regions. This interest in grass-roots level culture was instrumental in the foundation of the Higher Council for Arts, Literature and Social Sciences, which in 1970 organized the National Conference for Mass Cultures. As a result serious efforts were made to do research into the area of national heritage, thereby raising a consciousness of self-worth. Scholars were encouraged to go and live and work with the peasants (much as Haqqi had done many years earlier) so that this heritage should become an active part of the modern, westernized Egyptian's life.

When the Department of Fine Arts was dissolved in 1960, Haqqi was transferred to the National Library where he stayed for seven months as consultant. During this time he published *Antar and Juliet,* another collection of short stories, most dealing with town dwellers, with some sketches appended. The title story tells of two dogs, the mangy Antar and the precious Juliet. One day Juliet escapes her gilded cage. This, ironically, is the day that the officials of the dog pound are on the prowl, and by pure coincidence both dogs are caught. Juliet's mistress has hysterics and sends her husband to recover her darling. Antar's owners cannot even contemplate the thought of paying the fine that would set their darling free. This kind of irony can be felt throughout the collection to which this story has given its name. There seems to be no solution to social injustice, just bitter acceptance.

In 1961, Haqqi published one of his best known stories, "The Vacant Bed," in the literary journal *Al-Katib*. In a story heavily overlaid with macabre symbolism, he describes the career of a young man whose demands on life are so great that he is utterly incapable of giving of himself. Haqqi illustrates the young man's extreme self-centeredness through a detailed description of his pathological sex life. After failure at college, he decides that he should marry and, although his wife should be innocent, she should not be too naive, lest her initiation burden him with too great a responsibility. Accordingly, he chooses an Upper Egyptian girl whose husband had died three days after their marriage. The girl, despite her modest downcast eyes, turns out to be a wild thing, burning with desire. The young man recoils in horror and allows her to leave within two days. In search of a more passive partner, he goes to brothels where he finds, however, that prostitutes, too, can be demanding. Next he turns to homosexuality with a corpsewasher. The latter soon becomes demanding and finds that the only way he can hold the young man's interest is by offering the body of a bride who had died on the night before her wedding. With this necrophiliac act the young man finally destroys himself and is taken to the mental hospital. Such are the ends prescribed for those who cannot look outside themselves, those who are fettered by their desires.

From May 1962 until October 1970, a month after Nasser's death, Haqqi was editor-in-chief of the literary magazine, *Al-Majalla*. This period covers the Yemen and 1967 wars, and the vast growth in international economic cooperation leading to the opening of the High Dam. What is significant about Haqqi's editorship is that he introduced many young writers (e.g., Abd al-Hakim Qasim) to the Egyptian reading public. Without his initiative many of these writers might not have found an outlet for their works. However, he complained that this was a difficult period for an enterprising editor, since these young writers were so committed that their political convictions burdened their art. A young communist just released from prison came to him seeking publication. Haqqi agreed as long as the subject was not political. To his dismay the young man produced an article on Pavlov![36]

Again the environment was conducive to creative writing and in the years 1961 to 1972 Haqqi published nine books. In 1961 another collection of literary criticism appeared. *Stages of Criticism* comprises articles written between 1927 and 1961 (Lashin's *Irony of the Flute* until Mustafa Mahmud's *The Impossible*). These articles deal both with Egyptian writers and also with foreign authors such as Turgenev and Edgar Allen Poe. In 1962 and 1965 he published two collections of essays: the first was *A Thought Then a Smile,* a compendium of social criticism; the second was *A Tear Then a Smile,* a miscellany of witty anecdotes. *Come to the Concert!,* 1969, takes the form of a music primer. Writing for the uninitiated, Haqqi explains exactly what happens at a concert of western classical music, describing the various instruments and the elaborate rituals. He also makes some sophisticated criticism of certain conductors and violinists, displaying a wide and varied experience in classical European music. In the same year he published *A Suitcase in the Hand of a Traveler,* the tale of a trip he made to France. In a series of amusing tableaux he presents the reader with his perception of the problem of westernization. *People in the Shade* came out in 1971, a year after he had ceased to be editor of *Al-Majalla,* and two years after he had been awarded the highly prestigious state prize for literature. *People in the Shade* comprises sketches of servants, chorus dancers, street vendors, lottery ticket vendors—those people that inhabit the margins of society. 1971 and 1972 saw the publication of Haqqi's last books: two works of literary criticism, *The Scent of Loved Ones* (1971) and *An Anthem to Simplicity* (1972); and a collection of essays entitled *O Lail O Ain* (1972). *The Scent of Loved Ones* portrays literary personalities such as Jahin, Mahfuz, Haqqi's uncle Mahmud Tahir Haqqi, Mustafa Abd ar-Raziq, and Abbas Allam, and takes the form of literary reminiscences rather than analyses of text. The second collection of criticism, on the other hand, contains a number of technical essays on art and the function of fiction. He criticizes contemporary writers for poor style and slavishness to fashion. He is no longer willing to tolerate the increasing tendency toward abstraction and looseness of expression. And the final essay is a treatise on the Indian Muslim poet Ghalib. *O Lail O Ain* contains essays on cultural activities, and concentrates on the activities of the short-lived Department of Fine Arts.

Although his last book appeared in 1972, Haqqi did in fact continue to write articles and introductions to books by writers of the young generation. His last work was an introduction to *Bread and Silence (Al-khubz wa as-samt)* in 1977. Haqqi was most concerned that these short stories, written by a Saudi Arabian, be carefully introduced, and he was anxious to have the author read his introduction. However, the book with the introduction was published before Haqqi had been consulted either by the publisher or by the author. To his dismay, no one commented on the introduction. After fifty years in the literary arena he obviously regards this as a slight, and has written nothing since.[37]

Since 1970 Haqqi has more or less retired from public life, although there have been a number of radio and television interviews, and it is in this way that he has come to the attention of many people who may not have read him.[38] Fuad Dawwara has claimed that Haqqi is nowadays the most popular of Egypt's writers, and this is probably due to the personal warmth that he generates on the screen. In 1978 he adjudicated the awarding of the Pegasus Prize for Literature which went jointly to Sami Bindari with *The House of Power* and Sabri Moussa with *Seeds of Corruption*. He has also spent some time in Princeton University and in the University of Texas as a guest writer in residence.

Haqqi is regarded by some as the Grand Old Man of Egyptian literature, and many young writers turn to him for encouragement, if not for direct inspiration. The extent of the debt of the young generation to Haqqi may be measured by the number of introductions they have solicited from him.[39] Yahya Haqqi is one of the last *udaba*. A glance at his literary career, which spans more than half a century, immediately reveals the very wide scope of his interests and preoccupations. As literary critic, he has discussed not only the works of contemporary Egyptian writers but also those of western and Russian writers. As music lover, he has shown an appreciation of Sayyid Darwish, along with Bach and Stravinsky. As essayist and short story writer, he has written of peasants, of officials living with these peasants, of holy men, of beggars, and of the oppressed. He has described with evident awe—and caution (seldom despair)—the twentieth century, its wars, its cultural movements, its inventions, its political creeds. The list of his interests is endless and yet through them runs a connecting link—Haqqi's love for Egypt and his quest for the role befitting him as its literary custodian/harbinger.

Chapter One

COMMUNAL FAITH, PERSONAL EXPERIENCE, AND ART

> *. . . what a man thinks about religion is central to what he thinks about life and the universe as a whole . . . . To hope to reach any agreement, then, is perhaps to look for a consensus on ultimate questions of man, truth, and destiny.**

Islam is not only a religion, it is a way of life for a community joined in faith and submission to the word of God as mediated by His messenger, Muhammad. To be a Muslim is to bear witness to the oneness of God and to the prophethood of Muhammad, it is to pray five times a day, to act charitably, to fast, and to perform the Pilgrimage at least once in a lifetime. But beyond ritual requirements and community responsibilities Islam is the individual believer in search of God. And in Haqqi's works it is not a dogmatic adherent so much as this individual seeker whom the reader perceives: a man who believes ardently in God, in Muhammad and in the revealed message, but whose belief is tempered by the abuses that time has wrought on this message.[1] Like Sharqawi and Kamil Husain, his is a protest against the inability of established religion to help man find the truth that is hidden by religiosity.[2] Secularization has taught the twentieth century Muslim Egyptian that he should not submit unthinkingly to the rules of a contemporary religion, but should return to its roots, thereby systematically reviving its spirit. Darwinism had hit Egypt and with it had come the revolt of the young, of the Kamals,[3] against their parents, the bearers of a static religion riddled with superstition. Haqqi claims that, faced by this crumbling edifice, the new generation should engage in a jihad

> . . . not to gain land, nor converts to the faith, but to spread these noble principles (of equality) among mankind. This is the role that history imposes on us, and if we assume this role then religion will reveal all its virtues. Thus will Islamic nations move out of their stagnation and backwardness into activity and progress.[4]

*Wilfred C. Smith, *The Meaning and End of Religion* (New York, 1964), p. 21.

13

Established Religion as Obstacle to the Spiritual Quest

According to Haqqi, what is wrong with Islam today, as indeed with religion in general, is that it has frozen into a monolithic structure;[5] it is a whole that is either accepted or rejected, but which does not contain the flexibility to accommodate individual needs. Indeed, for those whose needs cannot accommodate this rigid block, the only way out is rebellion. But the rebellion that takes the form of "the religion of the individual isolated from the group, not the religion of the group of which the individual is proud"[6] Haqqi rejects as arrogance. The solution is not to be looked for in such heresy but in Islam newly-interpreted and understood. Such an Islam, despite rules and regulations, permits the individual to express himself freely. Haqqi wrote at length of the Indian Muslim poet Ghalib whose Islam was of a highly personal nature.[7] Once when in Mecca Ghalib spent the night next to the well of Zamzam. This appears to be a suitably religious way to behave, until we read that after his night of devotion by the well, he had to go and wash the wine stains from his pilgrimage garment. The reference to wine is transparently mystical and it allows Haqqi, without incongruity, to emphasize Ghalib's closeness to God.[8] For this was not a turning away from religion, but rather a total immersion in it, the realization of what Sufis call *sukr*.

As though to emphasize the individual nature of Islam as a belief possible to all, Haqqi draws a distinction between Islam and the Arabs: "Islam and the Arabs tried to attack the gates of Europe coming from the Far East"[9]—as though the two had joined forces. On another occasion he writes of the poetry that was written at the height of Islam *and* of the greatness of the Arabs.[10] This claim for the independence of Islam from any one national affiliation would seem to bless Ataturk's insistence that Turkish Islam should sever its links with Arabia. Mustafa Kamal's initial attack on Islam, says Haqqi, was not on Islam itself, but on its alienness, the emphasis on the non-Turkish origin and nature of the religion of the Turkish people. He enforced the use of translations of the Quran,[11] thereby integrating *Turkish* Islam more fully into the lives of his people by making them pray in the language of the state. Because Islam could not be abandoned without alienating the people, the only option open to Mustafa Kamal was to render it as Turkish as possible. What was vital was to eliminate every trace of Arab affiliation.

Ataturk's attack on Islam was, therefore, an attack on Arabism— *religion was the weapon he used.* Religion had become a means of identification, of recognizing oneself as a separate and distinct entity. It was a divisive force in a world that was looking forward to the exit from Babel—any attempt at reinforcing this difference was a factor of stagnation, even of retrogression.[12] This was true early in the twentieth century and it became clearer in 1948.[13] The emergence of Israel has shown that religion, integrated into a strict racialism, can become highly divisive; the religion of Judaism, redefined as Zionism, became a sacred ethnicity justifying the forceful establishment of an alien nation-state, excluding all who did not carry the right party card. Indeed, Zionism was no different from Nazism.[14] It was the establishment of this racio-religious state in the midst of the Arabs which awoke Haqqi to the threat inherent in organized religion. To progress, he argued, man must overcome religion as a system of identification. This need for difference, for exclusivity, is a primitive instinct prohibiting progress. Haqqi, indeed, echoes Radhakrishnan[15] in his insistence that the Zionist state's emphasis on religion had undermined hope of world harmony. The Palestinian problem has become humanity's problem;[16] it is not that Israel has made thousands of brother Arabs homeless, it is that it has forced itself onto a homogeneous mass which then turned in on itself to recognize differences and distinguishing features.[17] Each has become aware of himself as a Muslim, Christian, or Jew, *not* as a believer in the one true God; each regards himself as an Egyptian, Syrian, or Iraqi, *not* as a citizen of the world. The problem that Israel presents goes beyond the suppression of life; it is the suspension of progress. While death is a necessary part of the natural cycle, an arrest in the process of evolution is not.[18]

Islam as an established religion, however, seems to have lost its dynamism, or at least its throbbing heart has become hidden. Haqqi's description of mosques, particularly in Istanbul, is a good illustration. Beyond their *physical* grandeur and beauty they seem to have nothing to say.[19] They are a symbol of backwardness and stagnation.[20] Yet these silent monuments to strength and vitality once housed a force that could defy outside incursions such as the Napoleonic invasion.[21] Their history, if not their actuality, bears witness to a greatness against which man's weakness is delineated. What is this weakness? Not a negative feeling of inadequacy, but rather the recognition of imperfection, and then a positive striving towards the perfection of Muhammad, a perfection that is symbolized by the great Sultan Hasan Mosque. Though rooted in the earth, it seems to soar up to a dimension beyond. Its perfection Haqqi sees to be the result of the combination of contradictory forces: safety and danger, spiritual longing and intellectual scheming, promise and threat.[22] In its open courtyard, as in all of Cairo's ancient mosques, man is at one with God and nature, for here there is no veil between him and the heavens, between him and the whole of creation.[23] This meeting of opposites may also be found in the Aya Sofia in Istanbul—but what a cold meeting! In 1453 the Aya Sofia became a mosque within the walls of a church, and the two had continued concomitantly, each lending strength to the other. Such a union of religious architectures expresses eloquently Haqqi's longing for the union of religions—the recognition of mutual values strengthened rather than weakened by the breaking down of barriers.[24] But with time this house of God became a museum, and lost its spiritual warmth. The Aya Sofia had turned in on itself; no further communication was possible and, like a beautiful but dumb person, its smile to the world merely reflected a smile turned in on itself, "arousing pity not admiration." Stagnation pervaded established religion; everywhere the pattern was the same, stagnation and corruption.[25]

However, the fate of its external trappings could not affect its true nature: "Islam is a solid diamond that (Ataturk's) chisel could not crack."[26] It is the surface that must be hacked at, stripped to reveal the essence, as in "The Saint's Lamp," Mary "chisels" painfully at Ismail's fossilized surface to allow what was really him beyond education, beyond inherited beliefs, beyond all the weight of his past, to shine through.[27] Religion should not be a set of rules narrowly defining itself, says Haqqi; it should make room for the individual. As each man differs from his neighbor so will his way of believing and aiming at the truth differ.[28] For some, five daily prayers and a life led in accordance with the Sunna is the path, while for others it may involve apparent sins such as inebriation, as was the case with Ghalib.[29] Belief and the life led in accordance with such a belief, is, therefore, a matter of personal choice. It is essential that each man be free to choose the path he considers best suited to his needs. What angers Haqqi most are the mystical orders which enjoin on their disciples rigid doctrines as well as strict interpretations of sacred texts.[30] Freedom, which is the right and condition of true believers, has been usurped. Indeed, organized mysticism, above all other disciplines, is prone to divisiveness through misunderstanding; hence Haqqi denounces spurious mystics, dervishes whose practices involve climaxes such as foaming at the mouth, falling to the ground in paroxysms, fainting and claiming that wine when drunk by them is purified by their pure bodies.[31] Haqqi's morality, it would appear, derives from consensus; if a man has been acclaimed a great Muslim, despite apparently sinful behavior, then his sins become excusable in terms of the *seen* result; that is, since everyone adjudges him to have been a devout Muslim, therefore all he did must have been pure in intention.

Asceticism—an Alternative

To worship truly, writes Haqqi, one should be free of time, space, and particularly the body. This is the freedom, he says, which characterizes the true mystics, who struggle not for heroics in the battle of life but for the soul's deliverance from servitude to the body.[32] Ironically, as noted above, he sometimes views this freedom as heretical if it leads the individual to construct his own religion.[33] Yet this freedom is not a state acquired; according to Haqqi, it is a grace conferred. The pursuit of such a freedom leads only to further entrenchment in the prison of one's own limitations. Haqqi seems to be using a rhetorical device to resolve his contradictions: grace intervenes to provide the answer. If the believer has been favored, then his freedom with any possibly inherent deviations becomes sacred and the believer himself becomes a "friend of God." Where there is no such grace the believer is condemned to follow rules and regulations and cannot transcend his worldly prison; all attempts to achieve such a transcendence are doomed.[34] Haqqi's own case is eloquent. Having felt from the earliest age a deep spiritual longing, he had immersed himself in mystical literature—both Islamic and Hindu. He had embarked on a strict vegetarianism in consequence, as one of the "prescribed" steps on the road toward enlightenment. From his readings he knew what to expect, and whenever he seemed to have reached a particular state of consciousness, he would be filled with ecstasy, not the Sufi *wajd* but rather extreme self-satisfaction. This became clearer as he realized romantically that the innocent happiness that he had experienced as a child, when immersed in his thoughts of God, or while attending *maulids* or *dhikrs,* far exceeded the joy that he was now feeling.[35] Was it because he had intellectualized what was properly the domain of the heart and not the head? Each apparent victory over the body was just a reassertion by his body of its existence as something to be escaped. Torn between irrational, natural being and omniscient God, man in his ephemerality aims to merge with the ground of his being, the eternal. But how? By means of that which is the furthest from his rational self, his body, his flesh, that which brings him close to the animal: that which, in his ignorance, he sees as vile, as something to be overcome.[36] Each such victory merely serves to turn the key in the lock of a bodily prison.

Ironically, Haqqi's attempt at loss of self had resulted in a renewed affirmation of this self.[37] His vegetarian period had not only emphasized his ephemeral individuality, it had also resulted in fanaticism. When he had first turned away from his normal diet, he had expressed abhorrence at the thought of animal slaughter and meat eating. Are we, God's creatures, not all brothers? And yet he seems to have had difficulty accepting such a brotherhood—not only with animals but also with women (as wild a species)! And here it would seem that Haqqi's disgusted descriptions of women flaunting their sexual charms, although far removed from mystical love, is in some ways consonant with the ascetic mentality. In the words of a noted psychoanalyst,

> The ascetic literature . . . is preoccupied with sexual purity more than with any other single topic. The ascetic exists because he is tempted. And not once, but over and over. The only role of women in ascetic literature is as degraded objects, inspirers of lust and the horror of lust . . . . This phobic avoidance of women bespeaks an unusually intense desire for contact.[38]

Haqqi's horror of animal-like irrationality is vividly expressed in "Susu," where he describes the narrator's feelings of repulsion from the autistic mongol child. Haqqi makes the doctor say: "These creatures do not live long, as though nature wakes up from its negligence and wipes away its sins."[39] The sin here is the child. Is it mere coincidence that the beautiful, bewitching barmaid of "The Perfume Bottle" was also called Susu?

Haqqi's sallies into ascetic practices seem to be an abortive attempt to counteract the cultural limitations that he recognizes in himself. But with time he came to realize that his avoidance of meat had become fanatical, the polar extreme of what he had intended. The ascetic path is beset by dangers which lurk round every corner, ready to catch the unwary.

The Mystical Moment and its Communication

Haqqi's dilemma, therefore, is that personal experience, although the ideal, presents endless pitfalls, and institutionalized religion far from being a spiritual guide is an instrument to power.[40] Organized religion is the social relationship established among people who have seen religion as an expedient for some form of domination. But within Haqqi's idealistic system there is no room for religion that functions as an instrument of power. Religion for him is a personal matter: a mysticism in which all languages are the same, speech with God. The problem, it would seem, arises when this language is turned towards communication, when speech with God is turned into speech to man. The experience appears to be corrupted by the words which must be drawn from the material world, however cloaked in symbolism. Haqqi recognizes this corruption when he claims that the artist—the mystic who *expresses* the transcendental experience[41]—is born of the first woman to lie, for it was she who showed the first spark of intelligence.[42]

Although the transcendental experience is given (not going beyond the moment and having no motive outside itself), yet when it is subjected to the intellectual process, when it is expressed, we can see that it has a finality imposed on it, which is to *convince*. And it is in this will to convince that the experience loses what had made it personal, turning it into a tool of domination. When the religion of social contact is established, corruption has entered. The exclusiveness of an Israel, of a Turkey, is no different from the exclusiveness of a Nazi Germany where political ideology functions as a state-imposed religion. Power is a fact of life, and so for Haqqi's ideal world to exist it would have to be inhabited only by hermits.[43] It is interesting here to compare with Muwailhi: "Only hermits and ascetics may find peace in this world, only those who lead a life of seclusion and solitude find peace. He who lives furthest from men is the noblest."[44]

Intellectual Mysticism

For Haqqi, desire for truth is the condition of man, especially the mystic and the artist. To perceive this truth man must be pure—purified from the temptations of the earth, purified from his reason, that he may then find the purpose to his life.[45] It is in his use of imagery that Haqqi portrays most clearly his true, almost unconscious beliefs, as in the description of a Casino:

> Whenever I pass by an old, decaying house I am beguiled by this brilliant whiteness which gleams from the fragments of its hidden heart. I am amazed by its innocence and beauty. Then I am shaken by this contrast between beauty and decay, and I am filled with pity for this heart which used to live behind a veil, withholding its secrets from the world. Then, suddenly, it was forced to strip itself before the world. My mind then wanders, and presents me with the whiteness of a decayed corpse's teeth lying in the desert. Here, too, is beauty despite the ugliness of death.[46]

The interest which the house inspired is not a passing attraction but an inherent, morbid beguilement—"*whenever* I pass . . . ." The power of this fascination is emphasized by the unexpectedness of a casual passer-by finding himself enchanted by a gleaming whiteness. Whiteness, the symbol of purity—and here of beauty also—refers to the glittering fragments of the decaying *heart* of the building. The writer, at first passive, has been entranced by the magic of this purity and beauty, only to be torn apart by the contrast between beauty on the one hand and decay on the other. There follows the calm of sadness at the realization that what had at first seemed splendid was, in fact, the blinding flash caused by the *ravaging* of a heart's secrets. As the image draws to a close, Haqqi returns to his original passivity and simply witnesses the playings of his imagination. The whiteness of the building is reflected in the teeth of the corpse. It is this circularity which allows the reader to associate the ravaged heart with the teeth of the corpse; that is, with the part of the anatomy which is the most durable. At the end of the day it is the heart that will outlast the wasteland that is the body. *Its* beauty will shine out above, and even despite, the ugliness of death.

What does the heart do? It experiences. The reason merely processes the material provided by the heart: "Man's intellect alone digests the universe (*kaun*) whereas nothing in the whole universe digests man's intellect."[47] *Kaun,* the ground of one's being, of creation, is the level at which man unites with the creative process.[48] The resulting union is achieved by the perception that the individual spirit is identical with the universal self.[49] However, although it is the intellect that has made man master of the *kaun,* it would seem that this same intellect distinguishes man from the *kaun* he controls, and thus prevents him from merging (*indimaj*) with it: "If you ask God to save you from your intellect and grant you an ample share of innocence, know that I wish you well."[50]

Yet, despite his aspirations for a mysticism, a way of life in complete accord with the heart, in which he could experience the fullness of Being in the loss of his individual self, Haqqi's own mysticism is very much man-oriented. He has said that it is only those who have found favor in God's eyes—grace—who will truly gain a measure of awareness beyond that accorded to ordinary mortals. Others, and Haqqi seems to include himself in this category, may only catch glimpses of the sacred light which engulfed Sayyid Darwish's soul[51] and filled the Sultan Hasan Mosque. How difficult it is to perceive the light of God mixing with that of the human mind which created the arch surrounding the *qibla* and still raises the minds of those who contemplate it to its own level of light, of divine inspiration. Here is God's guidance, and even if those enlightened by God's grace—and those who gather the falling sparks—seem to have many tongues, their language is one,[52] the language of the Prophet,[53] as set forth in the *Burda,* the most sacred of all poems.[54] This poem is eloquent witness to the power of art which raises man (in this case, the reader or reciter) to the level of original inspiration.[55] From it emanates the light which other poor mortals do not normally see. To illustrate the darkness in which most people live one may use the image of the blind woman reciting the Quran on the occasion of Muhammad's *maulid:*

> Her open, protruding eyes, like gelatinous beings popping
> naked out of their shells and rising up out of the murky depths
> of the ocean-bed, came into contact with a world that was not
> theirs, a world containing something they did not know and
> which was called light.[56]

When writing of a friend who was passionately fond of the theater, Haqqi describes him under the bright lights in night-clubs, impervious to the uproar, as he drinks himself into a stupor.[57] The association of *dau, khamr,* and *yafqid wayah* turns this image into a mystical one, which is then extended as Haqqi extols this same man for his inner purity. He could be exposed to all the filth of the world and yet come out untainted.

As may be seen from the foregoing discussion, Haqqi's mysticism was not a point of meditative fixation within a state of unity, but rather a continued awareness of an *Other.* Might Haqqi then be compared to Freud's archetype of the ascetic who retires from the real world to live in a world of his own creation—a world peopled with prisoners to the ascetic's narcissism? It would seem not. Haqqi's reliance on others is more a vicarious spirituality that seeks out mediators. Busiri's ode could lead the soul to beauty, purity and innocence;[58] Ahmad Khairi Said purified the hearts of his listeners;[59] Haqqi loved Jahin's quatrains because "their juice (*essence*)[60] is the blood which has flowed in my veins since my birth into the cradle that held Hafiz, Jalal ad-Din, Rabia al-Adawiya, Muhyi ad-Din and Ibn al-Farid."[61] Through Jahin's quatrains Haqqi has identified himself with the great mystics of Islam: "Indeed, in the other he is looking for himself, that is the secret of the fascination of this other."[62] At a concert Haqqi describes how he watches the conductor waiting for the moment when the man will be lost to himself and then become an artist:

> The moment for which he was born, and although it only lasted
> a second, it was as though it had lasted a whole life-time. Before
> me was a man who was the incarnation of all the musical
> geniuses; their works had penetrated his soul to become a part
> of him.[63]

Haqqi looks to another in the hope of seeing there what he suspects but
cannot recognize or pinpoint in himself.[64]

In "The Mirror Without Glass" the narrator describes his anguish at not
being able to see his real self. In pursuit of this chimera he exposes himself
to the forces of nature "by land and sea." He searches out mystics,
madmen and the "dregs of the earth"—always in the hope of finding in
their torn hearts a mirror in which he might see his own face. One day, the
proprietor of a shop mistakes him for a certain Fuad Fahmi, a
photographer, to whom the narrator apparently bears a startling
resemblance.[65] Eagerly the narrator sets off in search of this longed-for
mirror. Soon, however, doubts and fears assail him. Which of these
identical men is the original, which the copy? Since the form God has
given each man is the expression of his personality, his life and
aspirations, what happens if this form is repeated? If there can be another
"I" surely one is redundant, for these two bodies must be endowed with
identical souls. The atoms of one of the beings must merge into the
unknown ocean out of which they had at first been fashioned—"just as
rain drops return to their source, the sea."[66] The meeting between the
narrator and Fuad Fahmi leads to a prolonged association, in which the
narrator feels himself at once attracted and repelled. It is as though his life
is being sucked out of him to nourish Fuad, who seems to be living for the
two. Then, one hot August day, the narrator poisons his wraith. The
parasite has been destroyed, but where does this leave its host? Although
he has seen his form in various aspects, he has come no closer to
understanding what he really is. Confrontation with "himself" has
engendered a bitter struggle for survival which he has finally, inexplicably,
won. Far from giving him a unified picture of what he is, this confrontation
has only succeeded in emphasizing his partiality, his multiplicity. What
part of him had at first allowed Fuad to feed off of him? What other part
had reversed the process?

Since the answer cannot be found in oneself, Haqqi's solution is to
turn to others. A master must be sought, and Haqqi's world is peopled
with such models.[67] He asserts that books about mystic masters—Hallaj,
Rabia, Ibn Arabi, Blake and Swedenborg[68]—draw him out of this world into
the world of the spirit; his stay in the land that had nurtured Jalal ad-Din
Rumi was instrumental, according to him, in his turning to things
mystical.[69] Haqqi's mysticism is not his own but a reflection of the
behavior of mystic masters. Why otherwise should he refer to himself so
scathingly as "this ascetic, spiritual, vegetarian Sufi who could not
convince anyone," let alone himself of his spirituality,[70] a spirituality based

on the illusion that answers can be found outside oneself.[71] Finally, in desperation at himself and at the enormity of the task undertaken, he dismisses mysticism and ascetic practices as a luxury for the affluent:

> At that time a fact became clear to me, a fact in which I still believe—and that is, that a millionaire is much more capable of asceticism than a poor man.[72]

And again:

> That day I wished to shake off my poverty so that I should become extremely rich, because I wanted to experience the joys of asceticism.[73]

These two examples shed light on Haqqi's evolved attitude to mysticism. As social critic he denounces mysticism, relegating it to the domain of the privileged.[74] England, Belgium and France can afford mysticism precisely because they are supported by armies and fleets which protect their dignity (karama). Egypt, however, is too weak—spiritually as well as militarily—to allow herself such a luxury.[75] This sentiment is echoed by Khalid Muhammad Khalid when he claims that true religion is only possible when social and economic justice exist.[76]

The Artist and the Individual Seeker

The result is ambiguity. On the one hand is Haqqi, the Egyptian, too poor for a spiritual life, and on the other hand is Haqqi, the individual, attracted to this life. However, since his focus is man he is torn: his ascetic practices cut him off increasingly from the material world, this world which is the absolute and only principle into which he can truly and joyfully merge.[77] And it is here that his personal crisis is situated. Ideally, he wishes to transcend the physical world, but reality in a country like Egypt draws him to his fellow man, and makes such a transcendence a cowardly escape, the abnegation of his duty, and ultimately of his predilection—to be with his people and to express their problems and aspirations.[78] His dreams are theirs. He dreams of a future in which understanding will be inspiration and when the language of the head and the heart will be the same.[79] He dreams of peace and equality, particularly between the rich and the poor, because then could the ultimate dream be realized, to evolve within a peaceful, economically sound society a communal spiritual life:

> I dream of a garden for all true believers from all sects . . . of a single language whose source is the heart, of a single race whose name is man. When there will be no difference between black, white, and yellow . . . when there will be no armies and all weapons will have been destroyed because aggression will have ceased . . . . I dream of the day when mankind will perceive the truth and will be able to act and speak freely.[80]

And:

> I dream of returning to vegetarianism when the soul shall have found its peace.[81]

The definite article used before "soul," and not the first person possessive pronoun, seems to indicate that although the subject of the main clause is "I"—Haqqi—the subject of the subordinate clause is general. The individual expression is thereby given a universal significance.

This need to express the dreams of his people forces Haqqi into a dilemma: he must choose between a devotional but lonely existence and a communal artistic mode with the corruption that this entails. The resultant dichotomy is partially illustrated in his discussion of the two Russians, Turgenev and Tolstoy. Turgenev is a natural mystic always open to inspiration: the first time that Haqqi uses the word *tasawwuf* in connection with Turgenev it is modified by the adjective *khashin,* a word that connotes roughness and earthiness.[82] Tolstoy, by contrast, is an avowedly religious mystic. Turgenev is described as annihilating himself in nature and the moon; Tolstoy is described as fighting his earthbound passions, exclaiming in dismay: "I am a prisoner of the clay." Whereas Turgenev went into the forest to observe nature directly, Tolstoy went there with one of Turgenev's books under his arm; so far had his religious zeal removed him from nature that he had to have it interpreted for him by an artist.[83] By exposing the vulnerability of the religious mystic, Haqqi has shown that the artist's spirituality is more total. Just before dying, Turgenev wrote to Tolstoy with whom he had had a bitter quarrel, and in conciliation offered him some advice: he should abandon asceticism and return to art for its own sake, for therein lay a deeper spirituality.[84]

Although all his longings as a child and young man had been for the world of the spirit, it was the earth that reclaimed her son. Haqqi had become a vegan eating only nuts, vegetables, and cereals:[85] a rejection of culture in favor of nature, of man in favor of Being. This urge to return to a primitive way of life uncomplicated by social norms and mores, may be seen as the natural accompaniment to a life of mystic devotion—a prerequisite on the road to self-realization. However, Haqqi repeatedly expressed his discomfort at this rebellion: "The danger of solitude threatened me, and I was afraid."[86] Finally, he returned to meat in satisfaction of the cultural urge to belong.[87] Here we see Haqqi responding almost unconsciously to the dictates of a modern life, that is molded by western values, and shies away from nature to experience it only at second hand.[88] In his criticism of Haikal's *Zainab,* Haqqi writes sympathetically of Hamid, who had realized that if he did not believe and worship as his family and friends did, then he would be ostracized.[89]

The Artist: Resolution of the Seeker's Contradictions

The dichotomy between the ideal and the real in Haqqi's thinking and aspirations is a reflection on what he considers man's estate to be:

> Man has his (alloted) span of life, but the soul, out of which
> arises the self, has no span . . . . Its world does not comprehend
> the concept of time; it is the heavenly world.[90]

Torn between his higher self (the human creator in touch with the universe) and his lower self (prisoner of the material world), man is weak.[91] It is this weakness that draws Haqqi to his fellow man, for in his recognition of another's weakness is his acceptance of his own impotence in the face of such incomprehensible forces.[92]

One the one hand, man is chained by his bondage to the world; on the other, he is still man, but this time free to roam in the higher spheres as the artist, the god-creator among men whose inner stirrings are those of the mystic. Even if society may seem to infiltrate the inner recesses of his mind, the true artist remains ultimately impervious, for he is blessed with the mystic's inner freedom. The artist soars up above the peaks beyond which the mortal eye cannot see.[93] Art and the life commonly associated with artistic creation—bohemianism—is mystical attraction, says Haqqi.[94] Like the mystic, the artist longs for beauty, ever searching in the world of the unknown, ever discovering and symbolically enlarging new horizons,[95] with words that are eternal since their goal is truth:

> Art is delusion, its goal is truth.
> It is anguish granting peace and contentment.
> Because it is temporal it is also eternal.
> It is a fanaticism that calls for moderation.
> Like prophesy it is a gift and a legacy.
> Like wisdom it is never satisfied.[96]

The resolution of human dialectics, art is most closely allied to the divine sphere; it is a gift of prophesy and wisdom. Those born with such a gift are sometimes called *majadhib,*[97] meaning "those drawn to God" but also "the mad ones."

It is interesting to look at Haqqi's use of the words for madness in connection with artists. After completing his greatest masterpiece, the artist is described as living "among men, speaking with wisdom, but hiding from them his madness."[98] The juxtaposition of wisdom and madness is interesting when viewed in conjunction with the previously quoted comment on art as wisdom and prophesy.[99] Madness, like prophesy, is a state somewhere between "rational" man and God, a sublime state which characterizes the fulfilled artist.[100] It is the cosmic consciousness of one who lives among men speaking wisely while living a level of consciousness, an "otherness," that he must hide lest he be branded a madman! For he is the visible branch of roots which reach down to primitive man.[101] At the moment of creating he is timeless, since he is drawing on that incomprehensible, inexplicable aspect of man that for most, if not dead, is certainly beyond reach.[102] He is outside the laws of nature. His day is our night. He can see what is darkness to the rest of mankind. He is dawn in harmony with night. Only he knows the purity of darkness.[103]

The true artist is, therefore, untouched by society: his motivation lies in himself and not in the money or acclaim accrued.[104] His audience is not an idol to be worshipped but the mirror of the artist's soul,[105] his unconscious reacting with his conscious. The audience response shapes the message; each is indispensable to the other. The writer, it would seem, has the obligation to establish as direct a link as possible with his reader; he must infiltrate the latter's unconscious, incorporating him into the creative process.[106]

According to Haqqi, the writer penetrates his protagonists, but not as a Hitler or a Freud—that is, moving from the outside to the inside of the person's psyche. The artist's penetration happens at a different level and in the reverse direction of the psychologist's: it is not the character's soul that is being observed at close hand from the outside, but the world outside that is being observed *from within*.[107] This other is analyzed by looking at the world with his eyes. Having established himself behind the protagonist's eyes, the writer is subject to a chain of swift changes which finally merge his identity with that of his object until he *becomes* that other. This ability to become the "other" is then transmitted to the reader through identification with the protagonist, creator/created. And it is in this relaying of the identification experience that Haqqi considers the power of the artist to lie, for art (and particularly fiction) is the only way to experience what it is to be someone else, to truly lose oneself. Psychological closeness merely serves to demarcate two individuals from each other until the gap between them has become paramount in the relationship.[108] As Haqqi says, it is only the mystical moment that resembles the artistic experience; but here it is not that the subject assumes the experiences of the other, *thereby* losing himself; in this case the loss of individuality is immediate and absolute. It is not a conscious, rational experience but rather an operation of the heart.[109] The creative expression is the intellectual demonstration of this mystical experience in reverse, but far from isolating the subject it serves to bring the writer close to mankind through his readers. True art, like the mystical experience, reaches man at his simplest, most basic level, where the individuality has melted into its essence.[110] What inspires true art is the eternal underlying the ephemeral manifestations of daily existence; "the artist's task is to strip away the transitory elements so as to unveil the essence."[111] The essence out of which arises a diversity that the writer shapes and behind whose contours he places the reader. Hence, we have the writer as prophet, the visionary, but with the power to make others "see" as he does, not merely understand what *he* sees.

The artist is the pure, untainted vessel of divine inspiration:[112] his creation is a disinterested reflection of his consciousness; but he is also the communicator, the son of the first woman to lie. Ideally, his work is the satisfaction of a creative drive, independent of the corrupting influence of power, the will to convince inherent in all communication. But in fact, the artist is "victim" of the need to communicate. In view of this paradox, how eloquent is Haqqi's statement that

> ... to penetrate into the realm of happiness ... one must pass through one of three gateways: faith, art and love. Love is the most attached to clay and fetid mud. Faith is the most ambitious for its goal is God not man. And so, art is left as the mean joining these two poles.[113]

Fetid mud and lofty ambition, these are the two poles which the artist seeks to reconcile; through him beauty becomes an experience and a creation.[114]

Haqqi's artist is an eccentric genius, the *majdhub,* who is in touch with the secrets and miraculous powers of creation. Understanding of the man himself is, therefore, the gateway to the understanding of his art.[115] Whereas an artist like Taufiq al-Hakim considers the creator to be secondary to his work, claiming that to know who fashioned the head of Nefertiti or the Sphinx would add nothing to our knowledge and understanding of the object itself,[116] Haqqi cannot see any work in isolation from its creator; the one cannot exist without the other. Art seems to be the development of that aspect which raises man above his finite, earthly self to share in the immortality of creativity, of creation.[117] Art is the nexus between man and the eternal ground of his self: it is the mind of the universe using the artist to advance its history. And Haqqi quotes Pasternak's description of the creative process:

> And at the moment he felt that it was not he who was creating the monumental work of art, but rather a hidden force which was above him and which controlled him. This force is the mind of the universe for which he is aiming, now and in the future. He also felt that what he was doing was merely a step in the history of this force, and that in its hand he was merely a medium, a tool and a focus.[118]

An interesting example of this interrelationship is Haqqi's discussion of the Pygmalion-like sentiments which writers may develop for their leading ladies; for example, Abbas Allam's love for Victoria Musa and Rami's love for Umm Kulthum.[119] This is not the normal love of a man for a woman but the artist's need for the work of art to "live." It is almost blind homage to the products of their function as realization of the synthesis of man's existential and essential selves.[120] But the synthesis of these two poles is not enough to make the man an artist. He must communicate; he must make another perceive this creative synthesis in an eternal renewal.[121]

The artist is artist to the extent that he transcends the man in himself to become the tool of a higher power. But he may also be artist in those moments when he merely experiences a flash of spiritual awareness that will be a constant reminder of something beyond this dull, material existence, bedevilled as it is by paradoxes and contradictions:

> If, for only one fleeting moment, you win the pleasure of the Creator . . . you will be at once amazed and saddened as you ask yourself why this fleeting moment should not last a whole lifetime? What is suppressing it? You promise yourself to hold onto it, but then you forget it in the heat of life's battle. It just slips out of your hands to remain in hiding until it should make another fleeting appearance.[122]

By rejecting the tenets of established religion, it would seem that Haqqi opens himself to alternative paths for spiritual fulfillment, e.g., mysticism. Mysticism, however, if not itself subject to rules and regulations that reduce it to the status of an established religion, does entail a life of devotion and isolation. By saying that he does not have grace, Haqqi has shown that the ascetic alternative cannot provide *him* with the spiritual fulfillment which he is seeking. And, in assuming the burden of the artist, to speak for and with his people, Haqqi has finally closed the mystical option: he cannot retreat but must throw himself into life so as to communicate effectively. It is in the act of writing itself that he finds the spiritual satisfaction that he rarely finds elsewhere, since art communicates a mysticism focused on *another*.[123] Art for Haqqi is the ever renewable moment of fusion. It is not the communication of a previous experience; it is the experience itself. Thus does Haqqi overcome the corruption of communication, for it is in the act of writing that he loses himself in another, and that the experience occurs. Indeed, it is through art that Haqqi resolves his problem as a believer. As artist, he cannot withdraw, and yet his need for annihilation of the self is constantly present. Through belief in the transcendence of the artist via his work, Haqqi finds a measure of release. The release he wants is a purging of the self, and this he gains through identification with protagonists: the more violent the portrayal of the character, the greater the violence done to himself. In this connection it is interesting to note his Malamati inclinations that not only made him search out a *qutb* (spiritual guide), but also induced him to write of characters that arouse universal censure. Could it be that Haqqi has after all espoused a discursive mystical path, the only avenue open to one who rebels against organized spirituality? In the act of writing he seems to be achieving catharsis through an exaggerated dive into the abyss of human degradation:

> Let the reader glance briefly over the edge of the precipice to gain an idea of its ugliness. This will prevent him from falling in, and will awaken his ability to live with others and to see what is beautiful in life. How wonderful it is to breathe in fresh air after

having stifled in toxic dens.[124]

In "As Though," a prisoner was being tried for the murder of little boys he had molested, and Haqqi constantly repeats the narrator's identification with the man in the dock.[125] Not only does this identification allow him to lose himself, but it also allows him to assume the sins of another, thereby arousing the universal blame that is a necessary part of Malamati Sufism.

*   *   *   *   *

Although Haqqi claims that Islam may be the fulfillment of the spiritual quest, he shies away from the monolithic structure that religion has become today. Since his goal is not religious reform, and since he cannot accommodate his needs to contemporary religion, he pursues his spiritual quest outside the confines of established religion. The paths to which this quest leads him are infinite, trailing off on to uncharted seas, far from the land. Out on the high seas, the fear of drowning seizes him, and the spiritual quest seems to be abandoned in favor of the security of social intercourse, i.e., a return to the land. It is on this land that Haqqi can begin again his quest, this time remaining within its boundaries. It is by means of that which he first spurned, social intercourse, that he will find spiritual fulfillment. It would seem that Haqqi has adopted a discursive mystical path: the act of writing is a meditation, it is direct experience of the highest order before being the communication of such an experience. Through his Romantic attitude to art, as that which elevates man above his human condition to share in the Divine, Haqqi has created for himself a mysticism which evades the issue of heresy or escapism; it is in the act of writing for and with others that he finds his own spiritual fulfillment.

Chapter Two

MAN AND MODERN SOCIETY

> *. . . man, conceived as being alone and without obligations . . . is without sin simply because there is no possibility for him to commit any . . . Adam is destined to fall into sin. Alongside this Adam there suddenly appears—not it is true an Eve . . . but a second Adam. And instantly Adam acquires obligations—and breaks them. Instead of treating his brother as having equal rights . . . he subjects him to his domination, he makes a slave of him.**

Haqqi's world is a harsh, intransigent one where survival is at the expense of others.[1] If man, as a social being, cannot escape the game of power, his only choice is how to accept the challenge that life throws out—how to fit into society's complex network of hierarchies. The people Haqqi seems most interested in—porters, vendors, servants—submit to, rather than accept, the challenge, since they are not equipped to wage the battle of life with any hope of success.[2] All they can do is dream. They are social victims condemned to remain within the web society has woven around them. These named individuals seem to be drawn from another level of existence, from an exclusive otherness that allows for the appearance into modern society of individualized outsiders, while itself remaining out of reach. This other level of existence, this nebulousness whence society draws its *individual* victims, is the Upper Egyptian *fellah*. Outside time, hence outside the mechanism that evolution has forced on modern man, this fellah is perceived as having existed independently of modern Egypt—part of ancient, eternal Egypt:

> Throughout its long life it has proved its ability to survive despite the obstacles in its path. There is no other nation like it that has remained within its boundaries and retained its distinctive features and characteristics since the dawn of its

*Engels, *Anti-Duehring,* quoted in Jack H. Abbott, *In the Belly of the Beast. Letters from Prison,* New York, 1981, p. xix.

history. The strength inherent in this land is the guarantee of its survival.[3]

The Upper Egyptian fellah is not only the last scion of the Pharaohs,[4] he is also primitive man in tandem with the land. It was during the period spent in Manfalut, 1927-1928, that Haqqi first became clearly aware of the otherness of this fellah. Not that each individual fellah was different from him, but that all the individual fellahs had merged into a unified block of opposition against all that was not fellah. Although Haqqi finally had to abandon the struggle to try and infiltrate the ranks of the fellah, their obdurate aloofness did not embitter but rather challenged him: it demonstrated the evil imposed on the good individual by society.

Social Intercourse—Source of Corruption

In the beginning was man, innocent and living securely in a concrete world of individual objects. And then, with the first spark of intelligence,[5] he was propelled into the world of cunning and deceit where reality could be twisted to suit personal needs. This twisting of reality was the first lie: the Fall. Thereafter man could conceptualize in generalized, total terms, and "unfortunately philosophy ensued."[6] This first lie was motivated by the incursion of an outsider on a couple who had until then lived in harmony. The outsider herself was not evil but it was association with her that had given rise to the evil.

At a microcosmic level it is possible to demonstrate how evil social intercourse is in Haqqi's eyes by looking at his treatment of friendship, where the friend seems to be more an insidious enemy! Since in the very act of communication Haqqi sees evil, it would seem that friendship is an impossibility. And Haqqi's stories of friends are a string of disappointments and bitter satire.

He relates the story of an old school friend who had become a dentist and in that capacity had taken vengeance on their vicious school master, Aqrab Effendi, years after leaving school. In cold blood and with much forethought, the dentist pulled every single tooth out of the partially anaesthetized gums. He then stood back gleefully and watched the blood flow out of the ashen face. This dentist then offered his friend, Haqqi, dental treatment whenever he should want it. Haqqi recoiled in horror— who knew whether this friend harbored some secret malice against him which he would satisfy in the dentist's chair.[7] Another friend invited himself to lunch with Haqqi and was then contemptuous because of the modesty of the fare. Several days later, however, he was lavish in his thanks to a mutual acquaintance who served exactly the same food, but on elegant tableware and served by a beturbanned *sufraji*. Then there are the friends who have perfected the art of smoking other people's cigarettes.[8] And the man who murdered his own wife with the help of a friend, which raises the question: what are the rights that one friend has on another.[9] And those who have risen above their former stations and no longer recognize old friends; for example, the Milanese priest who used to visit a simple holy man in the hills. After a number of years the Milanese priest became Pope. Hearing this, the holy man sold up all his belongings to buy a ticket for Rome to see his old friend. At the Vatican he was questioned endlessly, and then installed in the Pope's antechamber where he waited and waited. At last he was summoned into the holy presence only to be told: "You must learn that friends change with time."[10] Friendship for Haqqi is a liability, for the law of life is one of exploitation. Beware of the friend to whom you have been kind, for this kindness has lowered your defenses, opened you up to expose weaknesses of which this "friend" can take advantage. "Beware of your enemy once; beware of your friend a thousand times."[11] Friendship is a passing association between two individuals, subject to the whims of chance. Warned by a friend before going on holiday to a remote spot in Lower Egypt to steer clear of other holiday makers, Haqqi is swept away by the magic of sudden friendships: "Greetings turn into affection, affection into friendship, and then this friendship is sealed at the gambling table."[12] However, the point of the story is in the title: "Didn't I Tell You So?" When the friend heard that Haqqi had not followed his excellent advice, he gloatingly announced that he had told him so! Friendship is seen as a relationship of power; at best, the one is mentor, the other is pupil. But even the most exemplary, warmest friendship, such as the one between a Manfaluti policeman and a guard, could change in a flash into intense enmity and spite.[13] It is, therefore, scarcely surprising that Haqqi should make the sincere friendship between Yusuf and Amm Khalil, in "The First Lesson," end so soon and so tragically, before its innocence could be touched.

The Great Divide

Haqqi portrays society as a kind of caste system in which there is a basic division between the "haves" and the "have-nots"; the former are never described except in terms of their villains' masks, the latter are the stuff of which Haqqi's works consist. The distinction is complete—they are two different races, creatures of two distinct planes of existence between which there can be no real communication.

In "Antar and Juliet," Haqqi uses animals, two dogs, not only for what they are, but for what they represent—the contrast between two classes.[14] The one was Antar, the mongrel stray who roamed around his neighborhood as he pleased—all that was certain was that he was back home with Sitt Kaukab at dinner time. And the other was Juliet, a highly bred Pekinese dog. She was so refined and oversensitive that anything frightened her, shrinking away anxiously under chairs and sofas whenever her mistress screamed. In her heart lurked the greatest fear of all—the fear of life and its unknown dangers. This exotic being cowered away from contact with the great unwashed beyond the confines of the garden walls, living the endless repetitions of an existence that knows no willing. Fate brought these two unlikely companions together in the Black Maria of the dog pound. Juliet had perhaps, surmises Haqqi, succumbed to a moment's weakness, a second of curiosity to see what was beyond the confines of her prison. A slip that brought sudden and swift retribution in the form of the law. Juliet, however, was released before nightfall; Antar was doomed to stay forever, since Sitt Kaukab could not afford the two or three guineas necessary to recover him. The use of animals to represent the different privileges and conditions pertaining in the social hierarchy is particularly apt, for by using dogs Haqqi shows that it is not personality or academic education which makes us different, but environment, environment which suppresses the individual, and imposes on each one a situation. Haqqi's view of the world seems to be one in which vertical movement is inconceivable.[15]

In "The Spiral Staircase," Farghali is an assistant to a laundry man. Like many of the city poor he slept on the floor, walked the five kilometers to work and slaved away for long hours, surviving on the poorest of diets. Farghali is described as living in a world of his own, aloof from the grim reality of his miserable existence. The exclusiveness of the hierarchy imposed by society cannot be fought; it demands submission. But submission can take any form—in this case it entailed withdrawal into another world. One day as he was on his way to work he noticed that the doorman of the building where he was to collect some laundry was away. The marble steps, reserved for the masters and their visitors, soared up into the mysterious depths of the building, beckoning Farghali to taste of their forbidden fruits. With as much fear as though he were about to commit some dire crime, Farghali made his way up the three floors to Nafisa's apartment. He rang the doorbell, and then . . . all hell broke loose! The door opened and Rex, the dog who was never allowed into the kitchen (where Farghali normally went), jumped on the little boy and bit his hand—the system's spontaneous defense mechanism. Nafisa, the owner of the flat, was torn between her natural instinct to comfort the terrified boy, who had fainted with shock, and her fear of exposing herself to the danger of seeming too concerned, and thereby inviting demands for recompense from an untouchable—as had already happened to a friend of hers. Farghali left, and his hand soon healed—time and patience are the medicine of the poor, their only currency. What was most important was that he should return to work as soon as possible. He had, however, lost some time—money—because of the bite, and he finally forced himself to return to Nafisa in response to a weakly-stated offer of help, should he really need it. In his innocence, he had determined to ask for the exact sum equivalent to the lost time—he would absolutely refuse whatever extra she might offer; he had his pride after all, and was no beggar! However, when the cook returned with her mistress' response, Farghali was shocked. The apparent kindness, induced by fear and a guilty conscience, had misled him into temporarily believing that he had managed to bridge the gap between himself and the masters, and that communication was possible. Being within the social network, he had yet failed to understand its rules.

In "The Protest," Bumba was asked by her mistress, Sitt Khairiya, to sit with Hasan, the young tenant, while he was mending their chair. Bumba sat on the floor, from time to time coughing quietly and all the while keeping her eye on Hasan. Bumba was utterly exhausted—her eyes were drained of any spark of understanding, care or personality. Fatigue, claims Haqqi, can destroy even the strongest:

> . . . there was a clear struggle being waged in her eyes—a struggle that almost spoke. A glance that freed itself slowly and with difficulty from a harsh, choking grip. The struggle continued for quite some time, and then the glance cleared a little. The pure eyes, whose pupils were the color amber, spoke.[16]

The foregoing description is an illustration of the struggle sustained by those who have not been granted the strength necessary to survive. Those so oppressed by fatigue that they have lost the ability to understand, to care and to express a personality, those who have sunk into the morass of expressionless anonymity. And yet, although their voices are not *heard,* either individually or collectively, this does not preclude an unpublicized, private being. These silent masses are persons with feelings, victims of the hopeless struggle to communicate. A struggle which at times seems to climax in a form of expression: "the pure eyes, whose pupils were the color of amber, spoke"—here it is the color that speaks: amber, the stone used traditionally as a talisman to protect the wearer from evil and bad luck. Does this amputation from social intercourse protect these people from the evil wrought on man by social intercourse? Would not their audible voice implicate them in an evil existence?

Even though these people may live their own hidden lives, it is nonetheless true that they are curtailed lives that have never known the freshness of childhood. They have never known the imaginative, carefree world of discovery and games, the child's world which has no links with ours. Bumba was one such deprived person. Sitt Khairiya had inherited her from her own mother—chattels handed down from one generation to another. When Bumba had come into Sitt Khairiya's service, she had been ten years old, and then one fine day she had woken to find that thirty years had gone and that she was forty years old! That is, her poor old body had weathered forty years; her mind, however, had suffered a stunted growth. Fatigue had arrested its development and she had remained an old child, sticking her tongue out at her mistress' children, and licking their sweets. It is interesting to notice that Haqqi often compares his social victim to a child,[17] or indeed uses a child (Farghali) to illustrate their innocence of the games that people play. Mahmud, Sitt Khairiya's son, used to tease Bumba about her bad breath and filthy hair; although she accepted such insults without complaint, she was always deeply offended if anybody accused her of stupidity. Had she not been so tired, she would have realized that this resentment was born of a suppressed intelligence—stupidity was her *condition humaine*, her inability to transcend her exclusion from a society which relentlessly whips the outcast into submission, paralyzing him mentally and physically so that he shall never truly perceive what he is. Bumba had fallen in love with Mahmud and on his wedding night she was very upset, but of course, no one noticed—it was inconceivable that she could *feel* for anyone, let alone anyone so exalted in comparison with her own worthless self. It was not only Mahmud who attracted Bumba, but also the boy Hasan, for he had been the first to treat her as a human being.[18] When she overheard the family discussing Hasan's marriage prospects, she was deeply hurt—had she not been the one who looked after him? When Khairiya realized what Bumba's hopes had been, she was horrified, and accused her servant of madness.

Survival of the Fittest

Within the ranks of the poor are those who succeed and those who fail. For it is not only the rich, the obviously powerful, who exploit the poor and the weak, but the less poor and the less weak who use others to gain their ends. Haqqi seems to be illustrating the divisions at this social level in his description of the various categories of donkeys. The donkey-world, according to Haqqi, is divided into five: the *manure donkey*— untouchable and rejected, and living at the margin of the world; the *donkey for hire*—its strength drained like blood out of a sacrificial victim, fed according to its work output and not according to its hunger, its saddle hiding the traces of many vicious beatings; the *market donkey*—the first to be named, the first to be granted an awareness of a separate identity, of a Number One to be looked after at the expense of others; the *peasant's donkey*—good-hearted and humble, virtues which Haqqi attributes to the donkey's position as a member of the family, and the first to experience love; and the *"aristocrat"*—not born an aristocrat, but forced to become one by a tough trainer who makes sure that his pupil should walk as *man* wishes and not as God had originally intended. The donkey seems to be a symbol of man's exploitation by man. The foregoing classification would thus be equivalent to the social hierarchy of workers: the helpless excluded; the exploited; those who have risen to a degree of self-awareness and who consequently use others, however limitedly; members of corporations; and those apparently superior individuals who are, none-theless, nothing but the result of man's ultimate manipulation (the civil servant?).[19]

Ibrahim Abu Khalil in "Mother of Miracles" had spent his life switching from one job to another. At the point where Haqqi picks up his story, Ibrahim had established himself on a pavement selling radishes, cress and leeks. Soon Badr moved in with her two children, and Ibrahim's trade slackened pitiably. Nothing daunted, he determined to put his misfortune to good advantage, and he became friendly with his trespassing neighbor. Just as he was getting to know her, her husband returned—exit Ibrahim. After a considerable absence the narrator returned to find both Ibrahim and Badr gone. What had happened to Ibrahim? Ibrahim had a new job—and this one seemed specially cut out for him. Before the hustle and bustle of the day began, he went to all the shops in the square and spread incense. Unfortunately his incense was foul-smelling, and again he was ousted—this time by a Quran-reciting *brahmin* in a green turban. The "holy man" was hard-working and patient, but he was also resourceful and cunning (indispensable qualities in this fight for survival and domination). One morning the square was filled with the echo of a scream, and everyone rushed out, only to find the "shaikh" prone, paralyzed by a "mystical trance." As he recovered, people showered money on him, which he then collected with his heavily-ringed fingers. A despicable "con-man" no doubt, but successful, and what could an innocent like Ibrahim, who "knew nothing of life and people's natures," do to defend himself against such trickery? He could only submit, for in this life there is no room for artlessness. He joined the beggars who crouch around the Zainab Mosque—not in front with the others, but round the side—the manure donkey. He had abandoned all competition:

> He had become the inhabitant of a world that is not ours. A world which has no exit, which has only one door through which one enters, and above it is written: The Door of Farewell.[20]

It is interesting to note the difference between Haqqi's attitudes to the poor and those of another contemporary Egyptian writer, Lashin, as illustrated in "Mother of Miracles" and "Irony of the Flute." For Haqqi, a man like Ibrahim is the helpless victim of society; for Lashin, all, including the poor, are responsible for their destiny.[21]

The Bee Hive

Whether the individual is happy in his situation or not, one thing is certain, and that is that each one feels he must belong; but the problem is how to belong without losing individual identity in an institution. In his autobiography, Haqqi writes of the first day at work in Manfalut, when he had to sign in on arrival:

> It was then that I realized that I had gone to bed last night a man, and had woken an administrative assistant.[22]

For Haqqi this process of depersonalization is frightening: normal emotions are distorted as the stereotyped attitudes and ideas of predecessors are adopted. In this new situation the individual has lost that which made him a man, and has assumed that which makes him a function, a number. He will think along official lines: to the Cairene posted into the *rif,* the fellah is an obstinate being never to be trusted. Small wonder that no progress was ever made in government/fellah understanding with such a prejudice established.[23]

In accepting the function as ascendant over and above the personal self, the individual abdicates his history and, therefore, personality, to become part of "a living dough sucking down everything into its morass."[24] Each individual is struggling to rise up out of this morass, is desperate to assert himself:

> Talking about oneself!
> Oh, what an enchanting pleasure, what false modesty [to deny it]! . . .
> Most of our conversations—after no more than two words—change from the subject (whatever it may have been) to complain or boast about ourselves. It seems to me that this arises out of a single hidden inclination: the need to vindicate our existence.[25]

No kudos to him who criticizes such egotism, for such a critic will do exactly the same given the opportunity, says Haqqi. We are all obsessed by this one concern to affirm our existence to others: "I know that man's vanity is most gratified when he is called by name at a time when he least expects it."[26] At a party amid the uproar of thousands of conversations should we chance to hear our name mentioned, even if only in a whisper and across this crowded area, it is this conversation that will hold our attention over and above a monologue shouted into our very ears.[27] An instance of this need for self-assertion comes in one of Haqqi's sketches in the second part of the *Antar* collection, where he makes a brief study of readers' questions in *Al-Muqtataf.* Iliya Qandalaft had written to this magazine from Sao Paulo asking the editor how many hairs grow on a head. Haqqi immediately visualized the plight of this alienated Lebanese, living far away from home, and desperate to find confirmation of the value of his existence in a medium he could understand. Success in Brazil could not give him the assurance of his identity that publication of his question in an Arabic magazine could.[28]

Although the system suppresses the individual in the anonymity of the function, yet does the ego reassert itself as needing to belong, but to something else. Man is like the bee which derives its life from the hive; alone it cannot survive. In "The Postman," Abbas, the post office employee sent from Cairo to Asyut, was outside the hive of the village.[29] He was "dying" and all that could save him was to integrate himself insidiously and at second hand into the village out of which his function had excluded him. This he did through this very function by opening all the letters that passed through his hands. Finally, he only opened Jamila's and Khalil's letters to each other. It would appear that by mixing his fate with that of these two lovers he felt himself to be intimately part of the community out of which he had been excluded. He was fighting his exclusion by entering into the most sacred, into the otherwise inviolable privacy of the Upper Egyptian home.[30] He had left behind his personality in assuming the function; but by betraying this function he had transcended it. All that was left of him was an element in a relationship, but an element so strong and so important that it could no longer remain passive.

Jamila had fallen in love with Khalil, the brother of her best friend Maryam. The engagement was announced, but family affairs delayed the fixing of a wedding date. In the meantime, Jamila became pregnant. Khalil was teaching in Cairo, and since he had had to leave Kaum an-Nahl before definite plans had been made, the lovers had confined their affairs to letters. Jamila used Umm Ahmad's box number so as to keep her correspondence with Khalil a secret from her father. Time passed and with it the pregnancy advanced. Jamila began to implore Khalil to come to her aid. Khalil, however, had grown more distant and Abbas, the peeping postman, was horrified at his indifference, indeed his callousness. Finally, Fate intervened! When Khalil wrote to Jamila that he could not come before the summer, because he had been transferred back to Alexandria, Abbas kept the unopened letter to one side. The following morning, the messenger from the *umda* came to stamp and collect the outgoing mail. To his horror, Abbas saw Khalil's letter being stamped as coming from Kaum an-Nahl. The stamp could not be erased, and therefore, he could not let Jamila have the letter without incriminating himself. For four days Umm Ahmad came for the mail, and each time she had to go away empty-handed. Finally, on the fifth day, Khalil wrote from Alexandria, and Abbas awaited Umm Ahmad's arrival with impatience— but this day she did not come. On his return home that night he found a group of mourners outside Umm Ahmad's house: she had died that very morning! And so, Abbas found himself in the privileged position of being the only one to know what was going on. Jamila did not know that Khalil had returned to Alexandria, Khalil did not know that Umm Ahmad had died, and therefore he could not understand why his letters were being sent back. Abbas' intervention had made them both unavailingly dependent on him, and had broken their relationship at the moment when Jamila was in the greatest need. "Would Khalil have come had he received Jamila's last letters?" Abbas asked himself in anguish. The knelling of the church bell sounds the final note of the story, and seals Abbas' ultimate integration through his awful secret.

Outside Modern Society

Beyond the struggle for survival, for belonging or for progress, Haqqi perceives the fellah, particularly the fellah from Upper Egypt, "a good, believing modest people—maybe that was the secret of their aloofness from strangers, from officials like us."[31] He is not man in the previously defined sense of a modern social being nor is he animal;[32] he seems to partake of the natures of both—man before the Fall. He is close to nature, a closeness that is his birthright, and not a way of life that can be adopted by an outsider. In fact, Haqqi has described the effect that such proximity to nature has on outsiders:

> Their faces become coarse, their stomachs fat, their movements heavy, their looks animal-like. Their language is repeated obscenities, their wit is vulgar, their thoughts are mean and confined. When they return to the city their friends reject them, for their tastes have changes so much that it is as though they were two distinct races.[33]

His closeness to nature sets the Upper Egyptian apart: he is not merely a peasant working the land, but in a mysterious way he is the land itself, the land which produced the mighty Pharaohs, not subject to social evolution, he is outside time and the stranglehold of modern civilization. This merging of the fellah into nature is portrayed visually—the men in the fields seem to be at one with the earth, their muddy *galabias* camouflaging them from the eye of the outsider—and aurally—the fellahs' shouts out in the fields are described as being "some human, some animal, there was no difference between them."[34] Even when the Upper Egyptians come to Cairo or any other big city in Lower Egypt, their life remains pure and untouched by the filth of modern civilization. They maintain their traditions and life style in their songs, songs which penetrate the earth like seeds at sowing time, and are the expression of a life which spontaneously becomes part of the flow of nature. Each song, each life fecundates the earth to produce ever-renewed life, life that does not die (*la tafna*).[35]

However much the central authority may try to impose its will on these fellahs, they will always escape spiritually. Official after official has come from Cairo laden with documents, and the peasant is called from behind his plough to sign papers which are "stranger to him than wild beasts," and lo and behold! he is deprived of his land.[36] With time the fellahs were compelled to adopt society's weapons—cunning and deceit—to protect themselves. They would hide whatever wealth they had lest these government officials be tempted by it.[37]

During the Egyptian cotton surplus crisis the government ordered the fellahs to plant fewer crops. The peasants came to Haqqi, when he was in Manfalut, and begged him to reconsider their case and to make certain allowances. When they saw that he would not, could not, relent, they turned on him in frustration and accused him of not caring for their plight, all that he cared about was his salary. Despite his ardent desire to be accepted by these people as an individual,[38] Haqqi was finally compelled to accept that the gap between the fellah and officialdom was unbridgeable. Another instance of this distressing barrier is illustrated in "The Mosque Mat." The narrator, a government inspector, had just come to an Upper Egyptian village. During an informal meeting with the village headman and some villagers, the narrator suddenly became aware of a foul smell. When he tentatively mentioned this, the headman passed the matter off lightly. The mosque was the culprit, but it did not really matter because it was only rarely used for prayer. The narrator, however, had the headman take him to the mosque for the Friday prayer:

> As I entered I saw that the paint was peeling, cobwebs were hanging from the walls. On either side of the pulpit was a green flag weighed down by poverty and misery. There was dirt everywhere and the air was thick. The mat was a few sticks set at intervals, through which the filthy floor could be seen.

The narrator was so horrified by what he saw that he determined something should be done at once. He decided that the government should not be involved, and that the community should help itself. The first step in this plan for self-sufficiency was the purchase of a new mat. He assembled the headman and the villagers, and there was reluctant agreement that each one should contribute toward the new mat. The narrator pledged himself to a *riyal*. However, as he was about to collect the money, he was told quite unequivocally that there was no question of giving the money now. He would have to wait until the end of the harvest. The narrator, however, had no such excuse (he was paid at the beginning of each month after all) and reluctantly he handed over the promised sum. Time passed, the crops were harvested and sold, and still the narrator found himself before the wall of the peasants' surliness and aloofness. The headman assured him that by the time the government agents had finished bargaining with the peasants they were up to their eyes in debt. There was no hope of their contributing toward the mat. And so, in desperation, the narrator decided to have the mosque attended to officially.[39] There could be no relaxation of the barrier. The fellahs' and the headman's apparent cooperation had turned out to be a mocking, deceptive form of flattery. The headman had led the narrator to believe that there was hope when he knew there was none. Any headway the narrator had thought he was making was an illusion. After all, why should they bother to do anything for themselves when the government was bound to interfere at some stage? And in the meantime, why should they not enjoy themselves and tease this man whom the government had sent? And if he was stupid enough to give them money, so much the better!

Haqqi portrays a couple of government officials in such a way that the fellahs' mistrust is shown to be perfectly justified. One was an undisciplined, uncouth engineer, whose days were spent in the wine shop and whose nights were spent in the pigsty that was his home.[40] Another was the doctor. The doctor represented the ultimate in withdrawal and alienation from the fellah. This alienation was not a condition that he had submitted to passively, but rather a state that he had willingly adopted, and then elaborated. His house, furnished in the most elegant European fashion, was peaceful, dignified and clean. When Haqqi was invited to dinner, he was amazed by this opulence. It was as though the doctor and his wife had built themselves a sanctuary in the jungle, a sanctuary surrounded by barricades. Sometimes they would venture out beyond the fortifications into the thicket, where they would hunt. Once the hunt was over they would return, wash their hands, take off their hunting gear and savor the physical and spiritual luxuries of their civilized den. However, the atmosphere of predatory greed was so great that when Haqqi left, he felt as though his limbs had been torn off and seized by these cannibals. It is interesting here to note how Haqqi inverts the image: the doctor is first presented as living in a civilized sanctuary which is seen in stark contrast with the primitiveness surrounding him. Then, surprisingly, the doctor is compared to a wild animal—his home has become a den and is no longer a sanctuary. The victims which the doctor hunted so relentlessly were his patients. Peasants would come to him in agony, and he would refuse to help until he had the fee in his hand. On one occasion he was summoned to operate on an old man who had been attacked by his son. The doctor sat next to the victim and refused to move a finger until he was paid in full. By the time the wife had borrowed from all the neighbors the old man had died. Now, however, the doctor was ready to operate—more than that, he absolutely insisted on operating.[41]

Haqqi uses the visit of King Fuad to Upper Egypt as another example of the distance between the fellahs and the powers that be. When the king's forthcoming visit was announced, Manfalut was thrown into turmoil. The station through which the cavalcade was to pass was gaily decorated. The village attended in full force, and the prostitutes were brought along to ululate. The whole affair took on a farcical aspect when the prostitutes and the village notables mixed together in the confusion— the impending arrival of the monarch had upset their careful class structure. But when the time came, the train flew past with its shutters closed.[42]

No wonder then that the villagers should have no outside loyalties, that they should put their trust in charlatans who cure barrenness, and not in government doctors.[43] Without a trusted representative authority to protect their interests, law was an individual concern. Blood feuds were the rule, and a man was expected to assume responsibility for his honor, whatever the cost: he had to kill a dishonored daughter for fear of public censure were he to do otherwise, as was presumably the case with Jamila in "The Postman." Honor was a duty encumbent on all, and it justified even murder.[44]

We can see that Haqqi's account of the fellahs before the Revolution is not an analysis of their customs and behavior. The analysis lies at another level—it is the perception of the gap existing between himself as official and the fellahs as an indefinable mass which officialdom was exploiting. Although in *Good Morning* Haqqi has presented the villagers and their attitudes to the new process taking place in their village, there is still a feeling of complete alienation between these villagers and the powers that be. There was no question of rebelling against government injunctions; theirs was an acceptance of the inevitable. How unlike the rebellious peasant of Sharqawi, Fathi Ghanim, and even of Lashin are these inscrutable fellahs.[45] The answer seems to lie in a difference of perspective: these fellahs are not seen to be part of this life *to be able to rebel against it.* And the problem for Haqqi as individual lay in the fact that as an official he had had to adopt a mask that immediately set the limits of the gap of which the other extreme was the fellah. By the very nature of the game, he was here and the fellah was there, and ne'er the twain would meet. No official could establish contact with any individual fellah. Any relationship that was established, e.g., Abbas in "The Postman" and the narrator in "The Mosque Mat," is in some way unreal or an illusion. For the official, the outsider, can only belong through knowledge or information. Any desire to go beyond this alienation and to actively participate is doomed—Jamila's death is the ultimate prohibition on participation.

Discursively, however, this gap allows Haqqi to bypass all individual fellahs so that he may perceive them as a whole; he may use their elusiveness from *him* to illustrate their elusiveness from history. In their alienness they seem to be the material that Haqqi draws on for the delineation of innocent, exploited individuals in modern society. Each such named individual—Farghali, Ibrahim, Bumba—lives the fellah's exclusion, but within modern society.[46]

* * * * *

And so it would appear that Haqqi's primordial man is Rousseau's innocent who was corrupted by his association with another. Since the first lie was the first deviation from a simple, innocent awareness to calculated self-interest, it is presumable that this primordial state did not contain cunning: the first to enter Paradise, writes Haqqi, will be the simple-minded and the innocent, those who have not been afflicted with an undue measure of intelligence.[47] With cunning had come the realization by each individual that if he is to survive it must be at the expense of others. Thus evolved the game of power in which each individual is implicated *volens nolens;* the strong succeed, and the weak are gradually annihilated. By saying that each individual needs to belong to a social grouping for survival, Haqqi has shown how necessary it is for the official to belong, even to a totally alien fellah community. The impossibility of such a belonging has allowed Haqqi to draw the impenetrable line dividing the fellah from officialdom, from modern society. The fellah may thus be perceived as separate, elusive and nebulous, and as such may stand for an excluded otherness, a timeless affinity with nature.[48] Out of this unnamed nebulousness Haqqi models his particularized individuals on whom society tramples. They are too weak to engage actively in the struggle for power, and so we see them being driven to the edges of their social grouping. Yet by their very exclusion they are seen to retain a child-like innocence that spares them the corruption of social intercourse.

Chapter Three

EGYPT

The fellah, who has always been kept in ignorance and subjection, is the only pure Egyptian—those in power have been foreign ever since the Persian conquest of Egypt in 528 B.C.*

In this chapter I shall attempt to define what it is to be an Egyptian for one who has assumed the role of spokesman for his fellow Egyptians. Yahya Haqqi, the grand old man of Egyptian literature, has throughout his life represented Egypt to the outside world (while in the diplomatic service) and to itself (through his writings). And yet, he is of Turkish descent.

And so, what is Haqqi's Egypt? Is it a political entity? A geographically defined area? A people? The bearer of a history of a one-time greatness? "A tree that once flourished and now has withered?"[1] It is, of course, all of this, and something else besides: it is the spirit of a life force that transcends political, geographical, social, and historical boundaries. To Haqqi, Egypt is an abstract principle with which man may commune: it is nature in whose source he finds his own. In discovering his identity with the land, symbolized by the Nile,[2] the jugular vein of Egypt, man finds peace. In his autobiography Haqqi describes his own response to Upper Egypt:

> The hand of peace and serenity seemed to be stroking my brow, and I, a Cairene, felt as though windows in my soul, that had been shut, were opening for the first time. We were cut off from the whole world, delivered solely unto the land, the cultivation, the animals and the Nile.[3]

The land, the animals and the Nile are one—they are Egypt. Beyond the amalgam of its individuals Egypt is nature. Communion with it is a mystical experience, an opening of the self to the roots of Being. Sometimes, when wandering through the fields in Upper Egypt, Haqqi

---

*A.I. Dawisha, *Egypt in the Arab World. The Elements of Foreign Policy* (London, 1976), p. 80.

would feel a renewed connection with God. Here communion with the land goes beyond what Zaehner calls the natural mystical opening of the self to a greater principle—of which it is a part—to a communion with the divine.[4] To be an Egyptian, in the absolute sense, is to belong to the soul, not the history, of Egypt. And yet, it seems that it is only Egypt's great past that makes it worthwhile as a mystical principle, for it is in terms of its history that its infinitude is perceived. Egypt had always managed to keep itself aloof from foreign dominators; that is, as long as these rulers could be viewed as individualized exploiters, such as France and England. When, however, this Other shed its individuality and assumed the anonymity of modern industrialized civilization, the effect was so pervasive as to strike at the core of Egypt's being. Previously indestructible barriers were not so much destroyed as insidiously dissolved. What was emerging now was another Egypt, the nation-state that could no longer remain oblivious to the world outside. Until the middle of the twentieth century the nebulous Egypt of the Pharaohs, represented by the enigma of the fellah, had been the ideal, the non-changing, that which had preserved fresh and intact its splendid legacy. Now, however, ancient and modern Egypt were, *volens nolens,* joining forces to face the world united.

Baptism of Earth

After Ismail in "The Saint's Lamp" had failed to cure Fatima, he left his home to stay in a boarding house. He was torn between his desire to escape back to Europe, and his need to face the challenge presented by his society. Then came Ramadan, and suddenly it was as though the atmosphere had changed, and he became aware of something in the Egyptians that he had not noticed before: that which was eternal and unchanging:

> He did not believe that there was any people like the Egyptians
> who had maintained their characteristics and essential nature
> despite the vicissitudes of time and the changing rulers.[5]

Ismail had become aware of what Heidegger calls "the Same" in man,[6] the Same that is found in those who are close to the land, the principle of non-change. This is clearest in the peasant who is physically close to the land. To be *of* the land of Egypt is to be close to the non-changing ground of oneself. But in the first instance the essence of Egypt seems to be Islamic: Ramadan had awakened Ismail to the real nature of the Egyptians. A return to Islam was an essential step to overcoming the veneer of modern society; but the quest must continue beyond religion as a means of identity.

To be Egyptian is to be aware of that which is eternal and unchanging in Egypt: through this *awareness* Haqqi establishes his Egyptianness. He may well be of Turkish stock, but of what consequence is that in an Egypt that is much more than the lands held within its geographic boundaries?

Acceptance of, and subjection to, the power of the land watered by the Nile grant legitimacy to a claim of belonging more than genealogy ever could.[7]

His frequent references to his uncle, Mahmud Tahir Haqqi, are illustrative of his anxiety to show that Egyptianness is not a state into which you are born, nor one which is thrust upon you, but rather a state which may be achieved. Mahmud Tahir had been shaken, as had all "other" Egyptians, by the Dinshawai Incident and in 1909 he had written *The Virgin of Dinshawai*. This clash between the peasants and the British had given the dumb masses a voice—a voice in politics and in history. Even though their grievance then went beyond them to become a tool for nationalist aspirations—nationalism not being viewed as a movement of the "disinherited masses" but of the intelligentsia—the fellahs' voice in literature remained theirs. It had been immortalized in the work of one who was not Egyptian by descent, but who had certainly acquired naturalization through sympathy for one of the most potent Egyptian causes. Because of his response to this tragedy, his "new roots had sunk deep into the alluvium deposited since the days of the Pharaohs."[8] Haqqi quotes Qasim Amin when he says that Egypt's heart had beaten twice: once when Mustafa Kamil died, and once on the occasion of Dinshawai.[9] And those whose hearts had beaten then had acquired the right to call themselves Egyptians.

Haqqi explains that his uncle had chosen the short story genre because he wanted to use this new method of fiction writing as a tool for founding a truly Egyptian literature coming straight from the heart of the people. It was the first story, says Haqqi, to deal with the fellahs and their problems;[10] the first to tackle the usage of the colloquial in literature;[11] the first to introduce variety into the narrative; the first to attempt the inner monologue; the first to make fiction available to the non-specialist.[12] This extravagant eulogy for a story which has fallen—unfairly, Haqqi claims—into oblivion seems to have as its main purpose an apology for his own right to stand as spokesman for "his" Egypt. Again and again, he stresses the strangeness of the fact that a Turk could express an Egyptian consciousness.[13] It is not physical but spiritual affiliation that counts: Lashin is another who, although of foreign extraction, "was modelled from Egyptian clay mixed with Nile water."[14] When writing of Muhammad Taimur, he says:

> You feel that the source of (his) fiction is his sincere love for Egypt and its people. And it is not strange—as may at first be supposed—that one who can experience such love and who has borne the standard for a truly Egyptian literature is a young man whose blood is not Egyptian but a mixture of Turkish, Kurdish and Greek.[15]

Kosti Sajaradas, the head of the Greek community in Asyut, is described as having established his Egyptianness through his book, *The Virgin of*

Asyut, which displays humility, culture, and love of Egypt.[16] Another "naturalized" Egyptian is Muhammad Mahmud Ghali, of whom Haqqi writes:

> He was the equal of any European in his knowledge and culture and yet had he been squeezed, only Nile water would have dropped out. His being and knowledge were (closely) linked to our great river ... even though his ancestors were from Tunis.[17]

The Facts

But this ideal Egypt, this catalyst, is very different from the real one of the twentieth century, which is divided between the haves and the have-nots, where an impoverished doctoral student is more concerned about the fate of his sandals than about the outcome of his oral examination.[18] Having spiritually established himself as a true Egyptian, Haqqi, as an intellectual, stands in opposition to the established authorities of Egypt the corrupt nation-state: these authorities have not *become* truly Egyptian; they do not have the nation's interests at heart. Where were the great patriots like Muhammad as-Sadiq Husain who could give their government "a system of moral precepts indispensable for the correct organization of the nation?"[19] The Egypt of which Haqqi is now talking is the nation-state, a political entity trying to find a niche in modern society. No longer the ideal, but a contingent Egypt struggles to destroy the past to progress.

The decree of 28 February 1922 was a mockery, says Haqqi. Egypt has been declared independent, and foreign officials were to be replaced by indigenes. What in fact happened was that some of these foreigners claimed to have adopted Egyptian nationality! Foreign employees had been given three and a half months' holiday a year, if they spent the time abroad; this favor was now extended to all "Egyptian" officials—but, sighs Haqqi bitterly, who can afford three and a half months abroad? To hold power is to be, or to play, foreign; to be excluded from power is to be Egyptian. Egypt was not for the Egyptians—commerce was in the hands of foreigners; it was they who owned much of the agricultural land, most of the buildings in the cities, most of the shops. Signs were written in foreign languages; the taxi drivers were foreign; even the beggars were foreign! In the trams the ticket collectors were Egyptian whereas the inspectors were foreign, and in the metros both the ticket collectors and the inspectors were foreign (the metro was apparently of quite another class from the tram). Judges in the Mixed Courts, if not actually foreign, certainly never used a single Arabic word throughout the proceedings. When one Egyptian judge had asked for the use of Arabic as the offical language of the courts, both for the proceedings and for the writing of the laws, he was suspected of incompetence in French! Foreign judges would only respect someone who spoke French fluently—and the foreigners' good pleasure was the Egyptians' command. And so Haqqi had found himself excluded from the Mixed Courts because he could not speak another's language. He was only eligible for work in the civil courts. But the whole legal system, particularly within the courts, was a farce: judges would not listen and allotted arbitrary sentences. In one case, Haqqi writes of a judge who had asked a man, on trial for smoking hashish, whether he pleaded guilty to killing the goose![20]

Foreigners and their influence had infiltrated everywhere so that they even hired men to foment unrest and incite nationalist uprisings. Nationalism may, therefore, appear to be suspect, a tool used by the foreigners merely to emphasize their strength and authority as they suppress all opposition. In *Good Morning!,* however, Haqqi demonstrates that nationalist commitment may be sincere. While studying in the capital, the cripple's husband had been indifferent to political events until one day he had found his school surrounded by soldiers. These soldiers were eventually "provoked" into breaking into the building. As they surged through the corridors, a little boy was killed. The cripple's husband was incensed at the hushing up of the murder and funeral. From that moment on he became an ardent nationalist, attending all political meetings and demonstrations. Finally, he found the doors of academia closed to him, and he left the capital (Egypt as nation-state) to return to his village (eternal Egypt), where he threw himself wholeheartedly into the land. Introduction of western values had led to violence in whose name the unthinkable was made possible—the killing of one Egyptian by his fellow-countryman:

> A pure, innocent boy was killed at the hand of one of his compatriots, why? . . . there must be something wrong in the governmental apparatus which points, alas, to something wrong in the structure of the entire nation.[21]

Yes, indeed, there was something wrong with the nation as a whole. The ill stemmed as always from education—or, rather, from its lack. For a nation to be imbued with a sense of its worth, it must be taught from the youngest age what the nation is and what it is to be the son of such a nation. Haqqi complains that when he was at school, teaching was unrelated to the realities and problems of Egypt and individual Egyptians. When he was first posted to Upper Egypt, he could not even tell the difference between wheat and maize. Instead of learning other nations' legal systems, Haqqi wishes that he had been taught Hejazi law (as it had been before Islam) so that he might then understand the Sharia correctly.[22]

Haqqi's bitterness and cynicism at Egypt's corruptness and the general apathy about real improvement are well illustrated in the following story. After visiting a penal reform institution in Giza, he had been so horrified by the dreadful barracks and work houses that he had decided to give a lecture on abuses in social institutions. As he entered the lecture hall in the Law Club, the empty chairs grinned at him derisively—there were only two men in the audience. Should he use the dual or the plural form of address? No one cared about the abysmal state of social institutions. Let the schools continue teaching little Egyptians the arts and sciences of their foreign masters! What did anyone care as long as he was comfortable, and could be certain of a secure future for his sons.

Ironically, the only person at all interested in Haqqi's appeal to the public conscience was an opportunist. He came from a reform institution in al-Asfar and wanted Haqqi to come with him secretly—Haqqi having by that time acquired notoriety as a result of his well-intentioned speech. Delightedly, Haqqi gave his lecture at the penitentiary. Thirty people, including government officials, attended. His feelings of gratification were soured, however, by his ultimate realization that the man who had invited him to speak had quarrelled with his superiors and was using Haqqi to disgrace the institution. He had hoped thereby to have these men removed from office so that he might then take their place.[23]

> What was the use of struggling in a country like Egypt and with
> a people like the Egyptians who have lived in subjection for
> long centuries, and have enjoyed this subjection?

What indeed was the point, if one was only aware of the corrupt outer form? This was the case for Ismail in "The Saint's Lamp" when he returned to Egypt after his seven years in England. He looked at Egypt with the eyes of a foreigner, one who was cut off from the land, and who could not, therefore, purge himself through communion with the spirit of this land. It was not only that Ismail saw Egypt as being evil and corrupt, but that he saw it as actually corrupting: his Greek landlady was such a mean person that Ismail seemed to feel that it was Egypt that had coarsened her. Why otherwise could one not find such people in their lands of origin?[24]

Yes, there was something wrong in a nation where even the simplest activities were beset by cunning and deceit. In "The Ten Commandments for the Vegetable Market" Haqqi illustrates the skill and cunning required for the simplest daily routines, such as shopping. He had been invited to lunch by a friend whose daughter had just completed a domestic science course. For the first time in her life she was to shop for, and prepare, a meal without the help of her mother or servant. The girl finally returned from the market laden with her carefully selected booty. However, as she began to unpack, everyone witnessed the typical disappointment of the Egyptian housewife. The meat was cartilage, fat and veins, in the midst of which lurked the gem—a tiny piece of meat set in the fat.

To warn others against such deception, Haqqi drew up a list of commandments stipulating what the prospective buyer should beware of when he is out shopping—Egyptian vendors are a crafty lot who must be carefully watched! The customer should never buy in the dark; he should never hand the vendor a bag of selected fruits lest the latter surreptitiously remove one piece; he should beware of being called an old customer; he should not be deceived by fruit on display—if it is good, what he had been sold is probably from under the counter and rotten, and if it is bad then he is probably dealing with a cunning vendor who keeps his good fruit under the counter and will only satisfy the perspicacious, wily customer. How cunning one must be to beat these vendors at their game! Haqqi warns against sending for kofta or kabab from the butcher, and he complains of the lack of clean restaurants where one can eat good meat.[25]

Another grave problem was red tape. Haqqi relates the story of the Azhar-trained village headman who had made it his business to help a villager open a new shop. Finally, he had come to Haqqi proudly brandishing a rheumatism plaster (*waraqa lazqa wilkuks*)—how strange are the requests of the distant government, but who are we to question them?! Haqqi immediately understood the problem; the village headman had mistaken the *sad* for a *za,* and instead of getting hold of the stamped form (*waraqat lasaq*) had wasted days looking for a rheumatism plaster![26] On another occasion he writes of his attempts to file a complaint against a boy who had stolen his watch. There were so many formalities that he finally despaired of ever recovering the watch, and abandoned the case.[27] Taufiq al-Hakim's portrayal of a corrupt bureaucracy is more violent. He tells the story of a policeman who insisted on writing down all the particulars of a wounded man, even including the twisted cord on his trousers. By the time he finally asked who had attacked him, the man had died.[28] The media are also exposed to Haqqi's anger: why does the thirst for sensationalism drive the newspaper men to act in such bad taste?[29] Blown-up pictures of murdered men were always placed on the front page; in one case a corpse was photographed cross-legged, the head pushed forward into the camera—and it looked as though it were smiling. Although much of this latter section is written tongue-in-cheek, it does nevertheless reflect a deep concern and cynicism about the Egyptian nation-state which the Revolution had allowed to seep through into the heart of the *rif,* the symbol of the great Pharaonic past.

Good Morning!

This story illustrates the effect that the modern era has on a remote village. Blissfully oblivious to the threat which contemporary society held for the harmony of their lives the villagers saw no need to prepare themselves for change. The mooted, and then rejected, proposal to have the train pass through the village caused no alarm—just mild relief that their lives were, after all, not to suffer any disruption.[30]

The village through which the train was to pass is never given a name—it is at once general and yet particularized by its details. When the narrator returned after a considerable absence due to sickness, he bought a ticket for the bridge station. The ticket vendor announced, however, that the train now stopped elsewhere; and on receiving his ticket the narrator saw the name of his village—even at this tricky point Haqqi manages to avoid mentioning a single name.[31] Indeed, throughout the 154 pages there is not one name mentioned—even Cairo is referred to as "the capital." Lost in the depths of the country, the village had been out of touch with anything or anyone beyond the limits of necessary communication, and then suddenly, the inhabitants are faced with the specter of an alien element. The danger having been faced, the plan for the train is shelved, and Haqqi is now free to present the village in the immediacy of a recent past, and yet already imbued with romantic nostalgia. The villagers are aware of the existence, if not of the implications, of this innovation. The moment of discourse coincides with the occurence of the rupture.

Not only does Haqqi introduce the train in the first page, but on the next page he makes a passing reference to the *ustadh* (professor), the son of the late rich man of the village, on whose death the villagers had been left unprotected. It was, therefore, natural that his son—called "professor" because of the years he had spent in the capital studying—should be accepted by an otherwise suspicious people. He was regarded as their protector; whatever he recommended must surely be in their interest. Again, having mentioned the professor, the one who is later to implement what the train merely symbolizes, Haqqi abandons him until the end of the first half to concentrate on a number of interesting villagers—the tavern keeper, the butcher, the dwarf, the cripple and her husband, the aspiring artist, the station-sweep, the fireman, and the cart driver. These characters are not representative of the laborers, but are potential victims of modern society, those who are destined to leave the anonymity of "fellahdom."

The village is romantically represented as a symbol of innocence and solidarity.[32] Then everything changed. The professor's arrival is preceded by stage directions, as though what had come before were merely a backdrop for what was to follow:

> The stage had been set from the beginning of time for the promised moment. The bell rang and the curtain rose. The place: the station and the railway bridge . . . The time: just after dawn.[33]

Soon after his arrival the professor appointed a council of young men—not of old men or shaikhs, as had been the custom in the past. They initiated construction and closed down the tavern—a source of evil—and the train was diverted from its original course to pass through the village. The professor had achieved a resounding victory over the forces of stagnation, of non-change.

Under the impact of the train this integral, self-sufficient, inward-looking unit exploded to become part of an unfathomable whole on which it was now obliged to depend. The economy had become train-linked: the train had created new jobs (station-sweep) and had destroyed old ones (cart-driver). From looking in on themselves the villagers' eyes were directed outwards blindly into the desert around them. To maintain their sanity, they had to accept the rules of their new social grouping that preferred the community above the individual interests: "The individual can no longer be concerned with himself—this is the age of community rather than individual welfare."[34] This new orientation did not signify in any way liberation but rather change and disorientation: the villagers had suddenly become aware of the big bad world "out there," a ruthless world where old beliefs have to be abandoned as irrelevant, where attempts to find satisfactory substitutes lead to despair, where despair leads to anarchy.[35] The individual who no longer feels himself to be part of a "family" sees himself to be cut off from its spirit, and with his alienated perspective he sees this new community as that Other whom it is lawful to cheat. This new community has become the microcosm of society, whereas before the social grouping had been the macrocosm of the individual. Those who could not steal from the new community stole from the weak, the weak being forced to defend themselves by art and guile. There is nothing worse, sighs Haqqi, than for those accustomed to servitude to be given their liberty and to become responsible for organizing their own affairs.[36]

And yet, despite his intellectual appreciation of the situation, Haqqi found himself frustrated emotionally when faced by this inability of the fellah to adjust to the new circumstances. His frustration may be regarded as a reflection of the paradoxical situation facing the intellectual: the poor are defended as long as they remain distant objects; too close a familiarity breeds, if not contempt, at least annoyance. With the new system of land tenancy the peasants who had previously tilled the land of others now had to rent the land *and* provide the tools—a financial impossibility for many of them. The result was that many of them made agreements with their landlords, behind the village council's back, to continue the old system. Again Haqqi expresses his frustration: now that they have been given the freedom to choose between independence and dependence they have chosen the latter. The fate of the cart-driver illustrates most vividly the fate of those who have either voluntarily or involuntarily shunned "progress" because they had felt themselves to be so far removed from its encroachments as to consider its threat irrelevant:

> I had come to the end of life without taking into account (the coming of) the black day . . . Nay, I had mocked time, and hated ambition . . . Time is mocking me and ambition is taking its revenge, and God's compassion has left me.[37]

In this lyrical passage put into the mouth of the old, broken driver (now begging on the steps of the mosque), Haqqi is illustrating the dilemma of those suddenly faced by a new life whose reality they had never really had to acknowledge. The accommodation to these changed circumstances is seen to be each individual's responsibility—if he cannot, or will not, make the requisite adjustments he may find himself excluded, exiled, for he has proved himself unable to survive. This inability to adapt is also illustrated stylistically. As the narrator describes his reunions with his old drinking companions, he may use some form of the verb *hana* (to bend), adequately expressing thereby the effect which the new orientation has had on these individuals: "Finally I found him (the cart-driver) sitting on the threshold of the mosque with his back bent"; "the tavern-keeper's head was bent over his chest"—he had opted out by becoming the grave-digger, choosing the dead in preference to the living. And finally, the artist was found "sitting on a chair, bent over":[38] accommodation to the new situation had killed the artist in him. The oppressiveness of this new era on the villagers becomes particularly clear when viewed in contrast with the description of the professor standing on the bridge when he first returned to the village: "Straight-backed, he would bow only to God."[39] The villagers were not fighting back; they were surrendering to the split-up of old loyalties, and to the establishment of self-centered individualism. The dwarf's family previously owned some of the best land in the village— most of which had gradually slipped out of their hands due to mismanage-ment. Since the new situation in the village no longer made it possible to lead an idle life, the dwarf set about recovering the land.[40] His wife, who had previously given all her money to the poor, now joined her efforts to her husband's. Charity turned inwards, and her husband justified this new selfishness in terms of the futility of her former altruism. As the sense of solidarity is lost through the explosion of the sense of wholeness, so the idea of the individual becomes paramount: the individual is supremely important or he is nothing.

Through the loss of the significance of the individual in the eyes of the central authority, in favor of the universally more meaningful entity of the community, there, in fact, arises a renewed awareness of the self, but of a self that does not belong—the "outsider" consciousness. But outside what? The carefully circumscribed world of the past—the village—has lost its independent integrity. Its "walls" have melted and the village has merged into the nebulous Other, which is no longer Other but encompasses the village. The villager can no longer find reassurance in the fact of "belonging." His individuality is no longer defined by the village, and he is floating uncertainly between the desire on the one hand to find a *raison d'être* in service to the community as part of something else he cannot understand, and on the other hand, the irresistibly debilitating force of modernism which suppresses individualism. The cripple's husband has been hailed as someone whom the new situation has helped: now he has a job, a function (even though he had been flung into a dusty, cramped room whence he could no longer see the nature he so loved).

Haqqi illustrates, through the young artist, what might be regarded as a perfect adjustment to this new life. To his surprise, on his return from an extended absence, the narrator finds that the artist, who had planned to devote his life to art, had not left the village. The young man felt that the age of individual preoccupations and parochialism was past, and that now all had a responsibility to work in and for the community. He had decided to give up his artistic aspirations and, to his father's delight, had opted for a mercantile career. The cart-driver, on the other hand, had accepted the anonymity of modern society. He refused adamantly to adopt a new trade—he certainly would not work as a baggage attendant at the new station. Were he to compromise with the contemporary situation he would lose what dignity and worth he had once enjoyed (it is interesting in this connection to look back at the dwarf's original insistence on the fact that he had wanted to live in the village to be respected for his worth and ancestry).[41] The cart-driver's concern was that people coming to the station would not know what his past had been; their ignorance and disinterest would corrode this past. He preferred to effect a clean break, to eliminate any opportunity for comparison, to preserve the past as it had been. This beggar on the steps of the mosque was someone else, not the old cart-driver but a stranger receiving charity from strangers. Not only did he refuse the narrator's offer of help, but he did not even want to talk to him. By adopting the anonymity of modern society, he had, ironically, retained his links with the past and the memory of his individual worth.

The professor illustrates to what extent the central authority has taken over direct control of the fellah's affairs. When the professor first came, he delegated power to various members of the committee that he had set up. Within a year or so, however, he had retracted all power into his own hands. What had at first appeared to be a democratic system was merely an illusion to allow the central authority to instigate itself into the lives of the community unhindered. When it was well and truly entrenched, the mask was dropped: the professor had become a Big Brother—knowing all, controlling all. He even knew of the narrator's diary, let alone of his meeting with his old drinking companions. But this omniscience is not presented by Haqqi as a tool for arbitrary domination. The professor is described as aiming for what is right, with sincerity as his guiding principle, and it is this aspiration which set him apart from, and above, the others. What the narrator was questioning was what the professor considered to be right.

Aware of the narrator's disapproval of the new developments, the professor sought to excuse the apparent brutality of the system in the following terms:

> I cannot think of the individuals, but of the people of the village
> as a whole. If some fall by the wayside, and I stop to mourn
> them, then we shall never progress.[42]

He is aware of the toll that progress takes, but relies on spiritual justification. With the professor had come an enforced authoritarian Islam which judged wine-drinking to be a sin, and so we see that the tavern was closed—and the people approved. When the narrator talked to the butcher, it became clear that the latter's devoutness had led to a mystical withdrawal—a kind of escapism of which Haqqi disapproves in a country that is struggling to achieve material stability.[43] Haqqi makes a point of mentioning that the professor had called the first meeting of the council after the Friday prayer, thereby sanctioning what he was about to set in motion.[44] Official religion had come. Did the villagers feel that if they were to regret the closing of the tavern they would be showing themselves to be bad Muslims, and therefore bad citizens? If so, this is significant of the new orientation away from a purely peasant, nature-oriented, religiously undifferentiated mentality to an increasingly power-oriented religious consciousness. Haqqi comments that with the arrival of the train all the flowers had died. Religion may be used as a veil behind which material changes are wrought, but this veil is a thin one, for it cannot hide the results—culture has killed nature.[45] From now on it was only at the flooding of the Nile that all Egyptians could find respite from their material concerns, when ideal Egypt temporarily gained ascendancy over real Egypt. On the first day of the flood the people would rush to the banks of the Nile to see the dark red wave surge on, bringing life and strength and mysterious powers: "There would arise in us, the sons of the city, who have nothing to do with the cultivation and irrigation, a thrill of inexplicable joy."[46] But it was only at that moment that these new Egyptians felt bonded to one another, experiencing a communication that went beyond culture.

The train had brought the villagers into contact with an alien world into which they were being absorbed: the domain of the foreigner, of the rich, of those who had submitted to the xenomania of those who wished to succeed.[47] Service of king and country was the privilege of the rich: of those whose parents were wealthy enough to send them to foreign schools and then abroad; of those who had the necessary influential friends to hoist them up on to the next rung of the social ladder; of those who were concerned with progress and further westernization, not because of the general good that was thereby accrued but for their own personal benefit. This was a harsh, unscrupulous world in the hands of a corrupt government:

> . . . a government that wanted to hang on to the seats of power with all its might, and a nation of idle, foolish people who did not realize that they were playthings in the hands of crafty, sly politicians.[48]

The Real and the Ideal

Haqqi's problem is that he is compelled to see Egypt as two: it is eternal Egypt that had always held itself aloof from the world that changes; and it is Egypt that has become a part of this world. The break between these two Egypts had, of course, always existed, but before it had been easier to identify: unchanging, eternal Egypt was Upper Egypt, and it was represented by the fellah whose life style had not changed since the days of the Pharaohs; contingent Egypt was that area of land that had willingly bowed to the foreigner. This distinction can be seen in Haqqi's writings on his period in Manfalut, where he illustrates the unbridgeable gap between the official and the peasant. And then, with the Revolution, this distinction is blurred. As the fellah leaves the fields to occupy the seats of power, he ceases to be a wholly incomprehensible enigma. And in *Good Morning,* Haqqi, writing from the post-Revolution perspective, focuses on some villagers. The united front of the unapproachable fellahs has been shattered, and now Haqqi can talk of, and with, individuals. Egypt is no longer dominated by outsiders, but by a national government which has allowed the outside world to filter through to the *rif.* The fellahs can now be perceived individually for they are finally alienated from each other, from the community which previously had defined their very existence, and from the land: the two Egypts have merged. The question now is: has eternal Egypt been lost in this merging? If not, did this new united Egypt have the same mystical power to change a man's basic nature? Or was it now only in discourse, and in the knowledge that Egypt had once been great?

With each successive wave of foreign rulers Egypt had been modified and changed. Yet despite these changes, there had always been an awareness that beyond changing Egypt there was an eternal principle that allowed for the continuity of the spirit. This eternal principle had for long been the Pharaohs. Although a historical principle, Pharaonic Egypt was so removed in time as to lose its temporal dimension: it had become an almost arbitrary point in a line of continuity, in an eternal conscience represented by the land. But with the dissolving of the physical break between the symbol for eternal Egypt and the actuality of changing Egypt, this conscience was swallowed up in an amalgam of conflicting identities, each assuming greater importance in accordance with individual and temporal needs. The Copt was more Egyptian in that he was descended from the Pharaonic priests; the fellah was more Egyptian in that he was wedded to the sacred land of Egypt; the Arab was more Egyptian in that his language had been Egypt's for centuries, and had become the means for the expression of its self-image.

By saying that he is of Turkish stock, Haqqi has escaped the dichotomies of each individual Egyptian identity. By saying that he is of Turkish stock, he has dissociated himself from the Arab dilemma: it does not matter to him whether he is really an Arab or an African, whether he is black or white.[49] By saying that he is of Turkish stock, he has also refused Islam as a means of identity with other Egyptians, hence rejecting religion as a tool to shape a personal identity.[50] By saying that he is of Turkish stock, he has also gone beyond the disillusionment with a Pharaonic heritage that is being swallowed up into the Arab, the Muslim, and the modern nation-state, as its physical separateness is being corroded. By saying that he is of Turkish stock, Haqqi has thus opened up new horizons that allowed him to perceive that it is not enough to be a descendant of the Pharaohs to be an Egyptian; not enough to be an Arab or a Muslim; not enough to be born in the land of Egypt to be an Egyptian. Egyptianness can, of course, be any of these, but it is something else besides: it is a line of continuity which each individual identity merely serves to pinpoint. It does not matter whether one be a Copt or a fellah, an Arab or a Muslim. What does matter is that one be aware that there is a principle that cuts across all differences—a line of continuity that is the conscience of Egypt, that transcends and encompasses individual identities. By saying that he is of Turkish stock, Haqqi has given himself the liberty to look beyond accepted forms of Egyptianness to perceive and merge with this principle. To be Egyptian is to perceive, merge with, and thus perpetuate this eternal conscience.

Chapter Four

CONFRONTING WESTERNIZATION

> *Capitalism is not a philosophy but a reality. It is the surrender of man and his retreat before the things which he has created and produced.*[*]

In his capacity as diplomat Haqqi spent almost 20 years outside Egypt, and it is France that seems to epitomize the west for him. *Suitcase in the Hand of a Traveller* (1965) is a collection of essays that he wrote after a trip made to Paris and the north of France; and although the explicit subject is France, the implicit theme is the west and its different, at times unacceptable, value system.

When dealing with the west as the powerful, successful Other, Haqqi seems to be presenting the ultimate stage of a process that he sees to be taking place in Egypt—a process in which political conscience and social awareness begin to permeate all layers of society allowing for an upward thrust of previously excluded elements. The difference between Egypt and the west is that in the former this new process is basically modelled on traditional lines; power is still dispensed from the top.[1] In Egypt, certainly new people are being included in the system, but they are responsible only to those above, not to those who remain outside this burdensome burgeoning bureaucracy, which suppresses individual responsibility for the welfare of the community.[2]

But in the west things were otherwise, and again and again Haqqi asks: what is it that makes the western civilization so far superior to "ours"? He is aware of the changes taking place in Egypt, and yet he demonstrates the confusion felt by a society being wrested out of tradition into a world governed by different rules and values, in this case a world where materialism is seen to be the means to spirituality.[3] Although western values should not be adopted wholesale, Haqqi advocates a recognition of their importance, for confrontation with other cultures should not be regarded as a destructive but as an energizing force.

*[*]Michel Aflaq, *Choice of Texts from the Baath Founder's Thought,* Arab Baath Socialist Party, 1977, p. 46.

Politicians, economists, and sociologists may have felt threatened, but artists were aware of the significant constructive contribution made by the west in the cultural arena. It was from the west that writers had adopted and elaborated new styles and new genres. In the introduction to his collection of short stories, entitled *Miss Ihsan* (1921), Isa Ubaid recommended the assimilation of western ideas to counter the paralyzing influences of classical Arabic literature and unalloyed foreign borrowings. Muwailhi, on the other hand, does not acknowledge the possibility of partial assimilation. In *The Story of Isa the Son of Hisham,* he argues that the adoption of western values entails a break with the past, and hence with tradition and religion.

Western Superiority

The advantages and disadvantages of adopting the apparatus and philosophy of westernization are bewildering, for despite its many faults and drawbacks, the positive aspects of western civilization cannot be ignored in a nation struggling to progress. Haqqi used to envy the European students who could choose their field of specialization; in Egypt, the long arm of the government reached into the very heart of the educational system. Europeans were allowed at the earliest age to decide what they wanted to do and what they were competent to do; the Egyptians had abdicated their right for self-determination through centuries of submission to autocratic rule.[4] Like Ismail in "The Saint's Lamp," they had no confidence and looked outside themselves for moral crutches: "Religion and education were the pegs on which they were hanging their valuable coats." The lesson of the west was that these crutches were the supports of men who, if they were not careful, "would remain prisoners by the side of the peg, guarding the coat. The peg must be inside the individual."[5] Self-reliance was a vital lesson that Egypt had to learn, for self-reliance was the mainstay of the democratic system. The whole world could not run smoothly unless each part functioned independently and yet in perfect harmony. Should a Parisian have a question, he does not ask anyone but slowly and painstakingly gathers all necessary information from the source. Knowledge in the west is carefully collected, ordered and then distributed in an organized and harmonious form, thereby rendering people independent of each other while still dependent on a system. It is this order which pervades western society and which Haqqi feels to be a vital component in the superiority of the west over the east. Just as his praise for western organization is unreserved, so his censure of disorganization in Egypt is harsh: even if information in Egypt is collected in some fashion, it is practically impossible to locate. When he thinks of the west, there spring to his mind scholars and professors, factories and museums, activity and production; but when he thinks of Egypt, what he sees is total chaos.[6]

Haqqi's descriptions of tramdrivers in Egypt and Europe aptly illustrate the very different attitudes to work which these two peoples have. From childhood Haqqi remembers standing next to the driver when travelling by tram. The driver's eyes were wandering everywhere: he watched the women getting on and off, he conducted conversations with the ticket collector wherever the latter might be, he even got out to watch fights. In Berlin before the war, however, Haqqi had noticed that the driver was rigid as a pillar. Nothing short of a cannon could disturb him. His world was defined by the tram rails. He made no unnecessary movements. It was as though he had become a part of the machinery or as though the machine were an extension of him. Despite its weight the tram passed along the rails as though on silk, not iron. In Egypt the tram seemed to be travelling over gravel; far from being at one with his machine, the driver seemed to be struggling with it.[7] These views would seem to illustrate Haqqi's dual perspective—the outsider who has the distance which allows him to idealize, the insider who is hemmed in on all sides by facts, the components of his reality.

The diffusion of power in the west has not yet come to Egypt. A clear example can be found in the essay "The Committee,"[8] where yet another committee is being formed, only to be presided over by the same few people, most of them "gentlemen of leisure," and therefore able to attend all the farcical meetings. The system has not changed, just its names. Indeed, all that has happened is that some new people are being given positions, thereby extending the privileged sector.[9] Outside this sector are those whose voices are still not heard, those who still have no particular function or place. They are at best spectators: at the individual level they are totally dependent, at the corporate level they do not exist.

In *Good Morning!* we can see the effects which this new orientation is having at the grass-roots level. The cripple's husband was put in charge of the village storehouse. This new job had given him a sense of responsibility. It was important to him that he record everything that happened. With this new status he had become aware of his responsibility to himself as part of his responsibility to the system; he had experienced the birth of social conscience. As the artist had said, the time for individual preoccupations was past; now attention was to be directed toward the community, which integrates all of its members into an efficiently functioning whole. But Haqqi points out the dangers of this automaton-like harmony with work: in such a system people become machines; there is no allowance for human fallibility. For the entire network to run smoothly each link in this vast chain of activity must work uninterruptedly. Should even the most insignificant clerk, hidden away in the shadows of a dismal office, "stop for a second, the mountain would collapse." How imperative it is that each component member be aware of the primacy of the community, for it is only by placing the community above the individual welfare that the latter really benefits. Life must find its purpose and motivation in the service of others.

The individual may have the illusion of independence, but it is an independence granted by obedience to the rules of a society which demands of its members that they assume full responsibility for themselves so as to serve the community better. The advantages of this independence is that each person is answerable for the task with which he has been entrusted. He deals with all problems falling within his competence, without reference to a superior. Haqqi experienced directly the benefits of this system on a trip to France. In Egypt the wrong half of his ticket had been taken, and the mistake was only spotted on the eve of his return. Haqqi had been filled with anxiety at the thought of how long it would take to rectify the error. But after two quick telephone calls the lost half was recovered: no extended greetings, no flowery explanations—just the substance of the dilemma in one and a half sentences. In an organization with numerous offices all over the globe, each unit must be, and is, fully responsible for itself.[10]

1984

Utopia? Perhaps not. Organization is a great thing if it is not allowed to run wild. In Europe signs of this danger have appeared: electronic machinery which has rendered countless workers redundant. The system is taking over, and although each member feels himself to be independent and even omnipotent within his own sphere, this is an illusion, for each one is being insidiously manipulated within a system where order and organization are of paramount importance; yet if order and organization are taken to their logical extreme, they can become dangerous. The principle of systemization should be adopted—but only with full cognizance of the problem.

To have a system, to be organized, would seem to Haqqi to incur the danger of manipulation. Not so much by another human being—in which case the manipulation may be recognized for what it is and may then be rejected—but rather manipulation by a nebulous, unfathomable drive which cannot be perceived as a unit and therefore cannot be rejected as a whole. For this whole has become life as we know it; to reject it is to reject the very basis on which our civilization depends. Objects have strings attached, and we do not know who are the puppet-masters. Once upon a time they were the factory owners, the bank managers—those with the money. But now the system has exploded beyond the human sphere to become mechanized and totalitarian. The puppet-masters are now the scientists and the technicians. Power has diffused and the system has become strongly cohesive, and ultimately, all find themselves dependent on the electronic brain—the Big Brother who, in a mysterious and elusive way, represents the united front of the Manipulator.[11]

This system is robbed of any semblance of nature: people are gasping for contact with the non-cultural, the non-artificial, and they are given substitutes instead. In "A Glass House," two shops are described: one sells pets, the other plants. Imprisoned in their concrete jungles the clients come to these shops to partially satisfy inarticulate cravings for a lost nature. More oppressive still were the bookstalls on the banks of the Seine which sold books *about* animals and plants. On the right was knowledge, on the left was life—but removed from reality. Knowledge, far from replacing experience, creates a burning desire for it. Yet the system diverts these desires to its products, primarily useless luxury items to titillate the mind and prevent it from wandering uncontrollably to forbidden spheres, to nature itself. Should this temptation, however, prove too much to resist, there are always parks and botanical gardens, a second-hand reflex of nature.[12] With this loss of nature has come reliance on the system to provide a substitute, but a substitute which is necessarily lacking.

It is this very lack that induces the sense of dissatisfaction symptomatic of the new society, for culture cannot replace nature, and a civilization based on this lack is imperfect; it has divorced itself from God and the spirit, and it has handed itself over to the material realm. Although the material world is quantifiable and concrete, that which controls it is not. In a godly, spiritually-oriented society, this inexplicable is the "given" which cannot be questioned; it is the esoteric explanation for material phenomena. In a secular civilization this is unacceptable, and therefore nature becomes a terrifying enigma. Nature is seen to contain hidden, unknown powers that are at once enticing and terrifying, powers which destroy man's claim that he is the only cognitive being. Such powers seem to play with him. They give him the illusion of freedom but the illusion is soon dispelled, revealing the real imprisonment. And so Haqqi has subtly redressed the balance through the usual spirit versus matter polemic; the west may be ahead of the east materially, but Rostand is right: without nature, man is cut off from his spirit.[13]

Of Fustat and Thebes

Haqqi demands that his countrymen hold on to spiritual values because they arise out of a great past.[14] The Arabs (Haqqi goes beyond the Egyptian to the Arab heritage, so as to include the Arab world, at least for the present argument) come from the birthplaces of some of the world's leading religions, and echoing Afghani and Abduh, he reminds all Muslims that their religion already incorporates values of this western civilization that they are so anxious to assimilate.[15] Islam, "with its predisposition to a socialist system," would seem to contain within itself the germs of the very civilization with which it is seeking to catch up. But however much Haqqi may wish to idealize Islam, one fact remains: principles of freedom and equality do not suffice as the sole foundations of a *materially* successful civilization.[16] And it is this that Haqqi truly wants, because an economically sound society can afford to indulge in communal spirituality, while gaining the respect due it from the outside world, as indeed from its own people.

And Haqqi craves western esteem. Why does the Musée de l'Homme in Paris not give over half the building to the Egyptian collection? The only reason must be contempt! Indeed the west cares so little about the east that in 1967 the Sudanese Section of this same museum was called the Egyptian-British Sudanese Section! Such mistakes should be eradicated, says Haqqi, by recognizing the importance of education. If children were correctly informed at school, such negligence might be avoided, for the new generation would know its rights both at home and abroad. Under such conditions exploitation could not survive. And with their newly-acquired self-respect the Egyptians could change; they would thus project an image that was authentic, and not a poor copy of what they felt they should be in western terms.[17]

In his anxiety to prove the importance of the Arabs and thereby to restore self-confidence, Haqqi cites the common assertion that the Arabs were instrumental in the evolution of western society: they had translated from the Syriac into Arabic Greek and Latin texts which had then been translated into European languages. The knowledge thus diffused had become the basis of western civilization:

> From Rome they took their legislation, their inclination for colonizing and their road-building . . . From Athens they took philosophy (including scientific principles), the theatre, sculpture and aesthetics. And the strange thing is that, had it not been for the Arabs, the Athenian (legacy) would not have been fully incorporated (into western civilization). I am not saying that without the Arabs their modern civilization would not have come into being, I am merely stating that without the Arabs it would have taken much longer.[18]

This was small consolation in the face of western disregard of, bordering on contempt for, Arab/Islamic civilization.

Haqqi tries to lay much of the blame for western misunderstanding of the orient at the door of the Arabian Nights: all existing copies of it should be destroyed.[19] A European had once written to Haqqi telling him that she wanted to visit the Pharaonic monuments but that she was apprehensive because of all the stories she had heard of scorpions and harems.[20] He also writes of the usual questions put to Egyptian students by their host families in Europe: are women still veiled in Egypt? Do the men have four wives? Do they ride camels? What do they do with the crocodiles in the Nile? Do they run through the streets?[21]

This poverty of information in the west about Egypt, and the Arabs in general, Haqqi presents not merely as lack of interest but as part of a conscious policy of contempt, and by extension of power mongering: to know and describe the other in a particular way is to control it absolutely, unilaterally. The other cannot react to modify the image, because it is other than what it is perceived to be. Any incursion it may make on the ruler/ruled dialogue must be violent, drawing attention to itself as being outside that particular power game. But how was such a rupture to be effected when the west manipulated Egypt not only intellectually but also practically? Top students from teaching colleges in Egypt were sent to England—not to Oxford and Cambridge, which were closed to the "children of slaves," but to Exeter which England reserved for the indigenes from the colonies. All that they needed, according to the British, were the rudiments, enough to help them work efficiently as employees in their own countries' administrations—and this was called "cultural exchange."[22]

What Price Westernization?

However much Haqqi may malign the west, his love for its culture is irrepressible. Beautiful, exquisite Europe—the home of ballet, opera and concerts—represents a promised future, an unknown magic. Haqqi is lavish in his praise of western culture. Elsewhere he writes of the debt he owes writers in France, England, Russia, Germany and Italy, indicating the extent to which his literary tastes are western-oriented. Egyptian artists such as Sayyid Darwish are drawn upon not so much for their cultural as for their patriotic contributions. Egyptian writers—Mahfuz, Hakim, and Yusuf Idris—are tagged on to lists of foreign writers in a desultory attempt to introduce them into world literature.[23] And yet, like so many others, Haqqi accuses the "white race" of teaching the east the wars of annihilation.[24] Again, Haqqi has saved himself, and again he looks to Egypt's past for comfort. No monuments, he claims, are the subject of as much research. The Egyptian collections are the pride of all museums— their statues and mummies still retain the perfume of "our" valley. Haqqi writes of his visits to the Musée de l'Homme "to greet my fellow countryman—a skeleton in a glass case." How little does the west understand of this skeleton that it has encapsulated, but whose greatness is still clearly visible! While looking at the relic Haqqi sensed its dynamism, as though he were seeing himself for the first time. The object had become so familiar that it seemed to be his mirror image. It seemed to have become Haqqi. And yet, it remained mysterious for it was not Haqqi. Then, the process was reversed, and Haqqi felt as though he had become this mysterious object that encompassed, and yet was part of, his world.[25]

Herein lies the greatness of Egypt—its civilization is dynamic, not threatened by the uncertainty and ephemerality of the physical world. In the west people are taught to rely on themselves and on objects—books for information and machinery to simplify calculations and manual work. Matter has gained victory. Small wonder that western man is afraid because, having lost his soul, he has nothing beyond his possessions.

Elsewhere, however, Haqqi, feeling called upon as humanist, defends the spirituality of the west. One symptom is that *Time* magazine has a whole section devoted to religion. He adds that there are just as many pious people in the west as in Egypt. What has particularly impressed him are the great benefactors, the Lord Nuffields, who willingly gave so much to charities. In Egypt, on the other hand, if there had been no provision made for religious endowments in the Quran, then the practice of giving part of an inheritance to charity would soon have lapsed. There follows a surprising disclaimer: the distinction between the secular west and the spiritual east is false since man, after all, is man wherever he may be. A problem does arise in this connection. The distinction between east and west based on greater or lesser spiritual consciousness is indeed suspect, but what about his claim that it is only in economically sound societies that it is possible to lead a life of contemplation and mysticism? Is it perhaps because western civilization is based on science, and is, therefore, not threatened by anything so far outside its precincts? If so, material prosperity and secularization not only push the country concerned into the world arena, but also prepare it for a more fulfilling religious life. And, in this deflated mood, we see Haqqi visiting Europe. He has lost all thoughts of Egypt's intrinsic greatness. What is left is a feeling of sadness at the unfavorable comparison he is forced to draw between the two civilizations. Why was it that Europe was always looking for perfection and progress when Egypt was content with failure?[26]

The gap between east and west is well brought out by Haqqi in "The Saint's Lamp" through the contrast of Ismail's and Mary's respective attitudes to life: when Ismail suggested sitting, she was "raring to go"; when he spoke of marriage, she spoke of love; when he spoke of the future, she spoke of the present; his fear was of freedom, hers of bondage. By the time Mary had finished "educating" her acolyte, he was no longer dreaming of the beauty of some distant Paradise, but of the splendor of nature and its secrets. He had begun to live for the day, and no longer needed his guide since he had learned to rely on himself. Deep in himself had been uncovered the seeds of a possible renewal. Contact with materialism, or rather rationalism, had stripped away the veil of stagnation to open up new possibilities. Mary had made a rational man of Ismail, so that when he returned to Egypt the new set of values that he had acquired tore him apart. He was filled with anxiety as he faced the paradoxes of his new situation. The moment of "enlightenment" came with the perception that it is precisely by means of these paradoxes that one can overcome and resolve one's dilemma. When he, Ismail, had learned to readjust to what he really was, he was then able to view himself, his culture and his past objectively. He could rebuild with reference to the western values which had given him the necessary distance to *use* his past and not be bound by it.[27]

Eastern Woman, Western Woman

The paradoxes in Haqqi's attitudes to Egyptian and western societies are epitomized in the disparity between his conception of middle class women in Egypt and in the west.[28] The Egyptian woman idealized is the conservative woman who stays in the home and who is allowed out only if completely veiled. To idealize Egyptian woman he must revert to the mysterious being that the modern townswoman is not. He is writing of a woman who is outside the mainstream of life as known in the west, or indeed in *contemporary* Egyptian towns! And then there is western woman moving along on the high tide of progress and development. She is the one who pulls the strings and who judges man as her equal, measuring his culture and brilliance—to amuse her is to gain the esteem of others. She is the emancipated woman whose beauty is in her work and independence:

> Never would poets or lovers have dreamt that sweat and beauty could come together in one face, but I found that the face of this (French) girl, pouring with sweat, was radiant with beauty . . . I wish that you had been with me so that you also could have seen how her face glowed with a pride and joy that arose out of her work and self-fulfillment.

He had even seen women working as butchers, and he exclaims in awe:

> The symbol of beauty and tenderness has become the symbol of slaughter and bloodshed. Many of these jobs are very tough for women and yet they take them on with a courage that is admirable.[29]

Surely such extravagance is only possible in one who is idealizing from a very great distance. In contrast, there is the highly conservative Egyptian woman whose beauty is her mystery. She holds the potential for extreme beauty, yet a beauty that necessarily remains in the realms of conjecture: once she is known she is something else.[30] Both women, in effect, are idealized from a distance: western woman from a physical distance, Egyptian woman from a temporal distance.

*   *   *   *   *

The paradox of westernization is unresolvable: there is the need to progress in order to be the equal of economically powerful nations, but there is also the fear that loss of identity will result from the assumption of their values. The west, with its comforts and all the symbols of its material progress, brings an anonymity that reduces differences, particularly those pertaining to past greatness, to dull uniformity. The choices are clear: did the Egyptians want to be citizens of the world? Or did they want to be Egyptians taking comfort in a great, but dim and distant, past? Or did they aspire to be Egyptian citizens of the world? It is the critic who intervenes to bypass the contradictions of the writer: Haqqi the apologist resolves his own dilemma by citing the Egyptian citizens of the world—the Taimur brothers, Lutfi as-Sayyid, Aqqad, Haikal, Lashin and the Modern School, Taufiq al-Hakim—men who combine western scholarship with eastern sensibility. These are men who have left their "windows open to the world," both east and west, taking from each what they, as Egyptians, can use to help them in their unique quest for a progress that does not annihilate but accomodates the individual with his physical and spiritual needs.[31]

Chapter Five

THE SPIDER'S STRATEGEM: FEMALE ROLES, FEMININE IMAGES

> *Man has magic feelings of awe and fear,*
> *sometimes disgust . . . toward all things*
> *that are mysterious, powerful, and not*
> *himself, and . . . woman's fertile body is*
> *the quintessential incarnation of this*
> *realm of things.* *

Although it is true that Islam, as a religion and a law, played a positive role in the improvement of woman's condition, assuring her certain rights that she had not previously known, it is also true that Islam, as a civilization, gradually curtailed these same rights and imposed new restrictions. The Quran had not enjoined the wearing of the veil; yet altered conditions had rendered its adoption advisable.[1] As women came into contact with an outside beyond the confines of the tribe they were exposed to the eyes, and therefore the attention, of strangers. With time the veil was worn outside the home and also indoors when marriageable men were present. And by the Abbasid period most wealthy women were veiled and also relegated to the harem. This seclusion, far from being pejorative, was considered a sign of respect. It connoted the protection of something precious and vulnerable. It also conferred status. Originally only the aristocracy were veiled, but by the modern period the middle and even some of the wealthier working classes began to emulate the upper classes, keeping their women in social isolation. In 1957 Mahfuz published the first part of his Trilogy, *Bain al-Qasrain,* in which he deals with the family of the autocrat Abd al-Jawad. The latter is married to Amina who lives entirely in his shadow, only leaving the house once a year when she went to visit her mother, and even then she was accompanied by her husband. One day Abd al-Jawad had to be away from home overnight. Amina took advantage of his absence to go and pray in the Zainab Mosque. On her return with her son she was hit by a car, and she was compelled to stay in bed for three weeks. Abd al-Jawad, throughout the convalescence period, said nothing. As soon as

*D. Dinnerstein, *The Mermaid and the Minotaur: Sexual Arrangements and Human Malaise.* (New York, 1976), p. 125.

she was well enough, Amina got out of bed and resumed her wifely duties. She was expecting her husband to explode in anger, but without raising his voice, he told her to leave the house. Amina was horrified, but Abd al-Jawad was adamant. This was the first time he had ever been away overnight, and she had disobeyed him. There could be no forgiveness. It was not that he was impetuously harsh, for he had made this decision after three weeks' reflection. His inclination had been to forgive and forget, but his sense of honor would not allow him to follow his heart; he had to obey the rules of his society.

The veil was not seriously questioned until 1923. Huda Sharawi, the founder of the Feminist Union (1922), was returning from Rome where she had been sent as a delegate to a conference of the International Alliance of Women. On her arrival at Alexandria she dramatically tore off her veil in front of a stunned crowd and threw it into the sea. This symbolic act was the culmination of murmured protests that had been voiced already in the late 19th century: Qasim Amin, a Cairo lawyer, had claimed that the Muslim world was backward because of ignorance perpetuated in the family. Women, he claimed, should be educated, and their rights, detailed in the Quran but concealed by time, should be restored. Sharawi's act marked the beginning of a new era in which women were to play an increasingly important, although still largely invisible, role in Egyptian society. The veil as a social symbol was on its way out, but as a political symbol it was to recur throughout the twentieth century.[2]

By the 1950s, women in most Muslim countries had acquired some of the rights that had seemed so distant in the 1920s. Such reforms had been slow in coming. They had been preceded by years of literary protest. In the 1890s Manfaluti had lamented women's tough fate, subject as she was to man's unscrupulous desires; but he offered no plan of reform. Typical of the early writers on women, Manfaluti did not project solutions so much as expose situations.

By 1920, writers, particularly of the Modern School, felt that it was their duty to point out woman's invidious position. A favorite topic was the child bride. In "Hajj Shalabi" (1930), Mahmud Taimur writes of a girl married against her will to the old Hajj Shalabi. After a while the girl became pregnant, and her husband employed her as a wet nurse. At the first murmur of a complaint he divorced her, and returned to the match-maker for another young bride. And in "Shaikh Juma," Taimur speculates about the possible consequences of such a marriage. Shaikh Juma died soon after his child-bride had given birth to a son; the story begins seven years later. The elegant mother has lost all self-respect; her body is something to be used to get what she wants. She has run into debt with the coachman. The latter will no longer accept vague promises of later payment; he insists on immediate defrayment. She pays with her body, to the sound of her son's laughter as he watches the unlikely couple through the bedroom keyhole.

Another topic is man's brutality to woman. In his collection of short stories, *It Is Said That . . .* (1929), Lashin makes a direct attack on the reader in defence of his maltreated wife. In "The Ghost," a husband relates how his wife has woken up in the middle of the night, black and blue from a whipping that a ghost has apparently inflicted. And when the husband looked, sure enough there were the marks, "the color of which, you, of course, know!" says Lashin mischievously to his reader. And in "Fate," Lashin condemns the myth of honor. He tells of a young man who had asked his mother, whom he loved very much, if she could help an old neighbor, Urfi Bey. The latter was paralyzed and now needed their help. Years earlier he had bought some land from them, and he now needed the sale contract to clear up a border dispute with a new neighbor. In his search for the document, the son found love letters from Urfi Bey to his mother, and he realized that what he had thought to have been his father's inheritance was in fact money Urfi Bey had given his mother. The young man was horrified. The past now appeared to him in a totally new light. He forgot the years that the widow had lovingly devoted to her children. All that mattered was the tainted honor. He was so anguished that he wished his mother dead. Ironically, on his return he found that his mother was actually dying. And at the last moment he recognized her courage, and "absolved" her. So invidious is woman's position that her greatest sacrifice is decried. She is accused of sullying the family in her attempt to save them.

Haqqi does not approach literature with the same reforming zeal that characterizes the works of many of his contemporaries. Literature should at best point the way, he says, out of an unjust situation; it should not be a pretext for propaganda. And so, despite the prominence being given to the emancipation of women, Haqqi makes little overtly political comment. What interests him is woman's influence and visibility in society, and hence in literature.[3] But beyond a professed objective investigation there lurks the traditional view of woman—as chaste, or as vicious and vulgar.[4]

> Perhaps the greatest indication of woman's power over me is that because of her I never cease to grieve that the temple of poetry is locked and barred against me. I cannot enter into its hallowed heart, even through the servants' entrance. Too sublime for prose, she should be addressed in poetry sparked from her beauty and inspired by her gentleness.[5]

Who is this woman of whom Haqqi talks in such rapturous tones? Not the woman who is known, since the demystified woman suffers in her comparison with a deified, idealized counterpart. Haqqi's muse is shrouded in mystery: she is the passing glimpse of a flashing eye, the enigma of the body sold for the pleasure of others, the rumored innocence of the country maid, and she is mother. What is to be feared is the unveiling. Pygmalion-like he creates his marble beauty, but once infused with life she becomes a devil, a monster.

Juliette des Esprits

> It seemed to me that she took extra care to veil herself, so as to
> command respect . . ., because this veil symbolized her purity
> and goodness.[6]

It is as a spiritual being, and therefore when her body, her physical self, is veiled, that Haqqi and his contemporaries idealize women: women were no longer to be serenaded for their bodily beauty but for their souls. In "We Were Three Orphans," the meeting with Saniya is described as follows:

> It was the beginning of my life. What had come before was the
> dark age of ignorance, and what was to follow would be light
> and revelation.[7]

Saniya is the symbol of light; Haqqi uses her to open the narrator's eyes to the beauties of the world. It is to Saniya that he attributes his joy when he felt a brotherhood with animals. The sensitivity of the idealized woman brings out the essentially feminine aesthetic sensibilities of the man: "Every 'artist' is at once a child and an old man, and there is no harm if he should have the sensibility of the woman also."[8] Note the quotation marks around the word "artist," indicating, presumably, that it is not the artist as creator only to whom the reference is made, but also the potential, often unfulfilled, within each individual to artistic perception.[9]

Mary, in "The Saint's Lamp," is another such veiled person. She is veiled in that she appears only as a catalyst to direct and accelerate a tendency that is lying dormant in another. As it is only in her partiality that she is seen, there is no question of an unveiling, of an awful moment of truth when the thin veneer of the ideal woman is torn asunder to reveal the beast.[10] Woman here is the temporary incursion on a man's life which helps him to reach his goal. When Ismail went to England, he was adopted by Mary, the Scottish student. She taught him the values of this western society that was so alien to him. Through love and devotion she changed him from the weak boy he had been into a strong, independent man. At this point, when the crysallis first opened its wings, Mary turned away from her protégé—her task was done. Here is one of Forster's flat characters *par excellence*. Introduced as an entertaining expedient to achieve a desired effect, she was removed when the plot would have required her to change, to become something other than the fairy godmother Haqqi had designed her to be. From love of Mary, an intense emotion for an individual, Ismail could now abstract and project to the love of something supra-human, to the love of country, Egypt.[11]

Until the 1940s Russian literature had had a profound effect on Arab writers, in style as in content. And a theme that became popular was the prostitute as a symbol of innocence corrupted by man. Her salvation was the vindication of all corrupted innocence.[12] The prostitute may also be regarded as veiled, because in the act of complete physical abandonment to another she retains what is essentially hers. She has made a trade of an instinct.[13] Is it in this total separation of soul and body that Haqqi's fascination lies? The body, having been so denatured, cannot express the tremblings of the soul, and therefore it seems to have become the veil covering a soul which Haqqi can take and shape as he wills.

The prostitutes are as excluded as the poor in the city.[14] Prisoners of a system out of which they have been excluded, they are described as childlike and pure. A prostitute he had heard of while in Manfalut, Bahia, appeared to be oblivious to the world and all that was happening in it. In their exclusion from society and its corrupting influence, their basic goodness, and therefore innocence, is untainted. Salima, another Manfaluti prostitute, is veiled and therefore doubly removed: first by her veil (*malas*), and second by her expressionless body. She resembles a Pharaonic tomb dancer: tall, slim, long-necked, upright, almond-eyed, straight-nosed. Even the onion on her breath smelled sweet! She rarely drank, and when she did she became like a child; once she saw two photographs facing each other in a magazine, and was convinced that they were conversing. The brutality of society is emphasized in the treatment to which this innocent is exposed. Salima was once summoned to a private house, where she was told to arrive at the dead of night. On her arrival she found that her host had arranged a party. After she had been thoroughly abused, she was flung out on to the streets before anyone was stirring. This was certainly no exception, for Haqqi asserts elsewhere that many prostitutes spend their lives shuffling between threats and fears of treachery.[15] Such fears are founded in grim reality, as Haqqi illustrates in the story of the man who tired of his prostitute wife. He decided to kill her, but anticipating problems since she was very fat, he called on a friend to help. The latter felt no compunction in agreeing: she was only a prostitute after all! His collusion was a laudable act since he was freeing the world of an impurity. By his own reckoning he should be thanked, not punished.[16] In "The Truth of the Matter," Haqqi writes of a prostitute who was tolerated by her father and brother as long as she shared the proceeds with them. Later, when she refused to give them as much as they wanted, they killed her. The father who killed his own daughter justified this act to the judge as being the discharging of his duty: he had, after all, to defend his honor.[17]

Again and again Haqqi emphasizes the contempt and disgust with which prostitutes are regarded. The Manfalut prostitutes were herded through the streets to see the doctor for their weekly check-ups. Haqqi describes their strange gait; it was as if they were learning to walk for the first time. In the hall, they were quickly ticked off on a register and ushered out again. The doctor assured Haqqi that there was no point in actually going through with the medical examination—anyone going to a prostitute should be aware of the dangers. The whole operation seemed to be an exercise in humiliating the women. It was these prostitutes who had to do what no self-respecting woman would deign to do: they were marched up along the railway platform and instructed to ullulate as King Fuad's train passed through.[18] Another vivid example is the story of the Zarifa Mosque. While in Manfalut, Haqqi had come across this mosque named after a woman, Zarifa. Intrigued, he had questioned a number of people about the mosque's namesake. To his amazement, the only information he could elicit was that she had been a prostitute: her good deeds were forgotten, and her sad circumstances were gloated over.[19]

Describing the kind of life that the peasant woman leads, Haqqi can only know what, not who, she is, for again she is veiled.[20]

Haqqi tells of a friend who had spent a long time out of Egypt, and who had particularly longed to hear certain words out of the mouths of peasant women, words like: *akminah, ya daladi, ya nadasha, agruta.*[21] Although this is no less the language of women of the lower classes in urban communities, Haqqi does emphasize that it is the *peasant woman* who has created the nostalgic association. Haqqi's attitude now is not one of adulation of an ideal beauty, a muse, nor of sympathy for a victimized prostitute, but rather a wistful tenderness not for any particular woman, but for the state in which they live. Undifferentiated from each other, without personality, they are easier to idealize as principles of goodness. Their mysterious attraction and dignity lies in the unrealizable, though indestructible, potential for perfection. When the peasant woman leaves the country, however, she is exposed to society, and retribution is not long in coming. Haqqi writes of one such peasant woman who was pursued by her husband to the city. This man was driven to drink, theft, and finally murder: he killed his wife.

> This is the end decreed for all girls who think lightly of their chastity whilst living in the country; and if they reject this chastity, they may be certain of death.[22]

And then, there is the poor woman imprisoned in the city whose veil is not the one she wears but the one which her superiors have placed over their own eyes. In "The Perfume Bottle" the narrator's first impression of the beautiful barmaid, Susu, was of a nobility which raised her above her surroundings, and "enveloped her in a strange mysterious atmosphere."[23] Are they—Bahia, Samira, the mysterious Susu and Bumba[24]— victims of harsh fates which have not furnished them with the requisite defense for facing the battle of life? Is this weakness a blessing since, lacking the strength to compete in the struggle, they are outside the corruption of society?

> In my eyes my mother was a saint—innocent and pure—there was no one like her.[25]

Finally, it is to the mother that Haqqi turns for his ideal. Whatever her faults, woman has the potential to render a man innocent, for in her warm embrace he becomes a child again: the nagging woman becomes a mothering wife. In *Good Morning!,* Haqqi writes of the tavern frequented by all the men who were escaping their wives. When one of them got too drunk to walk home alone, his wife would come to fetch him. Although these women might be expected to be outraged, Haqqi describes them as enjoying the role of mother.[26]

Haqqi's pessimism about society is exemplified when he writes of the corruption that social intercourse can wreak on the maternal instinct. In "The Spiral Staircase," when Farghali was bitten by the dog, Nafisa forced herself to control her instinct to hold and comfort the frightened boy. In the opening sketches of *A Thought Then a Smile,* Haqqi delineates another townswoman. Lying on her couch and bloated from breakfast, she was interviewing a new maid. Callously she told the bewildered girl that if she were to come it must be without the new-born baby.[27] The gap between these two is accentuated by their different smells: the "lady" smells of sweat and incense, the peasant girl of rotting leaves before they fall to the ground. Surely, surmised the woman, this smell would go with a bath! Little did she realize that this was not dirt but the smell of the poor that, says Haqqi, can only be dispelled by a full belly. In "He Left and Did Not Return," Haqqi writes of a woman seeking a cure for barrenness. On her way to the hospital she came across a woman selling babies. Scarcely believing her luck she bought the trophy and rushed off in delight. On her return home, however, she realized her mistake: the baby had dysentery and would not stop screaming—the doctor's bills would be too great a burden. And so she returned the baby to the vendor, much as one might return a faulty pair of shoes, says Haqqi. What had happened to these women? How could a woman, a potential mother, sell babies? "Was this woman lower than an animal?" And how could this other woman return the imperfect baby? Society has so corrupted instincts that a woman cannot even rise to the level of an animal in the most basic of her instincts: maternalism.[28]

Madame de Farge

> This exaggerated worship of the *mother* is the very cause of their deep-seated contempt for *woman;* of their unconquerable distrust and yet hungry dependence upon them.[29]

In the struggle for survival the mother is lost in the woman: the woman who has passed child-bearing age, who has lost the charm of youth, and has become cunning and vulgarly aggressive, "as though an unknown enemy had stolen an unknown something, so that life was no longer worth living."[30] She hides her age in anguish when faced by those radiant girls in the first flush of youth who were kicking her out of the way No woman, asserts Haqqi, whether she be educated or not, can escape this anguished fury. Aggression guides her every movement and word. When a bus or tram arrives she elbows her way viciously to the front of the queue, eyeing the world with resentment. One day a fat woman boarded a tram with her huge son and tiny maid. She allowed the unruly boy to climb all over the other passengers; and in the street, the little girl had to carry the vast child. Had Haqqi been the ticket collector, he assures us that he would have given the girl a whole ticket for doing a job many adults could not have done, and a half ticket to the mother for being only half a human being. And then, there are those shameless wives who humiliate their husbands in public: the woman in the Louvre who dragged her spouse to the front of a group of tourists so as to be within easy spitting distance of the guide. The poor husband was grinning feebly and hiding in her shadow hearing nothing.[31] Haqqi has said that he wishes to be appointed *mufti* so that he might issue a decree (*fatwa*) legalizing the execution of such women.[32]

The most vivid example of ugliness in older women is to be found in a sketch entitled "Sale!!!"[33] It is only at such sales, Haqqi feels, that the full extent of their ugly tragedy can be seen. It is a tragedy at once sad and amusing. In the mad scramble for bargains individuals are lost in a crowd of sameness so that each individual tragedy is accentuated by the quantities of similar, desperate cases. What is oppressive here is not the crowds, but physical contact with this incarnation of the Tragedy. Where else can one see so clearly the covert battle being waged between the old and young? This battle has been suppressed for so long that its final explosion is the more vitriolic. Reason is lost, friend becomes enemy, looks become daggers! Suddenly, the onlooker understands. The women's attacks on the clothes are symbolic of the struggle to retain what is left of their femininity. Although they know that their struggle with the young is in vain, it is this very knowledge that makes them fight. One woman is described as having pillow-like arms, elephantine legs, a bent back, and her once beautiful cleavage stuck together with fat and flesh, all loosely covered with wrinkled skin.[34] In her right hand she clutches the household money. Her hair is dishevelled, her kohl rubbed, her lipstick smeared. Catching sight of a girl handling a dress she pounces on her screaming, "I saw it first!" The farce continues in the dressing-room where she tries on a dress that is much too small. Indignantly she declares that she cannot understand what has happened, since that had been her size last year. Finally, unable to find anything she stomps out, furiously dismissing all the clothes as old-fashioned!

Haqqi's feelings of revulsion for middle-aged women seem to connect with his anxieties about his mother. He viewed her as a coercive and oppressive element in his childhood. In Manfalut, he had still felt guilty whenever he came home late at night. Creeping into his own home like a thief, he was filled with apprehension about what his mother might say.[35]

In "As Though," the narrator seems to be putting the blame for his anguished view of women on his mother, this mother whom he had suddenly come to see as a woman. Although the narrator had once enjoyed reading about sex, when he realized that his "mother had suppressed much of her sexuality to protect her children," he no longer regarded sex as something pleasant but as something evil and violent.[36] Woman had become a graphic example of viciousness and vulgarity:

> Her face was distorted by so much angry, mad frowning. Her eyes bulged tensely, her teeth stuck out like daggers, her gums were exposed like the belly of an obese person. Her lips were bloated, her voice was gypsy-like, her language was obscene . . . Her fingernails scratch the flesh that approaches in search of caresses and tenderness, until it bleeds. She is an octopus, whose thousand tentacles miss nothing . . . When she has caught her prey there is no one more powerful than her to hold on to the strangled (victim), and then to eat it. Sex became confused in my being and in my mind with the act of strangling . . . I hated my mother and because of her I hated all women.[37]

The emotions here are not related to the young girl nor to the older woman, but are directed at Woman, that terrifying being that the narrator's mother had refused to be.[38] The state of childhood engendered by a *mother who refuses to express her womanhood* is traumatizing. This mother had provided sanctified refuge, sanctified, that is, until she was perceived as woman.[39] This would seem to be the Oedipus complex of the immature male whose separate individuality is threatened by the octopus-like hold that this mother-figure represents—she holds him while he is unable to hold her; she is the incarnation of his impotence. This dragon on a tram, or beast at a sale is probably the revered head of a family: her sons feel that they owe this "angelic" being a great debt; to her grand-children her lap is heaven; to her husband she is a trusted companion. How evil is man's lot that his instructor, comfort and companion is in reality a vicious but wounded animal! Licking her wounds, she sneers at the girls in the street, censuring their immodest behavior. And here, suddenly and unexpectedly, Haqqi intervenes on her behalf: "For the first time I will say that she is right, because this is an embarrassing, degrading sight."[40] When, asks Haqqi, will these girls realize that their charm is spoiled by their reliance on the animal in them?[41] And so women are animal-like when old because they feel cornered and their only defense is to kick and scratch; and animal-like when young because of their unsuppressed sexuality.

The Woven Womb

Who are these nymphs who arouse such indignation? In "The Perfume Bottle" Haqqi describes the lovely barmaid Susu whose beauty had attracted a wide and loyal clientele to the bar where she worked. When Sami, the narrator, first went there, he had met an impoverished school-friend, Abd al-Karim, with whom he then spent many drinking days. As the story progresses, Sami is increasingly caught up in the web that Susu's beauty had spun around him until he is finally enmeshed. When Abd al-Karim told him of Susu's rumored prostitution, Sami was outraged, and he wanted to assure himself of her utter degradation, perhaps to free himself of his obsession with her.[42] But however much he tried to satisfy himself of the depths to which she had fallen, he could not forsake her. At the first hint of her innocence he eagerly forgave her. What had originally attracted Sami—the inviolateness of her beauty (the veil)—had gone; he was no longer *attracted,* he was irrevocably *trapped.* He now saw her innocence and nobility as having been besmirched by her environment—*she* appeared to him as victim, and it was in this capacity that she held him: the tyrannical victim.

In "A Photograph" Shauqat tells the narrator of a photograph that had captivated his imagination. The subject was a beautiful heavily-veiled girl. Copy of reality and veil—double mystery and distance. Shauqat became obsessed with this girl. Months later he saw another photograph of this same woman, this time unveiled. She was still beautiful certainly, but with the veil had gone the mystery. She is now described very differently:

> Her thick lips were parted to expose gapped teeth. I shall not elaborate on the kissing . . . that this thirsty mouth could not achieve.

He was filled at once with desire and loathing. Ugliness lurked at the corners of the mouth, and in disgust Shauqat had run away. But, as in "The Perfume Bottle," the spell had been cast, and the victim could not escape. When Shauqat met the narrator some time later, he admitted that he had not forgotten the girl. It was now that strange vileness that was holding him. And he says:

> Maybe ugliness is the principle from which human nature had to gradually evolve . . . until it achieved beauty. Is the fascination of ugliness a longing for the past?[43]

This is Shauqat's justification for his continued attraction to a woman whose beauty he now sees to be somehow vile and ugly; it is an attempt to understand a state of abject subjection. But this statement would also contradict Haqqi's thesis of man's original goodness, since he is looking back not to a Garden of Eden, but to an original ugliness from which man had to evolve to beauty. This may be explained by the fact that it is not man but woman with whom this ugliness is associated; woman, that is, as a sexual being. Haqqi's condemnation of the sexual impulse may be regarded as a denial of the will-to-live. This rejection confirms his pessimistic view of a world in which man is condemned to evil by evolution. His choice of the mongol child (also named Susu) as his principle of survival is significant: cut off from the world, and not the product of the narrator's loins, he was doomed to die before that which he was supposed to perpetuate died.[44] And he asserts that even if he could find a paradise on earth, he would not wish to have his son experience the chore of living, as though to quote Maarri, the archetypal pessimist: "This wrong was by my father done/ To me, but ne'er by me to one."

What disturbs Haqqi is woman's calculated mastery of man—the hold of the temptress.[45] Since woman was the first to lie, the first to awaken the intellect to its capacity for abstraction and manipulation, it is she who is responsible for the opening of Pandora's Box.[46]

In "A Story from Prison" Haqqi uses a gypsy girl as an agent of the devil. Ilaiwa, a fellah, had been put in charge of a flock of sheep and told to take them along the Ibrahimiya Canal to Minya. On his way he ran into a group of gypsies. One of them, a woman, lured him away from his flock so that her band might steal one of the sheep. The gypsies had taken the precaution of poisoning Ilaiwa's dog, so that it could not warn its master. Haqqi describes vividly the dying convulsions of this loyal animal—the final agonies of a will that the gypsy girl was stifling. Ilaiwa was finally compelled to join the gypsy band, and there he had to acquire a new set of values. From the basic level of man as a social being,[47] he was reduced to the basic level of animal.[48] What mattered now was the moment. Woman had brought him to this low ebb. And in "Abu Fuda" the reader sees that it was Narjis who deprived Jasir of his need for freedom—he needed to possess this evil woman more than anything in the world: "Sometimes she was filled with desires for evil, the extent of which circumstances did not allow her to know."[49] It might be argued that critics like Sharuni,[50] Mustafa Ibrahim Husain,[51] and Naim Atiya,[52] have over-emphasized the role of sex in Haqqi's works. For them this urge within each *man* is responsible for the loss of will and direction in life—woman merely acts as the trigger to a process that is somehow independent of herself. This is true also of Ghali Shukri who, however, considers Haqqi's view of sex to be a positive impulse; it is the drive for life, and he attributes the fall of men like Ilaiwa and Jasir to their desire for *life,* on behalf of which no sacrifice is too great.[53] These critics do not seem to have paid attention to the evil that Haqqi sees in certain women. Haqqi lays the blame on the woman: she is the one who is fully conscious throughout of what is happening, while the man is bewitched.

In "The Holy Man is Not Confused" the daughter of a rich man, with whom the holy man and his followers were dining, had taken a particular interest in the prince-turned-fakir. With consummate cunning she analyzed his acseticism as being a suppressed will-to-power. He had lost his mother as a child, and now, she told him authoritatively, he was searching for this lost sense of his own importance. His humility was pride, his asceticism extreme ambition. She was attempting to seduce him by exposing the falseness of his position, and by analyzing his behavior in terms of a mother complex. Now she could present herself as the ersatz-mother figure and fulfillment of his desires. Through this maternal gateway she promised to introduce him to the ecstacy of love, for only after such love could he truly experience love for God.[54]

In "The Awakening" the narrator tells of his trip to France and of his affair with Blanche. He had invited her to dinner a number of times and when she told him one day that it was her birthday he gave her the watch that he had bought specifically for his sister, inviting her to dinner at the same time. With some reluctance she set a time and place for the rendezvous. When she did not turn up, he went to Pigalle, and there, to his horror, he caught sight of her in another man's arms. He escaped to a bar where he sought the dubious comfort of a tête-à-tête with a toothless crone—her physical appearance according well with Blanche's personality. On his return to the pension where he and Blanche lived, he determined to recover the watch. Tiptoeing downstairs he made his way stealthily into Blanche's room and stole the watch. A woman had driven him to theft, as indeed she might drive him to any vice:[55]

> Her man is her prisoner day and night, whether she be present
> or absent, whether she be loyal or false. How many secrets has
> a trusted man told a woman in the hour of passion.[56]

In *Good Morning!* we are told of a girl who had ruined a man's life. While virtually engaged to her cousin, the butcher, she had run off with the clown of a circus that had stopped briefly in a nearby town.[57] Many years later she returned with two sons and a daughter. Her husband, the clown, had died and she had nowhere else to turn. The butcher forgave and forgot, knowing that if he did not then no one else would. However, before long she ran off with the miller's boy leaving her children to the butcher's care. Haqqi compares her to a strange bird (cuckoo?) which lays its eggs in the nests of other birds—the mother had sacrificed her children for the sake of passion.[58] Here it is certainly sex that is destructive, but sex in a *woman*. It is sex in a woman of which Haqqi writes with such awed horror in "The Vacant Bed." This is the story of an apparently innocent, shy girl who was chosen by the hero for these very qualities. However, on the wedding night this innocent became a ferocious animal: her eyes shone like a hawk's, and "had she come near a match she would have lit it—there would have been a fire that all the waters of all the holy rivers could not have extinguished." Her passion was so intense that it seemed to set itself up as a counter-system to religion and to belief in the supremacy of the soul, defying even the waters of *holy* rivers.[59]

Haqqi is longing for the ideal in the mother and in the woman, but he can only see this ideal when it is placed at an impossible distance: the angelic mother of the child *not* of the man, the sexless beauty and the working woman. But how much can be said about something that exists so far away? Was not the moon also the symbol of beauty while it was still distant? And did not man's curiosity and thirst for knowledge turn it into a lump of rock in the skies? It is only in divesting himself of his knowledge that man can once again perceive the moon as beautiful. And this is Haqqi's case: at rare intervals he will draw back and half-closing his eyes will imagine perfection in woman; but his need to go beyond mere superficial description brings him up against the facts, against his fear and suspicion of the real woman, this being of flesh and blood who constantly intrudes upon his dreams.

Chapter Six

THE CRITIC IN SEARCH OF HIMSELF

*All criticism must include . . . an implicit comment on itself; all criticism is criticism both of the work under consideration and of the critic . . . it is knowledge (connaissance) of the other and co-birth (conaissance) of oneself to the world.**

"The Irony of the Flute" in *Kaukab ash-Sharq* (February, 1927), Haqqi's first article of literary criticism, appeared at a time when the critic was still more or less exclusively concerned with explaining a text, or with justifying the rival merits of "ancient" as opposed to "modern" literature. In 1921 Mazini and Aqqad had published their *Diwan: A Book About Criticism and Literature,* which constituted a significant step away from the traditional mold of literary criticism. A primary motivation of this method appeared to be an attack on the neo-Classical trend exemplified in the poetry of Shauqi, Hafiz Ibrahim and Ismail Sabri. The Diwan School, as it came to be called, required that the poet express his true feelings in an imaginitive way without resorting to pure description or stereotyped imagery confined within traditional poetical forms. The inspiration for this new move away from traditional literary criticism of the Ibn Qutaiba variety were English poets and critics like Hazlitt, Wordsworth, and Coleridge. Yet this new criticism had not only a literary but also a political motivation; and it is particularly in the work of Aqqad that one can detect such political overtones—the universal preoccupation of the 1920s and 1930s with the affirmation of a national consciousness. Just as Aqqad was calling for a literature that was human, Arab, and Egyptian,[1] so the Modern School (at its height between 1917 and 1925) was calling for an authentic Egyptian literature which should arise out of the awareness that Egypt—her peasants, her men-in-the-street, her bourgeoisie and her national rulers—was one. Literature, particularly prose fiction, had come to assume a new function; not merely a work of art, it was also a social and revolutionary tool. Both elements had now

*Roland Barthes, "Criticism as Language," in Lodge, *op. cit.,* p. 64.

81

to be present for the work to succeed. Equally imperative was the need for a critic to make sure that the writer was communicating.[2]

The Apologist

Haqqi is fully aware of the significance of his seminal role at a time when the individual identity of Egyptian literature was tentatively taking shape. Assuming the burden of literary progress on his broad critic's shoulders, Haqqi accuses other critics of irresponsibility: by indiscriminately censuring enemies and praising friends, they were perpetuating a poor literary output.[3] His own feelings of responsibility for the progress of literature require him to make honest assessments of his fellow writers.[4] If Egyptian literature is to become universal, having bypassed the individual expression, then it must be subjected to constructive criticism.

In his anxiety to prove Egypt's inherent greatness, and to reveal its literary potential, Haqqi turns on the west, attacking its unfair material advantages. They could afford the luxury of the novel. In fact material worthy only of a short story, says he, was often extended into a novel, since the author was avid for gain! For example, H.G. Wells' *The World of William Clissold* came out in three volumes. It could easily have been abridged into one, he feels.[5] In Egypt, by contrast, the only outlets for prose fiction were newspapers and magazines.[6] Although he complains that this necessitated the pruning down of subjects that should have been given much more space, he does not remain blind to the fact that Egyptian writers also have suffered from prolixity. He accuses Mustafa Mahmud of verboseness in *The Impossible,* recommending that it be shortened by two-thirds. But then his apologetics intervene, and he moves on to the redeeming feature which more than compensates for the just cited fault: Mustafa Mahmud is forgiven because he displays skill, sincerity, passion and intelligence.[7] Again, when writing of *The Irony of the Flute,* Haqqi commends Lashin's direct, careful observation of life and effectiveness of plot, his humor and his use of the colloquial both in the dialogue and in the narrative, all of which more than compensate for the work's short-comings: unlikely imagery, occasional verboseness and passionate romantic outbursts that are more likely to elicit laughter than any other emotion.[8] In the case of Aziz Abadha's *Al-Abbasa,* Haqqi excuses whatever faults the play may have had by commending the unbiased portrayal of the struggle between two characters. The audience, he feels sure, will end up being divided in their sympathies between Abbasa and her brother, the Caliph Harun ar-Rashid.[9] And in *Return of the Spirit,* Taufiq al-Hakim is forgiven for his faults—for instance, using a Frenchman to sing Egypt's praises rather than an Egyptian—because he had written in a clear style, and with assurance as well as passion of Egyptian rural and urban society.[10] Sometimes, however, Haqqi is forced to admit defeat, as was the case with Taufiq al-Hakim's *People of the*

Cave. Voicing a common dilemma, he claims not to be able to judge a work that conforms to two genres—drama and fiction. If it is a play written for the stage, then it is impossible to assess it except in terms of audience acclaim, and so it is as fiction-to-be-read that he goes on to criticize the contents. After briefly praising the dialogue, he complains that the work plunges the reader into a state of confusion between reality and illusion, between waking and dreaming. He finds himself to be in a state of transcendent, abnormal consciousness, where time loses its reality. Taufiq al-Hakim, says Haqqi, lures the reader into his own escapist world. Since the new reality here portrayed is of a non-material world, it is dangerous because it draws the reader away from normative reality—to a weakly understood escapist mysticism. The only mitigating circumstance for Haqqi is the fact that a work of such erudition has limited circulation, reducing its potential danger.[11]

Literature—A Political Barometer

Usually Haqqi tries to assess the effectiveness of a story, whether derived from its oratory, its need to convince, or from a distinctive style and structure. Styles such as Iryan's, says he, are of the old school—pure limpid water. The dust must be shaken off the classical language, and a fresh breeze allowed to blow through. Since the new country is entering the international political arena as an independent entity, it should also enter the cultural arena, for its political status remains uncertain if it is not paralleled by cultural status.[12] His constant quoting of western influence seems to be an attempt to enter into a wider, universal literary tradition in which revolution is no longer necessary and individual experiences can be expressed. As is now well known, Haqqi divided foreign influences on Egyptian literature into two stages: the first, the "intellectual" influence, was European and American;[13] the second, the "spiritual" influence, was Russian.[14] Russian literature was concerned with spiritual freedom and saw itself as fulfilling a mission to liberate mankind; Haqqi goes so far as to link the political significance of literature in Russia with the rise of Communism.[15] By enumerating many foreign literary figures and suggesting familiarity with their works, Haqqi, as teacher, seems to want to bring to Egyptian consciousness an awareness of what is great in the west. Translations and borrowing are permissible preliminary steps, and he himself freely admitted to borrowing the subject of "Irony, or the Man with the Black Face" from Edgar Allen Poe.[16]

But it is not enough to cite influences. Haqqi as nationalist wants to secure a place for Egypt in the circle of international literature. And so he proceeds to compare writers with western literary and artistic figures—a proof of intrinsic greatness and a qualification to belong to a literary heritage greater than a merely inward-looking Egyptian one. Although this may seem to contradict what was said earlier about Haqqi's aspiration for a purely national literature, it is in fact complementary. For a national literature to become great it must be allowed to surpass itself, without at the same time losing its individuality. Just as some of Sharuni's sketches are reminiscent of Dali, so Mustafa Mahmud is comparable with Somerset Maugham and Georges Duhamel "who also began their careers as doctors."[17] Hasan Mahmud's work is likened to a Schubert concerto.[18]

Aladdin's Cave

What Egypt needed, according to Haqqi, was powerful writers with their feet on the ground and their eyes to the heavens, combining all that is great in western literature with what they offer as Egyptians. But who are these powerful writers whom his country needed so badly? Dotted throughout Haqqi's works are such names as: Lutfi as-Sayyid, Muhammad Abduh, Qasim Amin, Ismail Abadha, Shauqi, Hafiz Ibrahim, Yakan, Ali Yusuf, Muwailhi, and, of course, all the members of the Modern School. Nor is it only literary men who are exhumed out of this national goldmine; one also finds songwriters like Abd al-Fattah Mustafa, Fathi Qurah, and, above all, Sayyid Darwish, due to whom alone, Haqqi maintains, Kishkish Bey was made famous—a harsh blow to Rihani's reputation.[19]

But particular praise is reserved for the doyens of modern Egyptian literature—Haikal, the Taimur brothers, Taufiq al-Hakim, and Najib Mahfuz. Haikal is described as master of his emotions, unlike Lashin whom, we have seen, Haqqi sometimes criticizes for his over-indulgent sentimentalism. *Zainab,* Haqqi claims, was not the result of artistic fervor but of a cool, rational, critical spirit; its passionate scenes could have been penned by an Azhar shaikh.[20] Haikal had been taught control, firmness of logic, commitment, and, above all, courage, by his teacher Lutfi as-Sayyid. Haikal is even referred to as his *murid,* the novice in search of enlightenment from the master, and it is, therefore, interesting to note that Haqqi attributes to Haikal a mystical insight into the universal beauty of nature: while in France Haikal had come to see through the ephemeral manifestations of beauty to their essence. Each manifestation served to trigger, for him, a memory, and in this moment of recovery he discovered the depth of abstraction that had previously been missing.[21] In contrast, Muhammad Taimur is presented as a prey to the fever of art: "He did not arrange his flowers into a bouquet but scattered them as he picked them."[22] Through his enthusiasm, says Haqqi, he did much to break down the barriers which Arabic literature had built up around itself. Najib Mahfuz is lauded for his style. But it is for Taufiq al-Hakim that his greatest praise is reserved. Rarely do the fates bestow such talent; powers like his are restricted to the few who live in the upper sphere of divine inspiration.[23]

Thus does Haqqi see his literary heritage safely in the hands of the gods; its present greatness is merely waiting to be uncovered. But it is not to be the literature of the ancients, which precluded individual expression and style. Nor is it to be an irrelevant linguistic literature of biographies, *Arabian Nights* and *maqamat.* The Arab/Egyptian is sad, meditative and emotional. He is, in Haqqi's view, the son of the desert with his eye always on the horizon; it is, indeed, his privileged position *vis-à-vis* nature which excited the Arab's first creative impulse.[24] This seems to be an attempt by Haqqi to reassess Arabic literature and with it, of course, Egyptian literature as having an inherent predisposition to thematic profundity and not to the mere linguistic acrobatics of which it is usually accused.

The Dawn

Romanticism was the first reaction against the artificiality that had suffocated the true nature of the Arab mind. But this trend soon took an unhealthy turn, and Haqqi often condemns Romanticism as rendering emotions ridiculous. The next stage was Realism, also a reaction. For a writer like Taimur it was enough merely to describe a person or a place.[25] But such descriptions were usually of strange, eccentric people. Haqqi compares this stage to the few drops that precede the fountain of oil which, once liberated, gushes forth in luxurious abundance. This stage is a didactic one; no story could be written for its own sake alone; it also had to instruct or moralize. Literature was no longer an individual exercise, but was now a corporate responsibility to create a national literature. Financial gain was not the motivation, nor was personal fame. Literature could be and should be a selfless search for a national identity.[26] Such literature would then achieve universality through an intensified awareness of the particular.[27] With this new self-consciousness form would give way to content in the emergence of a truly national Egyptian literature.

Commitment

Such literature now had to be "local and true in its expression," not concentrated in the desert (a mere theoretical construct of the *jahiliya*), nor in the west (a blind imitative construct), but in itself. Haqqi recommends this direction despite his paradoxical misgivings that local literature could not stand comparison with western literature.[28] The author must first of all closely observe life around him and then "surgically analyze" the human soul, noting down carefully what he finds. Yet throughout this process the writer must be aware of the universal dimension of his work. Why? Because each writer is responsible for the evolution of his nation's literature, and by extension his nation's welfare. Lacking such an externally-directed dimension, his work is intrinsically doomed. Taufiq al-Hakim may be held up as the exemplar of such a synthesis: he based *Return of the Spirit* on a legend taken from the *Book of the Dead* in which Osiris, here signifying Egypt, is resurrected; similarly, while he based *People of the Cave* on a Quranic *sura,* his major concern was with the resurrection of Egypt.[29]

For Egyptian literature to become universal, each author must apply himself to all levels of society. It is here that Rihani failed, for he had limited himself to one class, the petty officials. Though he faithfully records of their activities, Haqqi accuses him of creating stereotypes guaranteed to elicit laughter, while remaining in their narrowly-defined framework. Haqqi also complains that Rihani's picture of Egypt is very negative; any goodness that is allowed to shine through seems to be presented as stupidity or empty moralizing. Haqqi compares Rihani to a foreigner visiting Egypt for the first time; he sees only the surface.[30] Nowhere had he portrayed the helpless individual faced by an unjust and hypocritical society, though the condition of the oppressed loomed large in the writings of the Modern School. Literature, for Haqqi, had to combine commitment and imagination, so as to draw the work out of its particular associations. Its success could be judged by the spiritual response evoked. Haqqi quotes as an example Mahmud Tahir Haqqi's *The Virgin of Dinshawai* (1909). The test of its literary merit was its ability to move a subsequent generation by the author's rendering of a national incident remote from their own lives.[31]

Each writer is responsible for the evolution of Egypt's literature. Indeed, whenever Haqqi senses an author's distance from Egypt, he criticizes this distance as destructive. With Isa Ubaid, he stresses the importance of the short story in the founding of an authentic Egyptian literature to illustrate Egypt's progress and maturity in the political arena.[32] Literature should combine and compare observation and memory so that descriptions evoke more than the present. Crucial is the ability to hint and suggest without overworking the theme. Isa Ubaid, for example, is accused of subjecting his work to a theory, at the expense of developing any imaginative element.[33] Literature should suggest, but also proclaim. If it does not ultimately serve a patriotic function, if its drive is not political, it has failed. Whatever aesthetic criticism Haqqi may make, there lurks behind this artistic facade an insistent call for commitment.

And so we can see that the writer, in Haqqi's eyes, is a tool of change. He is the individual voice expressing the desires and aspirations of his people. This neutral reflection plays a positive part in politics, as is illustrated by Russian literature.[34] Turgenev, he claims, helped in the liberation of the peasant, since he was the first to write of him as a person and not as an object.[35] Turgenev wrought his effect not through direct incitations to revolution or violence, but with the "sting of his poisoned dart."[36] Calm, committed writings seem to Haqqi to be more effective than conferences and overt political activity. Turgenev and Tolstoy are compared to elucidate what Haqqi considers to be the two functions of literature. For Turgenev literature exists for its own sake; if it can have repercussions, all the better, but its aim is not political. Tolstoy, on the other hand, required that literature express an ideal: even though he admired the literary quality of works like *Hamlet,* he deplored them.

Haqqi stresses the importance of a revised language to express a new political, social, and economic reality. He insists that the author be fully aware throughout of his intention. His language should be carefully controlled, not submitting to the hypnosis of sound.[38] With the rise of intellectual literature, where even plays, like *People of the Cave,* were no longer designed to be heard but to be read, verbal manipulations had outlived their usefulness.[39]

It is to the Modern School that Haqqi turns for a model of what literature during a period of change ought to be. These early writers, he says, loved Egypt, and longed for a classless society in which spiritual and intellectual harmony prevailed and it is in this aspiration that can be seen the relevance of the revolutionary literature from 1919 to the needs and demands of 1952, as indeed to all periods of turmoil and struggle for national self-affirmation.[40] To prove this point, even if only at a linguistic level, he quotes a passage by Ali Abd ar-Raziq which he claims no reader would believe had been written at the turn of the century. By reappraising these works of the pre-1919 generation, he can show their relevance to present conditions, thereby proving their worth as tools for revolutionary reform. At the same time, he is showing the vision and literary skill which allowed these men to rise above the material to the non-material, and thus to universalize their struggle for independence and authenticity.[41]

Methodology

Haqqi has himself called his style of literary criticism impressionistic.[42] His approach is highly subjective; his is a recording of impressions made on a sensitive reader, for whom the function of literature is nationalistic as well as aesthetic. As realist, Haqqi recognizes that life should be portrayed as it is, the object being a "truthful exposition" of society; as committed artist he must show that "truthful details" are accidents and that beyond them lies hope.

The impressionistic style that Haqqi adopts is due, he maintains, to a lack of literary training. Should he criticize according to established literary norms or subjective reactions?[43] By his own admission he is thus guilty of the two cardinal faults he continually emphasizes: instability or dilution, and superficiality. When he criticizes Taufiq al-Hakim, he admits to not knowing which of *Return of the Spirit* and *People of the Cave* had been written first, but "thinks" that it was probably the former.[44] In his discussion of Aziz Abadha's introduction of a chorus into *Shahrayar,* he first enthusiastically acclaims this innovation, but then admits that Salama Hijazi may have already used a chorus. He excuses himself on the strength (weakness?) of not having the relevant texts at hand.[45] When discussing Kosti Sajaradas' work on Upper Egypt, he excuses a foreigner for writing about Egypt—a practice he usually deplores—because this Greek was born in Egypt—or at least he thought so.[46] After exhorting writers to control their passionate expletives, because of the danger of ridicule, he suddenly concludes that what he has said makes it obvious that Romanticism deprives a work of any value, in the final analysis.[47] Such an affirmation is not the logical conclusion of a well-reasoned argument. If the observant reader thinks he has chanced upon some Marxist literary criticism, it will be found on closer observation to be borrowed, for no Arab has truly understood Marx![48] Again, when writing of Taufiq al-Hakim he asks the reader's indulgence: he is not going to make a comprehensive study, but is going to describe Hakim within the "framework of his age." He begs forgiveness for one, himself, who is distant from home, and who yet ventures to criticize; in the same breath, he deplores the empty praises showered on Taufiq al-Hakim by the literary men in Cairo. What criteria, one might ask, does he use to measure the validity of his praise, coming as it does from distant Istanbul, in contradistinction to that of others? He finesses the question; and in a moment of gay abandon salutes fiction, lauding it as the most suitable medium for artistic expression since it has not exhausted its potential.[49]

Haqqi tends to project and make general his individual reactions. For example, after reading *People of the Cave*, he assumes his confusion and anxiety to be a common dilemma. Having summarily dismissed biblical and ancient themes in modern literature,[50] he nonetheless quotes Goethe approvingly when discussing the use of ancient or legendary themes in modern fiction: Goethe had said that "had he been able to start again he would have chosen ancient stories and supplied them with contemporary significance," concentration being on style and literary skill rather than on the plot.[51]

Haqqi is aware of his preconceptions, but does not seem to regard them as faults so much as facts. Before reading *The Death of Cleopatra*, he had feared that Shauqi was going to write as a poet and not as a prose writer, and he had been pleasantly surprised.[52] His negative criticism of Lashin's "At the Bottom of the Pit" is based on the preconception that young people do not want to run away from home. He then accuses Lashin of inconsistency when the girl changes her mind at the last moment after thinking of her mother. Haqqi's argument that no child thinks of running away from such a home may be valid if the structure of the text does not allow for such a thought pattern, but he has not indicated that his criticism is structural rather than functional. And he claims that Lashin's introduction of the mother as an escape deterrent was an afterthought: Lashin must have suddenly imagined what his own feelings would have been. Another criticism is that Lashin describes the drunken father as sending his daughter out into the "icy" rain to buy alcohol. Haqqi seems outraged that such a preposterous statement could be made (ice in Cairo!); the atmosphere, he declares, must not depend on such a departure from reality for its effect.[53] In a similar vein he criticizes the image "the full moon was like a dirham on blue brocade." Haqqi maintains that for this image to be at all effective the brocade *must* be black; he also censures all images using Pleiades because this constellation cannot be seen.[54] The inner logic of the text which he had previously emphasized seems to have disappeared.

And yet whatever the mood of his criticism, Haqqi's style is lively and picturesque. Works are discussed informally, opinions offered, suggestions made, preferences stated, and all in a style that is polished and sometimes flamboyantly imaginative.

Above all can be sensed his eagerness to inscribe Egyptian literature into a major plan where all literary works are motivated by clear-cut intentions over which he has set himself up in judgment. But this preoccupation with the author's imputed intention can lead to dissatisfaction and lack of understanding. Haqqi criticizes *Return of the Spirit* for not fulfilling its "intention" of showing how the 1919 revolution not only united Egypt and returned it to life, but also placed it in sight of its goal.[55] The question is: did the revolution put Egypt within sight of its goal? And even if it did, was Hakim interested in anything beyond the unification of the Egyptians? Since Haqqi had begun his reading with a question that remained unanswered at the end, he could not understand the motivation behind this work, and felt that his misunderstanding was a common dilemma.[56] In Mustafa Mahmud's *The Impossible,* Haqqi's search for intentions has led him, he freely admits, on a wild goose chase. Details, seemingly pregnant with significance, are ultimately discovered to have no importance beyond themselves. Haqqi's concern with meaning and intention is so great that he cannot submit to the text enough to allow what may seem to be extraneous characters and incidents to work at another level—atmosphere, for example.[57] He has even called upon authors to state their intentions at the end, so that there be no ambiguity in the message.[58] But what is the message? And if there is one, has he not himself recommended that it be the reader who sift it out?[59] As he says, reality is something different for each one, so that however a work is presented it will mean something different for each one.

"Criticism is subject to chance and illogical tendencies"[60]—thus does Haqqi justify the neglect that *The Virgin of Dinshawai* had suffered. Haqqi's tendency to generalize puts him in charge of the whole literary situation, and makes it possible for him to fit Egyptian literature into a wider framework, so that any rupture can be explained away in terms of chance. "Unfortunately" many writers had friends who did not mix constructive criticism with their praise. "Fortunately" he had read *The Olive Branch* immediately after reading *The Virgin of Asyut,* both by Kosti Sajaradas: the combined literary quality and patriotism (even in a Greek of doubtful origin) had restored his faith in the future. The coincidence of the two readings has justified an otherwise unfounded optimism. The positive development of the short story is also "fortunate." Whereas a passing glance at Europe might have driven the new generation to a rejection of the past with its poetry and linguistic acrobatics, Fortune had intervened and chosen a birthplace for the short story which precluded any such danger: this birthplace was the Café al-Fann where a group of aspiring young writers—"fortunately" of different temperaments—met under the leadership of Ahmad Khairi Said. "Fortunately" the form of the first novel was mature and therefore worthy to exist and to be a forerunner—it could just as easily have been "hideous" and "malformed." "Fortunately" Lashin rid himself of his faults as he matured, since he moved from rhetoric to calm, though emotional, analysis, and stopped borrowing from western literature. "Fortunately" when the short story was in its infancy it required no incidents, just description. Haqqi claims to have chosen Mahfuz as his model for the contrast between "static" and "dynamic" styles, because "fortunately" he had moved from the one style to the other.[62]

The cure-all to such arbitrariness is, says Haqqi, a scientific method, removed from the whims of chance. Elaboration of such a method does not, however, seem to go much beyond a verbatim transcription of Isa Ubaid's recommendations in his introduction to *Ihsan Hanim* (1921). Briefly, such a method requires good, accurate description, "as nature is not improved by linguistic jugglery"; not only the beautiful but also the ugly must be described; truth should be the writer's inspiration; Egypt must find its independent place within Arabic literature, since Arabic is its language; secondary conversations should be written in standard Arabic with a few colloquial expressions; the colloquial dialogue should be treated with circumspection.

The faults to be guarded against are: abruptness, as each step should prepare for the next; "padding out" poor material; the over-use of conjunctions; exaggerations; over-simplicity, in that the work should contain the double dimension of an internal and external layer of meaning; *baina baina,* or the aimless floating around the core of the meaning; tediousness; pandering to the reader's whims; and finally, and most importantly, the writer must always keep in contact with the world.[63]

Another critical "system" that Haqqi adopts is the division of literature into "static" and "dynamic" styles. "Static" literature depends on a linear progression; there are no flashbacks, no dreams. The style is a careful, balanced construction and the language is Classical. The "dynamic" style, on the other hand, slips easily from one time sequence to another. The "dynamic" has rid itself of the stolidity of the "static," and the colloquial is used as much as possible. Haqqi has devised a scheme for the correct usage of the colloquial in literature.[64]

Concluding Remarks

Haqqi insists that an Egyptian literary identity can only arise out of the Egyptians' positive attitude to themselves.[65] He is very bitter at the contempt of the west for the Oriental, as evinced by books written on the eastern mentality without due knowledge. Sarcastically he comments on the physical state of the author of *White and Non-White,* Francis de Croisset: the poor man was on a convalescence trip when he wrote these memoirs of his time spent in India, and so he must have been too weak to make an exhaustive study.[66] Once Egyptians have regained a belief in themselves, their literature will then derive its inspiration from a national consciousness. The reason that literature had failed so far was that Egyptian authors had been cut off from the spirit of Egypt.[67]

But with the affirmation of such an Egyptian identity will come the need to find a place in the world. And so it is interesting to note that by the late 1950s Haqqi seems to be signalling a development. In his lecture at the University of Damascus in 1959 he is calling for a united front, a united *Arab* front. Egyptian literature it would seem has established itself, sufficiently for it to be able to join forces with the rest of the Arab world. The period of extreme self-centeredness has passed, and Egyptian literature can now incorporate itself within a wider field, a wider struggle. The Arab world must be prevented from splitting off into innumerable vernaculars. An *Arabic* literature must be retained, and with it a united political identity.

Along with concern for the universal, for that which was greater than the sum total of individual traits, came Haqqi's realization of the insignificance of each individual writer in the face of the communal task which contemporary literature was presenting. Haqqi actively demonstrates this subordination of the individual through his own method of literary criticism. And this he does by placing himself in an inferior position to the authors he is criticizing: he had been blind to Taufiq al-Hakim's genius when they had been in law school together. He emphasizes his abjectness in comparison with the object of praise through this Chinese proverb: Confucius said that those destined to "blindness" will never see.[68]

And finally we come to perhaps the most significant aspect of Haqqi's achievements as a critic, and that is the "recoverer" role. He is not only conscious of the recognized geniuses but has a keen sensitivity to potential. In his introduction to the 1964 edition of *Ihsan Hanim,* Abbas Khidr hails Haqqi as the recuperator of Isa Ubaid's genius that might otherwise have remained forever unknown.[69] Haqqi's importance as a critic does indeed seem to lie in this role. He expresses surprise that little mention is ever made of the literary magazine, *As-Sufur,* in which the early works of Haikal, Taha Husain, Ahmad Daif, Mansur Fahmi, and Ali and Mustafa Abd ar-Raziq had first appeared.[70] Had it not been for Haqqi's discussion of Lashin's novel, *It Is Said . . .* in *Fajr,* where he enthusiastically acclaims the maturity of these short stories written in the 1920s, the world would probably have been deprived of a story like "The Village Story."[71] Renewed interest in Lashin's third novel, *Eve Without Adam* (1934) is also due to Haqqi's discussion of it in his introduction to the 1964 edition of *The Irony and the Flute*.[72] Another person whom Haqqi feels that he has restored is Mustafa Abd ar-Raziq, whose collection of essays on the Azhar, *Memoirs of Shaikh Amir al-Fazari* (1914), should be reappraised as a collection of literary sketches. However, since there was no response to this "challenge," as Haqqi put it, it remains uncertain in what capacity Mustafa Abd ar-Raziq has been restored: merely as a critic of Azhar or as another Egyptian writer saved from oblivion?[73]

* * * * *

And so we see that the role of criticism for Haqqi can take three forms. First, it may be socio-political; with judicious criticism, not only literature but also society is bound to progress. Secondly, it may be apologetic: compensating for what is bad in contemporary Egyptian literature by the complementary discovery of what is good, and thereafter inscribing this literature into a wider literary field. The third role of criticism is archeological, to mine the Aladdin's Cave of undiscovered genius—the Ubaids, the Lashins, and the Hasan Mahmuds. "I hope that I recovered for some of them rights that were due to them, and had been neglected."[74]

But beyond the "intention" can be detected another function of criticism—criticism for Haqqi seems to be not so much the revelation of an author's work as its covering up; it is another prism through which he views the world. An interesting example is his study of Jahin, a man who had announced that he wished to be considered among philosophers and mystics. His quatrains, Haqqi tells us, contain a pervading sense of sadness, arising out of the contemplation of the universe and its secrets. His is the grief of someone looking into eternity—the grief is not his own, but that which he sees reflected in the eyes of others. Haqqi constantly points out how Jahin is longing for beauty and hence for God. He is filled with love and understanding of man's weakness—and this, despite his relentless criticism and satires.[75] How like Haqqi is this description of a man who ideally loves his brother man, but whose idealism is hemmed in on all sides by facts which he can only dispel with a bitter smile. The heroes of *Zainab* and *The Virgin of Dinshawai* are seen by Haqqi as educated peasants who are suffering from the struggle between their newly-acquired moral code, which has replaced religion, and their traditional environment: if they announce this code, it will be regarded as blasphemy and will lead to their amputation from their past. Moreover, since they are not totally convinced of this new code, which opens up prospects of loneliness and isolation, they do not make the break, because they cannot find harmony in themselves. This analysis can be seen to restate the dilemma in "The Saint's Lamp," where science and religion are originally regarded as mutually exclusive systems. Ismail's acceptance of the oil is the acceptance of belonging, and a recognition of sacrifices that must be made if harmony, that does not exist *a priori,* is to be achieved. As if to solve in certain measure his own dilemma, Haqqi wishes that Haikal had made the hero in *Zainab* break through this barrier and make a decision for, or against, tradition. Haikal had, however, merely made Hamid disappear without explanation. Here as elsewhere, Haqqi is not so much concerned with aesthetics as with his own predicament, and for this reason it is often through careful attention to his literary criticism that the reader can better understand Haqqi's own views.

Chapter Seven

THE STYLIST AS HUMORIST

The comic is possible only when it is accompanied by a momentary anaesthesia of the heart. *

Haqqi has been aptly compared with Jahiz in his satirical exposure of society.[1] Humor is a tool, not an end in itself. Although Haqqi often provokes a smile, the reader is rarely tempted to laugh; absent is the distance necessary for ribald satire. Unlike Mahmud as-Sadani and Muhammad Afifi, to whom he dedicated *A Thought Then a Smile,* Haqqi does not contrive humorous effects. His aim is never farce, but rather a controlled subtle perception of the absurd, a play on the discrepancy between appearances and aspirations. Though Haqqi deplores bitterness,[2] his works nonetheless display an ill-disguised cynicism which even the artifice of self-mockery cannot mitigate. Haqqi is always conscious of his reader as student and of his own responsibility as teacher toward this student. While entertaining him, Haqqi must also educate him and increase his moral awareness; laughter is a luxury not often indulged in.

Self-Mockery: A Device

It is for his period spent abroad in the Egyptian foreign service that Haqqi reserves his most biting self-criticism. This period is seen as a betrayal of himself: he had forfeited the sense of who he really was in favor of pursuing what he had liked to think he was. While posted to Istanbul, 1930-1934, he had agreed to join a group of diplomats who went to the Aya Sofia Mosque, not to pray but to watch Muslims pray on the Night of Power.[3] At the moment of accepting the invitation, Haqqi knew that he should refuse, and that instead of watching from the balcony, he should be down below praying with his brothers. Yet, if he were to do so, what would his colleagues think of him? Would he not have violated diplomatic etiquette? He even agreed to join his pro-

*Henri L. Bergson, *Laughter, an Essay on the Meaning of the Comic,* trans. B. Claudesley and F. Rothwell (London, 1911), p. 5.

fessional associates afterwards at a night-club: despite his feelings of guilt, he had to continue to assert himself through his function.[4]

> You have no idea how much I valued the diplomatic passport which allowed me to bypass the customs . . . pass through military barriers.[5]

From a perspective of thirty years beyond that period and its activities, Haqqi can perceive quite clearly the gap between what he knows he should have done and what he realizes he did do for "low" motives. He smiles wryly. Then came Rome, 1934-1939, and Haqqi finds himself looking back to still another period marked by the same naïve need for recognition. He describes his first visit to a concert. He had been warned not to sit in the front rows, lest he be overpowered by any one instrument. However, weighing up his aesthetic and social priorities, he found that the latter were preponderant.[5] Humor is introduced here by Haqqi's admission of his own foolishness and simultaneous recognition of the foolishness of such behavior in others: it was, after all, a group of Italian officials who had insisted on displaying their importance by sitting in the front row of the concert hall! This "schizophrenia"—being locked in his function, while at the same time being able to rise above and view it from the outside—grants an edge to Haqqi's humor: he faults others but also, willfully, cuts himself.

In this connection we should take another look at "The Mosque Mat," where Haqqi derives comedy from his perception of the gap between the official and the individual. Haqqi allows the reader to share the narrator's concern and anguish, showing the futility of any attempt to try and overcome the barrier between the fellahs and the officials. In amusing detail he describes the meeting between the village headman and the other villagers. It results in the general verbal agreement that each man should contribute a certain amount toward the new mosque mat. Then comes the loss of the *riyal.*

> Although I felt that if I were to pay I would lose the esteem of the villagers, before I knew it my hand was in my pocket. Then it was out again with the *riyal* between its fingers. Then it was touching the village headman's hand. The *riyal* melted out of the hand which then returned empty.[7]

Yet harvest came and went without the slightest hint on the part of any of the villagers that they were about to hand over the money they had pledged. They all claimed to have incurred crippling debts. Finally, the narrator was posted elsewhere, and as he was bidding the village headman farewell, he was still wrestling with the same old problem: should he reclaim the *riyal* and restore his standing as an individual worthy of respect, or should he regard it as a kind of official alms for the village? He was not allowed to resolve this problem, for at the crucial moment a she-donkey rushed past and Haqqi's donkey set off in hot pursuit: "Perhaps most of life's problems are resolved by just such she-donkeys."[8]

The secret of Haqqi's comedy is his ability to be at once actor and witness, participant and bystander. On the one hand is the individual attempting to see himself as part of a group, any group, and on the other is the observer who cynically points out the inanity of such behavior. It is in the simultaneous perception of these two attitudes that Haqqi defines a gap and elicits humor. In Istanbul he had gone to honor the Mosque of Abu Ayyub al-Ansari, but when he arrived what he asked for was Pierre Loti's café! This was no pious mission but the eternal quest for recognition. He had really come to sit where Pierre Loti had once sat, so that he might, like so many before him, regale dinner guests with the story. The same motive drove him to the Café de Flore in St. Germain des Prés, which Sartre had once patronized,[9] and to Greece to ride around on a donkey as Robert Louis Stevenson had done; and to climb up the San Marco bell tower. In this last case punishment came swiftly, since the bells began to clang thunderously, as though each one were intent on hitting his head![10]

A heavy smoker, Haqqi portrays the petty vices inherent in this apparently innocent practice. With undisguised cynicism he shows how cigarettes have assumed a ritualistic aspect. Just before leaving the room, for instance, a man may surreptitiously leave behind a pack of cigarettes as a bribe. Had the equivalent in cash been left, this action would have provoked indignation. It is the perceived gap between the ritual act and its underlying reality that elicits humor, or at least irony. Cunning schemes are devised to "sponge" cigarettes off others. For example, one man always had a pack with two cigarettes ("as though he always bought special two-cigarette packs") which he immediately offered to his guest. When the latter remonstrated, his host would reply that he would send for more. Hours—and many of the guest's cigarettes—later, the second pack had not appeared; it apparently remained "in the realms of the unknown." Again, Haqqi tells us that European women, though they had suffered unbearable deprivation during the Second World War, could not endure being deprived of cigarettes; they were prepared to do anything for a cigarette. It is through the dramatic tone which he uses to disclose such "plots" that Haqqi evokes much of his humor: thinking that he had had a lucky escape from a would-be sponger Haqqi is disconcerted to hear the friend, who had at first refused a proferred cigarette, announce that he would after all do Haqqi, just this once, the favor of taking the cigarette. Haqqi is not laughing at himself because he smokes, but rather he is using his "insider's" view to expose a reprehensible situation: "Were it not for man's weakness and stupidity there would be no market for this thin, despicable item."[11]

In condemning the Egyptian penal system, Haqqi also illustrates his point by a sketch directed against himself.[12] The anecdote is related in a racy, sardonic manner, and it is only on reflection that the full impact of Haqqi's cynicism is felt. Again, during his short period as a lawyer, Haqqi had to defend a boy who was accused of putting zinc into some bread dough. Haqqi argued the boy's case and won. Yet, thereafter whenever he bought a loaf, he opened it to make sure that there was no zinc in it.[13]

In "The Perfume Bottle" Haqqi relates Sami's adventures with a woman in Tahta, a village in Upper Egypt, where he had been posted as prosecuting attorney. This woman had originally come to him in peasant garb, selling *masli* (cooking butter) and eggs. After complaining of her trouble with the police, she seduced him. Sami proceeded to lavish a great deal of money on her. All his spare time he spent with her. Finally he had to leave, and although he had been perfectly well aware throughout of her whorish past, he had, nevertheless, determined always to act the gentleman. He never told her what he knew. The most important thing, in his view, was to maintain his dignity. He kept their liaison a secret. Months later, however, a dissolute dignitary from Tahta, whom he chanced to meet in Cairo, told him the amusing story of a woman who had gone to the new prosecuting attorney, wearing peasant garb and selling *masli* and eggs . . .! Surely Sami knew this woman! Haqqi makes the irony of the story more poignant by having the man repeat this question a number of times with disbelief, and each time Sami vehemently denies her acquaintance. The whole tone of the story is bantering: even the name Sami means "superior one," he who thought himself to be above all those around him who were doing as he did.[14] Haqqi has crafted the tale in such a way that much of it may be regarded as autobiographical: the true spectacle is Haqqi laughing at himself, at his inflated sense of self-importance, at his pettiness.[15]

Self-mockery, however, has its limits: Haqqi does not convey an inordinate sense of his own ridiculousness, either at the physical or at the psychological level.[16] Rather, Haqqi uses himself as a medium through which to convey ironic condemnation that goes beyond himself to embrace the generality of which he forms but a single instance. In his capacity as author he stands outside himself as a man, and seems to see others through his own weaknesses and despicability. Having established himself as the butt of his joke, he has set the requisite distance between the reader and the object of ridicule. The former can view the situation as funny precisely because he has not been compelled to identify; he has been spared the pain of perceiving himself as the target. Having removed the reader to a perch of pseudo-objectivity and detachment, Haqqi can then attack "himself" viciously, while the reader smiles indulgently at the spectacle of this austere self-critique.

Society Rebuked

Not all Haqqi's humor is self-deprecatory. Part of it stems from the ills which attend the establishment of a new order boding a complete break from the Egyptian past where man and nature could apparently live together as part of an eternal cycle. With the disappearance of the colonial exploiter, the 2,000-year-old dream seemed to have been realized: Egypt was at last returned to the Egyptians. The barriers between the Egyptians and the ruling elite were also removed: the one had ceased to be clearly demarcated from the other. Yet now dreams could no longer be viewed as fulfillable in some future world—the future had arrived, but the dreams remained unfulfilled. In facing the reality of disappointment, in looking at Egypt as it actually had become, there lingers the ideal vision of what it should have become. This interstice—at once individual and corporate, private and social—provides the source of tragedy but also comedy in Haqqi's writings.

The doctor whom Haqqi had known in Manfalut had once delayed operating on his patient until he had the fee in his hand. When the money was collected, he insisted on operating on what had by then become a corpse![17] Again, after the fellahs in Manfalut had spent much time and energy preparing for the king's arrival, they were not even granted a glimpse of the royal profile, as the train flew past with the shutters closed.[18] On another occasion, while attending a Friday prayer meeting in a mosque in Istanbul, Haqqi had heard the *imam* eloquently imploring his congregation to use rose water for the ablutions, and there at the door, much to Haqqi's amusement, stood a man selling rose water.[19] Humor in these cases lies in the ironic twist at the end of the anecdote: the doctor's macabre insistence on operating on a corpse; the hectic preparations leading to the pathetic farce—prostitutes lined up on the platform ululating, the row of dignitaries in full array and then the blurred vision of a disappearing train; the *imam's* hortatory plea—which turns out to be motivated by mercenary interests. In each story the bitterness is temporarily slaked by the pitch at which the satire is set.

Elsewhere, Haqqi appears to make a joke of the appalling eating facilities in Cairo, but the true intent of his humor transpires. It is not the food itself which he is criticizing but the social conditions that it betrays. On the one hand, you find heavily overpriced meals in restaurants where a smile from the foreign "garçon" will cost you a shilling; where a menu, twelve pages long, is produced but the waiter announces that only ten items are available; and when you go to wash your hands in the corridor next to the kitchen these ten items are further reduced to four large pots containing: boiled potatoes in one, fried onions in another, chunks of meat in another, and finally some red broth! On the other hand are the sandwich shops. But lest we mistakenly imagine that the sandwich is the answer to a cheap meal, note that each sandwich, instead of being a loaf, is a bite, and that the whole is accompanied by pickles tasting only of vinegar! Haqqi's professed objection to such a meal is that it is very soon over: at its conclusion, he must hang about in a café to while away the midday heat, waiting for the afternoon cinema to open. There are, of course, the omnipresent *ful* and *tamiya* shops for the cheapest, most nourishing meal in town, but

> . . . sometimes when I approach the door I am stopped as
> though with a blow, the blow of great sadness, of a frightening
> oppression . . . And then this blow turns into spit in my face and
> I feel as though, were I to enter, I should be burdened with all
> the cares of the world.

This statement comes directly after a comic description of pepper which is
so old that mountains of it must be added for any hope of flavor, of salt
which has turned gray by the sweat of nicotine-stained fingers, and of
beans which are as hard as brass.[20]

Yet it is in his treatment of women that we see some of Haqqi's most
virulent satire. This may be noticed in the ironic contrast presented at the
beginning of A Thought Then a Smile between his adulation of women
and the four ugly sketches that follow.[21] Alas, the door of poetry was
closed to him and he laments his inability to give eloquent expression to
his admiration of women. But then, without further ado, the reader is
plunged into the sordid, heartless world of vulgar, egocentric women.
Humor lies in the suddenness and violence of the dichotomy presented by
the lyrical lament and the contrasting sketches that follow it. As Luis Awad
has said, Haqqi is not smiling in this collection of essays, but frowning.[22]
Again, in "Sale!!!" the reader is made clearly aware of the dichotomy
between idealized woman, the mother in this case, and the real,
"unveiled" woman. From the incompatibility of these two concepts of
women emerges the irony that borders on humor.[23]

The last sketch in Mother of Miracles, "The Artist is a Visionary," is a
very short, skillful expression of the absurd incongruity of art's mechanical
precedence over nature. Haqqi relates the construction of a poem by an
infatuated poet. His head was ringing with all the exquisite phrases which
he wanted to write down. But he had no pen! As he was standing under a
tree and brooding over his dilemma, a dove dropped down and offered to
help. They agreed that the dove would give him one of her feathers. The
poet began to write, but soon the feather had broken and he had to take
another, and another, and another, until the dove—in her devotion to the
artist's genius—was denuded of all her feathers. But the poem was
complete. Now the dove asked the poet full of love and tenderness: "What
did you write?" And he replied, "I sang of the beauty of birds as they float
in the heavenly sphere."[24] Discourse has replaced life. In expressing the
beauty of flying, nature was distorted. The feathers, the instruments of
flight, have served to describe their own function, thereby losing it. Where
is the beauty of flying? It has been stripped of life; it has become fossilized
in discourse.

Haqqi is not condemning artistic expression for its own sake; he is
satirizing its assumed capacity to replace life. When it is art itself that he is
condemning, his criticism, though overlaid with a varnish of humor, is
cutting. He read some recently published works of fiction but was

disconcerted by the complexity and heaviness of the language. To the author he commented: "Since I lost five kilos reading your work, you must have lost ten composing it!" Much to Haqqi's disgust the author replied that he had written it with the greatest of ease. The confusion and disjointedness did not even have the dubious justification of being intentional.[25] Indeed, some writers indulge in such heaps of verbiage, says Haqqi, that publishers would do well to print only the first word of each phrase.[26]

In his humor Haqqi often reveals a deep sympathy, particularly for the fellahs, whose behavior and reactions are so different from the Cairenes' as to arouse a smile of surprise or indulgence. Some fellahs had once invited Haqqi to share their lunch of rough bread and onions. One of the peasants cracked open an onion for him and presented it as though it were some great delicacy. Haqqi ate the "feast," and the smell of the onion continued to permeate his mouth, tongue and throat until the next day. He felt as though his stomach were boiling, and throughout the following day he remained in a bad mood: "If that was how I felt after one such meal, what state must they be in since this is their daily fare?"[27] Again, in "The Mosque Mat," a group of fellahs had collected outside the village headman's house to hear a government proclamation. There was an epidemic among the chickens and the government had announced that it would innoculate chickens free of charge. The fellahs were amazed: what did the government have in mind?

> Are chickens human? Last year they gave me an injection that
> made me ill for a week. What on earth would happen to the
> chickens?[28]

Again, while standing at a bus stop in Cairo a fellah had once asked him whether this was where the "bus going forward stopped?"[29] Of a different order is Hilmi Effendi in "The First Lesson." He is a gray, flat character, living in a world of his own, not communicating with other individuals, not even his son, Yusuf. Hilmi did, however, have one redeeming feature, and that was the love he felt for his chickens, pigeons and geese. Haqqi suggests ironically that the reader may now be prepared to forgive his neglect of Yusuf.[30] At first sight this might appear to be merely a sarcastic condemnation, but in fact the comment does reveal sympathy.[31] In the new world that the train has brought to Dasunis there is little use for relationships at a human level. Individualism has reached its peak, and the fact that Hilmi does find joy in communion with nature, however domesticated, is a mitigation of self-centeredness. It is particularly in *Good Morning!*, however, that the reader becomes aware of Haqqi's attitude to, and sympathy for, the plight of the fellahs in their new situation. The first half, dealing with the village of the past, is full of gay vignettes of village life, where everyone knows everything about everyone else. Consider the dwarf: he insists on paying for everyone's drinks—after quarrelling yet once again with his wife—and is personally offended if anyone refuses! The second half lacks the light-hearted wit of the first, being a series of dry sketches interspersed with ironic cynicism. Its tone is exemplified by the bar-keeper. Important in the past, he has now become a grave-digger since, ". . . it is only in alcohol and in death that the true nature of man is revealed."[32]

A Sense of the Ridiculous

Issues beyond the confines of morality and society also spark humor in Haqqi. He is quick to notice the absurd in a situation which he can then depict in a witty and sometimes comically melodramatic style. Although he has attended numerous concerts and has a thorough knowledge of the meaning and also of the structure of western classical music, this does not prevent him from criticizing the ritual involved. What particularly arouses his amazement and mirth are the outfits that the members of the orchestra and the conductor have to wear. How could this cultured society encourage the continued use of clothes from another age, clothes which today turn the wearer into a caricature! Most of the tailcoats he saw looked as though the owner had either put on ten kilos since buying it, or as though not enough material had been bought when it was made. Such coats would more appropriately be worn at carnivals.[33] As for that lowly vehicle of public transporation, the bus, it is, in Haqqi's eyes, a mine of amusing anecdotes and comical situations. Although he was quite prepared to forgive the bus conductor for bumping into him— indeed, he would be happy to see him enter Paradise—he could not forgive this whistle that split his head in two. On the same bus he notices with amusement that the beggar, who had asked him on his way into Cairo for contributions toward building a mosque in Heliopolis, was now asking for contributions for a mosque in Giza.[34] A woman had once sat opposite him and on her clothing he had espied a vast brooch: the only value of the size was to indicate how little she had paid.[35] While waiting for the bus, Haqqi had come to the conclusion that the human race is divided in two: those who believe that if they leave the bus-stop for one second they will be struck by disaster, and the others, free souls who roam around carelessly at a distance from the stop, only to rush panic-stricken at the last moment.[36]

Sometimes, if annoyed, Haqqi will indulge in a mildly vengeful act that will give him much amusement. When asked by some queue-jumping matron to buy her a cinema ticket, his only revenge is to buy himself a ticket as far from hers as possible.[37] The only victory he can score against luxury restaurants is to steal every toothpick he can lay his hands on.[38]

Tourists are a rich source of entertainment. How strange are those creatures whose happiness is exactly correlative to the mileage covered, and who will find supreme satisfaction in Egypt, a land where men of old obviously had these very tourists in mind when they erected their most splendid monuments not on the sea, but as far south as possible.[39]

Haqqi chuckles merrily at the outcome of his idealization of a Roman violinist. One day, having caught sight of him in the street, he decided to follow him. They finally came to a café opposite St. Cecilia. As he sat there observing his mystery man he noticed to his dismay that no girl came to meet him; not even a cat approached. He just sat there chatting endlessly with the waiter and an old woman. What seemed to preoccupy him were not spiritual, aesthetic concerns, but the latest horse-racing results. And suddenly, Haqqi saw the musician's long hair not as an expression of bohemian adandon but as a sign of poverty: he had obviously lost his money gambling. The final insult was that he was called Napoleoni.[40]

Each observation of the ridiculous provides material for a vignette of Egyptian life. The fat man who has to push his *fez* to the back of his head to restore his balance.[41] The sausage shop next to which is sold men's hair dye.[42] The judge who asked the hashish addict if he pleaded guilty to stealing the goose.[43] The piles of papers that bureaucracy produces and which only serve as travelling museums of the various kinds of Egyptian calligraphy.[44] The assistant policeman who greeted his friend warmly by squeezing his shoulder as though checking a watermelon.[45] A rather more grim instance of Haqqi's humor is the description that he provides of a turkey. This turkey was bought to celebrate a boy's success at school. As soon as the turkey was brought home, it looked as though it had both epilepsy and eczema—it could scarcely move. When it had been grabbed by its legs, out poured the pebbles, corn, mud and beans with which the crafty vendor had stuffed the unfortunate animal before selling it. As it became somewhat more steady, it looked as though it were about to belch and ask for a fizzy drink.[46]

*   *   *   *   *

Haqqi's works are full of such examples of wit and humor. To Haqqi humor is essential to literature, for it provides the sparkle that momentarily deflects the author's ironic perception of the contradiction which he pinpoints with a smile. How cynical is his description of Nafisa, in "The Spiral Staircase," comforting Farghali after he had been bitten? To soothe him she gave him three fancy sweets; Farghali ate one but tucked the other two away in his pocket so that he might enjoy them later. When Nafisa noticed what he was doing, she asked anxiously if he were not worried lest he dirty his clothes! Haqqi does not achieve humor by farcical caricatures, as is the case with Mazini, but through his keen attention to the telling detail that has struck him and which explains so much.

In his works of literary criticism Haqqi will often mention whether the author he is criticizing has used humor, this being regarded as a great virtue. Already in 1927 he had praised Lashin's works for their humor. Lashin's use of humor, however, is much heavier than Haqqi's, and much more obvious; e.g., in "Hello" we are told of a young man who had only married for his father-in-law's money, and on the very day of his impatient divorce the old man died. Similarly, in the "Ghost Story," he "accused" his reader of beating his wife.[47] Salah Jahin is another author whom Haqqi cites for his sense of humor, and an ability to perceive and point out good-naturedly what is amusing in people's behavior. But what is most important about his humor, in Haqqi's view, is that it arises out of a deep awareness of the pathos of the Egyptian situation.[48] This analysis of Jahin's humor is equally valid for Haqqi's,[49] and it is interesting to note that Haqqi seems to be pinpointing the source and function of his own humor through commenting on that of another. At the same time, he stresses the importance of controlling humor lest it be used vindictively.

Haqqi has two eyes: the eye of a child looking at the world with amazement and amusement, and the eye of the artist seeing the world as ever new and changing. Because of his double vision, he sketches his country and his people with a gaiety and freshness that still, however, betrays an underlying strain of sadness or pity for the weakness of men and women. Humor is the tool for prying open the reader's awareness without burdening him unduly with rebuke and bitterness.

Chapter Eight

THE STYLIST AS CRAFTSMAN

The intellectual links now pertaining between civilized nations make us share in common conceptions and similar ideals. Despite differences in history, natures and languages which separate people, the human spirit drinks at the same source— as God alone knows. This explains how the literature of one nation, despite its local nature, can embrace the whole of humanity.*

The particular should serve to highlight concerns that cut across and transcend linguistic and national barriers. The book expresses our difference from each other—as thinkers, as individuals, as nations, as races—and yet at the same time it facilitates the discovery of our oneness.[1]

From the Particular to the General

Yet how is it that the mere description of an incident, the characterization of an individual, can inform beyond itself? For Haqqi the answer seems to lie in the writer's awareness of the universality of the particular events he is presenting; without such awareness the work remains flat and uni-dimensional. A man directly transposed from life to paper will not come across with the same forcefulness as one who has been molded and grafted from several living models. Only after an author has analyzed a number of individuals can he deduce common features, free of spatial and temporal dimensions.[2] These features can then be molded to form a new being which, however fictive, is firmly embedded in reality.

In "People . . . and People," Shaikh Mahdi is described in a comical fashion reminiscent of some of Jalal ad-Din Rumi's satire. Haqqi assures the reader that the first impression of this shaikh would have been olfactory—the smell of spat-upon wool, sweaty slippers and mud mingled

*Khutuwat, pp. 216-217.

105

with the perfume of clover and guavas.[3] Everything about Shaikh Mahdi was rough; his clothes, the touch of his hand, his facial features, his parchment-like skin, his voice, even his stick was gnarled and thorny. Although in this passage *khushuna* (roughness) is used only once, and *ghaliza* (coarse) twice, it is as though each word has been reported many times. The vividness of the description and precision of the details render repetition unnecessary. The old man had a long, solitary black molar which fascinated the boy narrator. He noticed how the old man put food between his thumb and forefinger, and then carefully placed it on this tooth. The little boy could not only see, he could also hear the shaikh sip his water "with a loud echo." Never had he seen anyone enjoy food and drink as much. The latter part of the passage is filled with active, transitive verbs to produce a series of impressions: separate sketches to be recalled in the future, when the memory has been triggered, perhaps by a hint of the old man's smell?[4] Shaikh Mahdi is at once typical of all peasants (his smell, his dirt, and his roughness epitomize the land and peasants), and yet he is individualized beyond possible comparison with any other peasant. This is also true of Haqqi's other protagonists: in "The First Lesson," Hilmi Effendi, the typical government employee "with a pencil behind his ear," had an extraordinary love of birds.[5] The school boy in "Aqrab Effendi," who had felt the normal anger of a pupil toward his vindictive teacher, actually exacted his due many years later by pulling out all the old man's teeth without anaesthetic.[6] In "The Postman," the post office employee sent to a village from Cairo actually succumbed to the common temptation of opening the villagers' mail. Each character is presented as typical either in his function, his emotions, or more directly in the particular descriptions: the common juxtaposition of turban/fez, galabiya/suit, squatting/sitting, which alone are sufficient to hint at a dichotomy in the society and more particularly in the situation being described.[7] Other signal descriptions are: "pencil behind the ear" for Gogolian civil servants, "fez pushed to the back of the head" for idle men, "unkempt hair, rubbed kohl and smeared lipstick" for women, "bent back" for the oppressed. Having established the typicality, Haqqi introduces the twist, that added element which makes the typical real.

Precision

But such a construction is not possible unless each detail be correct, for validity is dependent on precision.[8] The following passage illustrates the effectiveness of the carefully chosen word:

> Finally this struggler realized that with the effort expended he
> had bled all faith out of his heart . . .: bled it by depriving it of its
> will through his own doubts; and also bled it simply through
> exhaustion and ennui.[9]

The verb "to bleed" (*fasada*) in association with the loss of faith conjures up pictures of complete ineptitude and impotence. No other word could have illustrated the process of psychological debilitation so vividly, and the repetition of this word serves to emphasize what would otherwise have remained a vague impression: the sap of this man's life has been drained out of him. Without this precision shades and tones of meaning are lost, and the writer cannot penetrate beyond the surface. In another case, Haqqi writes of a group of men who had, as students, decided to meet annually on the anniversary of their graduation from law school. With the passage of time their numbers were reduced, and this year from the nineteen original members of the group only six remained:

أصبحوا الان ستة • الاجدر أن يقال: امسوا الان ستة، لانهم جميعا أوغلوا في مساء العمر . ١٠

This conscious precision is a didactic reminder of the potential of the Arabic language.

Haqqi accuses Salah Jahin of looseness when he writes of the *andalib*, the nightingale. Haqqi would have preferred it had Jahin passed from the *bulbul* (nightingale) to gliding birds and then back to the *andalib*. The reader would then know exactly what aspect of the bird Jahin was pinpointing, and by choosing the *andalib* he would have made his point with greater force. As it was, Haqqi complains that Jahin obviously had no idea what this bird was; in fact, he seemed to think it was some kind of legendary bird. The reader, says Haqqi, is confused: what is the author trying to say? Why did he choose the *andalib* in preference to the *bulbul?*[11] This example illustrates the value Haqqi sets on precision, and his familiarity with, and command of, the intricacies of the Arabic language. J.G. Hava, *Al-Faraid: Arabic-English Dictionary* (Beirut, 1963) and Hans Wehr, *A Dictionary of Modern Written Arabic* (London, 1966) give only "nightingale" as a translation for both *bulbul* and *andalib;* Lane's Lexicon renders *andalib* as a "bird of 1000 notes, voices or tails, of the passerine species. Said by some to be the *bulbul* (nightingale) or a certain melodious bird resembling the nightingale." To write well, to create effective images, the writer must be in command of so rich a vocabulary that he can describe any kind of bird, showing that he is familiar with the nuances and shades of meaning behind each different word. Precision is the secret of true communication.[12]

The choice of a particular derivative form or of a quadriliteral may have a significant impact on the sentence. In the following example taken from "A Strange Creature" Form V verbs and quadriliterals combine to produce the tension and heaviness of the room in which the feverish child was tossing and turning:

إنه يفرفر من الحمى، يتقلب على الجنبين، يتطوح بدنه على الفراش من اليمين الى اليسار
ومن اليسار الى اليمين بلا توقف، كأنه يتقلى في فرن. ١٣

By the very nature of its structure the quadriliteral is heavy and deliberate, precluding ambiguity caused by the incorrect positioning of diacritical marks and by fluidity of meaning.[14] The writer who chooses a quadriliteral in preference to a triliteral verb does so consciously; he is pinpointing a *specific* action or state.

كانت تصعد السلم ذات صباح ...،، محنية الظهر، تكحكح فرأت ابنها يخرج من الحجرة مهرولا. [15]

The onomatopoetic quadriliteral *kahkaha,* meaning to cough slightly, is here used of a mother timidly announcing her approach to her callous son. In a single phrase a whole series of actions and moods is enacted—of the last eight words three are active verbs and one an active participle: from the timid announcement, compressed into a single verb, to the quadriliteral participle *muharwilan,* of the son rushing off after stealing his mother's gold and silver.

In *A Tear Then a Smile, A Thought Then a Smile,* and *Leave it to God,* there are 131 quadriliteral verbs, of which only 43 are repeats.[16] This in itself is an indication of Haqqi's rich vocabulary and the precision of his language. The quadriliterals chosen are by no means common ones like *itmaanna,*[17] which occurs only twice in the three books studied, but rather *safsafa* instead of *abth,* and *nahnaha* and *kafkafa* instead of *harama.* He makes extensive use of onomatopoetic quadriliteral verbs: *jaljala* (rattle, ring, clatter); *taqtaqa* (rattle, crackle); *khashkhasha* (rattle, clank); *dandana* (hum); *kharkhasha* (scratch); *nahnaha* (clear the throat); *tamtama* (mutter).

In this search for precision artifice must go. The melody of language lies not so much in its sound as in the images it presents to the mind's eye or ear. There are rare occasions, however, when Haqqi will use rhymed prose when it is consonant with the meaning, as for example:

تستخلص منه العصارة، وتلفظ العكارة. [18]

Memory, he says, is like the stomach; it digests what it is given, extracting the sap and expressing (excreting) the dregs—the rhymed prose (*usara, akara*) provides the phonetic expression of the symmetry described. Haqqi also uses metathesis for closer identification, as for example in his description of Naima kissing the tomb of Umm Hashim in "The Saint's Lamp":

ليست هذه القبلة من تجارتها، بل من قلبها. [19]

Or, by careful repetition, he will create a most effective word-play:

أصبح السيد عبدا لعبده والعبد سيدا لسيده. [20]

In these few words are summarized the stages in the development of a relationship between an actress and her playwright.[21] Such devices are not mere rhetorical flourishes, but indispensable aids in the quest for precision.

The accumulation of details is a feature of Haqqi's style.[22] When describing Ilaiwa in "A Story from a Prison" as he entered his cell, Haqqi uses four similar expressions to indicate his confusion and stupidity: *ibtisamat al-irtibak, barid, sakhif,* and *balaha.*[23] The chorus member in *People in the Shade* is described as *mumtali, malfuf,* and *madkuk,* and yet he was energetic.[24] To emphasize the skill of contemporary writers at plagiarism, Haqqi uses a theft image and employs seven different expressions to illustrate the diversity and ingenuity of these writers' thieving tactics: *khatf, fath al-kahzain, qabd, taiba, nashl,* and *tadliya min an-nawafidh*—six words in apposition to the proposition: *makhtufa ghadran.*[25] When describing the various stages in a man's laugh, the accumulation of details is most effective: *dahka* to *hashraja* to *buhha* to *sula.*[26]

The writer, says Haqqi, must plumb the depths of language to discover its hidden treasures. An example of such care may be noticed in a passage where Haqqi describes a novice watching the movement of a master tight-rope walker. As though he himself had just seen this performance, Haqqi meticulously details every movement:

كيف يطبق بطن القدم على الحبل اطباق فك على فك، كيف يتم التوازن، تتأرجح الكتفان مع وثبات الوسط، كيف تمتد الذراعان، والى اين تصوب النظرة. [27]

The cognate accusative, *itbaq,* introduces the second half of the first proposition to complement and balance the first half; then there follows *yatumm at-tawazun,* which the reader has been led to expect from the very structure of the preceding clause. This phrase merely completes the balance. The staccato of the quadriliteral *taarjaha* interrupts the steady beat of the sentence, thereby illustrating and contrasting the movement of the shoulders—steady feet, rocking shoulders.

It is such powers of observation and intricacy of detail that achieve for Haqqi the precision he values so highly.[28] With precision of language Haqqi feels that there comes precision of thought, and he quotes Confucius' saying that the cure to social unrest and moral decay is the placing of words in their exact context.[29] Haqqi writes admiringly of Flaubert who had once asked a friend to check some medical fact in the Rouen Library. Although this information would not constitute more than six lines of his novel, he had nonetheless felt it essential that this detail be correct.[30]

Yet precision in detail does not mean photographic reproduction: each detail must serve a particular purpose, and every word must be significant in its particular place. To achieve precise placing a sentence may have to be rewritten up to forty times; yet precision for its own sake should be avoided lest the writing become cumbersome.[31] For example, one cannot write of a servant bringing in a cup and then taking it out again unless this repetition serve a particular purpose.³² In Manfalut, Haqqi had known a dissolute engineer who had allowed his house to degenerate into a miserable hovel:

> Within no time at all—can you imagine what the situation must have been after three months—the place had become a playground for mice, spiders, vermin and dust. Wine glasses were strewn along the corridor from the door to the bed, newspapers were flying around and there were piles of garbage everywhere. Yet the engineer, who was responsible for the tidying up of the whole village, was delighted with his life.³³

It may appear that Haqqi has recorded all he has observed, but on closer examination it will become apparent that only the salient details have been chosen: nature and man are cohabiting. In "The First Lesson" the station not only serves a remote village but is itself remote from the village, dozing in the fields. Its platform, the stage for the whole action, is bordered by clover, buffaloes and cows. So remote is this station that not even the slow, dirty trains stop there, they merely "linger" (tarayyatha).³⁴ Every detail emphasizes the dreamy lethargy of this idyllic setting. No contrived hints of the future drama. The routine of one long doze interrupted by sporadic activity as a train is announced. And in *Come to the Concert* Haqqi describes the members of the orchestra "trickling" into the concert hall, some carrying their instruments, others making their way to their drums or basses. The players then sit down, adjust their music stands and arrange their scores, sometimes with their hands, sometimes with the tips of their bows. Before the conductor arrives, suppressed coughs can be heard; there is a sense of great anticipation throughout the auditorium; and then the conductor rushes in.³⁵

In "A Story from a Prison" the reader is immediately informed of the status of gypsies in rural Egypt, and that through the reaction of a sergeant to his "gypsy" prisoner:

> Routine had deadened the sergeant to compassion for the men he threw into the cell. But with this particular man he was annoyed; his lips curled, his grip tightened viciously and he enjoyed cursing him and slapping him on the nape of the neck. Not because his nose had been offended by a horrible smell emanating from the filthy blue galabiya which was patched all over in dark colors—he was used to all this from the peasants who passed through his hands. No, the reason was that ever since he had known that the suspect was one of the band of gypsies whom the police were chasing, he had regarded him with aversion. It was not the look of one man to another, but the averted glance of a superior species to an inferior one. Whenever his hand fell on his shoulder, he was overcome by a disgust close to nausea. Gypsies! Were they really human?³⁶

The description is direct and simple: annoyance, curled lips, vicious grip— *mutadajjir, multawi al-fam, qasi al-qabda,* three participles alone indicating the sergeant's reaction: awareness of anger, to its expression on his lips, to action in his grip. Through three participles the whole process has been enacted. How loathesome are gypsies that even the tedium of routine cannot mitigate aversion for them! The vivid description with which Haqqi regales his reader is not an exercise in cinematic effects but a hint at what is to come. Only with an appreciation of the gypsy's other-ness can the reader hope to understand how confused, indeed how traumatized, Ilaiwa must have felt: a simple law-abiding fellah was seduced by a beautiful gypsy girl and suddenly he found that he was no longer a fellah, but a being who could arouse nausea in an emotion-blunted man. His confusion is well illustrated by the contrasting description that immediately follows upon the sergeant's reaction. This is no wicked gypsy but a pathetic, disoriented peasant:

> The gypsy entered the cell, on his lips a smile of confusion—a smile that was weak and inane and increased in stupidity and length when he caught sight of a boy sitting in the corner, and saw that he too was smiling.

Confusion, weakness, inanity, stupidity—each epithet lending force to the one preceding it. Strange attributes for a gypsy, for that is how Haqqi introduces Ilaiwa. The scene has been set in these few lines, and Ilaiwa's otherwise unaccountable behavior which follows has become perfectly plausible.

The description is simple yet powerfully evocative. And this is a fact Haqqi has often stressed. Simplicity is a virtue when it has been achieved through an awareness that it is not merely expressing itself but something else. Hence, its own meaning must be crystal clear so as to allow the perception to go easily beyond it. Simplicity should not be achieved simply, for that would entail a lack of appreciation for the function of language.[37]

Having introduced his story with, for example, a lyrical description of a bucolic backdrop or a vivid portrayal of his protagonist, Haqqi then plunges into action. Introductory passages, as in "The First Lesson," are often slow, drawing out the reader's interest by withholding the principle information until the end. In "A Story from Prison" the sergeant was described as perturbed not because of the prisoner's smell and dirt but rather because (and then Haqqi introduces the main proposition of the first paragraph and the theme of the story) of the horror induced in him by the gypsies: were they human?

In purely descriptive passages Haqqi does not complicate the grammar and structure, for he is interested in an effect that can only be achieved through richness in vocabulary and imagery.[38] The sentences are short, sometimes even staccato in effect:

ووصلتهما كلماتهم واضحة، وضحكاتهم كلها. [39]

تهجم الخيل، ويقع السوط، ويوضع القيد في اليدين. [40]

A precise picture is being painted—this is the backcloth that must be clearly defined so that it may then be taken for granted as patterns appear on it. Even the sound of what he writes is important:

نعجة هزيلة، لها من كل مأمأة جواب، فيه نداء حنون تخفي تحته ولع الام وجزعها. ⁴¹

Notice the soft, sad, nasal and liquid sounds. In this whole description there is only one active verb—*tukhfi*. This seems to indicate the ewe's impotence: all she can *do* is hide her pain and grief.

After Ilaiwa had spent the night with the gypsy, he went off in search of his dog, and finally found it dying from poison that the gypsies had administered:

> Its body was shaking convulsively. The dog stared at its master, a gleam of hope shone in its eyes. Then quickly a deep silent grief extinguished this light. Never before had he seen eyes weep as those glassy eyes wept. They spoke to him, saying: "Is this the last time you are going to see me?" Then it opened its mouth . . . But Death had already come and put his hand over this mouth so that it could not bark. Instead of a cry there poured forth a stream of viscid saliva which had welled up from the turmoil in the animal's stomach—pain such as no one knows . . . Gradually the dog's trembling grew less until it ceased altogether, and the flies ventured on to its mouth and eyes.⁴²

The naturalist attention to detail (i.e. the flies) makes this passage at once vivid and touching. Instead of a cry (*sarkha*) there poured forth a stream of viscid saliva (*suyyul min luab lajiz*)—from the harsh sibilant and guttural to the liquid and fricative. The death of the dog, which may be viewed as the death of Ilaiwa's will, is never actually expressed. Gradually all movement ceased, intimating not so much a change as the culmination of a process.

Stylistic Devices

Nothing in Haqqi's style is fortuitous; all is carefully weighed and planned. Haqqi has said himself in his autobiographical introduction to *The Saint's Lamp* collection that he has always been very conscious of style and has been anxious to use new devices.⁴³ He claims that "The Postman" is the first example in Arabic literature of the use of flashback, and Ismail's seven years in Britain are dealt with purely in flashback.

A stylistic device that Haqqi uses to great advantage is the Proustian parenthetical clause—the introduction of one proposition within another to build a complex structure, where attention may be drawn to a thought of perhaps secondary importance but which sheds light on the text at hand as also on an aspect of the writer's world view. The following passage from "The Turkey" is a good example of the cumulative effect of such a construction:

> My wife reminded me—how powerful is a woman's memory
> when it comes to annoying matters—she reminded me of the
> vow we had made that night in the middle of Shaban—it had
> slipped my mind, I had forgotten, or rather I had pretended to
> forget—how easy it is to forget vows—one is full of good
> intentions to fulfill them, but when it comes to it one escapes
> just as one escapes repayment of all debts—the man one loves
> the most is the creditor who asks for help, the most unbearable
> is this same man when he demands repayment. . .[44]

A couple had vowed that should their son pass his examinations they
would celebrate. This vow leads to a digression on vows in general, vows
which one intends to fulfill, but which then start to weigh as heavily as
debts. This then leads on to a further digression on creditors. A third of
this sentence is matter and two-thirds is digression. The value of these
digressions lies in the weight they lend to the passage: the reader is made
aware through the heaviness of the sentence just how onerous the vow
has become to the father. This introduction leads into a dialogue in which
the wife insists that lamb's trotters would not be a suitable feast to
celebrate their son's academic success. The homily on vows makes the
reader fully aware of the father's state of mind: he had taken the vow
seriously, had tried to forget about it and now pretended to his wife that
he did not know what she was talking about. Each digression, seven in all,
serves to create an atmosphere rather than to provide direct information
necessary to the action. Another example of the use of the parenthetical
clause is in connection with a proverb which Haqqi had learned at school:
"There is nothing like your own finger to scratch where it itches."[45] This
leads him to talk of his Sudanese nanny who liked him to scratch her back.
From the nanny, Haqqi moves on to a young couple who metaphorically
scratch each other's backs. The success of this sentence lies in the ultimate
resolution of the apparently contradictory nature of the parenthetical
clauses. In the first part of *Good Morning!* there are many parenthetical
clauses which serve to accentuate the slow tempo of life in the past. These
heavy clauses contrast well with the brisk, almost syncopatic style of the
second part which is nearly devoid of description. In *Leave it to God*
Haqqi allows his pen to wander from the "charm of oratory" to Hilbawi,
to speeches in general, to speeches in the mosque, to a speech that was
given on the occasion of the flooding of the Nile, ending up with the recital
of his own experience in oratory—the only link between all of these
wanderings is the word *khutba.*[46]

Repetition is another important element of Haqqi's style and serves to
provide a signal: "The house of the poet is full of excellent things, but he
does not know the art of stacking (*tastif*)."[47] The use of the word *tastif* acts
as a signal and refers the reader to *A Suitcase in the Hand of a Traveler*
where Haqqi has written an essay on the virtues of *tastif,* "which is
virtually unknown in the east." Thus, this *literary* criticism acquires
cultural overtones. In "The Chorus Member" Haqqi repeats three times

the phrase: "He is at the back in the shadows, content not to take a single step forward to stand in the light." This repetition and the use of the image of a queen bee and her hive serve to underline the message conveyed by this sketch: the man in the chorus finds his joy in belonging to a nebulous, but collective, anonymity. What is to be avoided is the loneliness of the lights.[48] In his long critical essay on the works of Ghalib, Haqqi repeats five times that Ghalib was always upright before his Lord. What is implied by this repetition is that however irreligious his life may have appeared, he had in fact been a pious man.[49]

Author or Narrator?

Although it is certainly true that Haqqi's main concern is with the perception of situations, it is also true that he has the ability to make the reader share in the actuality of such situations. This reader participation is achieved by means of a careful choice of narrative techniques, alternating between first and third persons, and an effective combination of both.

Through first person narration the reader, in an identification with the narrator, experiences the fact, not the theory, of a situation and is left to judge without obvious manipulation on the part of the writer. In "Mother of Miracles" the narrator describes Ibrahim climbing down the last rungs of the ladder of life: he was selling radishes on the pavement and suddenly he was faced with high-powered competition from Badr. As Ibrahim was adjusting to these unfortunate circumstances, Badr's husband arrived. At this point the narrator was obliged to absent himself for some time. On his return the narrator, and therefore the reader, is immediately presented with the effects which Badr, and presumably others such, have wrought on Ibrahim. He has become an incense vendor. And then again he is ousted, this time by a charlatan; and what had originally appeared to be the bottom rung of the ladder of life has turned out to be illusory— there are further rungs. Since the story is written in the first person, the narrator's absence at a crucial point has obviated the need to detail the stages in Ibrahim's decline. The reader is merely presented with Ibrahim's inability to withstand opposition in a fiercely competitive society. Even beggars compete, and Ibrahim is finally excluded from this struggle: the last picture with which the reader is left is of Ibrahim sitting on the side steps of the mosque. Such people are indeed at the mercy of the winds of life, to be abandoned by all, just as the reader, through the narrator, ultimately abandons Ibrahim.[50]

In *Good Morning!* Haqqi is again narrator, the observing insider on the margin of his society: the professor accuses him of speaking of the surface and not of the heart of what is happening. As in the preceding story, Haqqi can use the narrator's absence to allow the crucial events to take place. The full impact of developments is felt without any mellowing transition period, and finally we see that even the most important quasi-outsider is dragged in: he has brought news from the outside and acts as an increased stimulus to discontent.[51]

Although Haqqi's works could not as a whole be described as existentialist, in a number of instances he does evince a concern for the problem of identity. And this problem he tries to solve by attempting to perceive himself as two distinct elements, so that in the position of narrator he may observe his other self and by delimiting what he *sees* come to some understanding of what he *is*. But the problem is that we cannot define ourselves by what we are but by what we are *not,* and so Haqqi finds that the "mirror technique," far from enlightening, clouds the issue even more. In "The Mirror Without Glass"[52] Haqqi tells the story of the narrator's discovery of his double whom he eventually has to destroy to survive. As his relationship with his Doppelgänger progressed, the narrator began to feel that he had become food for this other. With this realization came revolt, and to save himself the narrator destroyed this other. Again the narrator is alone but with his identity even more shaken than at the outset of his quest. The anxiety of the lost soul and its ultimate disorientation is very clearly illustrated through the use of the first person, for this is a problem in which the reader must participate through identification with a narrator, and not merely witness through the eyes of an author.

Although Haqqi tends to prefer narrative in the first person, he does sometimes choose the third person perspective for objectivity. In "The Saint's Lamp," using third person narration, Haqqi retains a distance from a story that might otherwise appear autobiographical, and not therefore have the necessary philosophical impact. In "Antar and Juliet" Haqqi again retains the impartiality and omniscience of the author. To present a clear picture of the backgrounds of these two dogs which fate throws together, the writer must be able to rise above the plot to perceive both clearly. His sympathies must not be seen to lie on either side if the irony of the situation is to have its effect.[53]

At times Haqqi may combine these two narrative techniques so that the reader can look at the world through the eyes of the hero, and may then be wafted aloft to look down on a world in the making. This technique may be most clearly seen in "A Story from Prison" where Haqqi has established a break between the narrator, as hero, and the commenting author. The effect is to produce a double dimension of narrator-memory which shapes the past, and the rectifying principle of the author in an eternal present. When the interest of Ilaiwa as narrator in the gypsy girl was growing and his description was becoming more subjective, the author intervenes to draw an objective picture, as also to make concrete a feeling Ilaiwa must have only dimly perceived and certainly would not have been able to render so concisely and precisely. With the clear picture established, Haqqi allows the narrator to take over again to introduce the action.

When the gypsy threw her arms around Ilaiwa's neck, he was too confused to realize that she was not excited; but it is important for the reader to know that at no point did the gypsy lose control. Everything she did was calculated. The narrator, however, was too naive to be able to analyze his feelings and to reconsider what his emotions had *really* been then and when he had looked at her for the first time. At first sight he had not consciously found her attractive (the author tells us), but in hindsight he was reliving the past *as though* it had been charged with emotion. The author adds another dimension that allows the reader to understand the source of the narrator's confusion. This is particularly clear when Haqqi deals with Ilaiwa's dilemma concerning his feelings for the gypsy. What could he do about the attraction he felt for the kind of person he had been taught to hate and fear? This is the clear articulation on the part of the author of a quandary which Ilaiwa faced—the triumph of instinct, in this case sexual, over reason.

An event like the dog's death must be described by an omniscient author, for the process that this event symbolizes—the death of Ilaiwa's will—cannot be apprehended by the subject. Turning points can only be assessed in hindsight, when ordinary moments are invested with a significance they had not originally had. By intervening the author can highlight the occasion without impairing the validity of the narrative.

On another occasion the author intervenes to clarify what to Ilaiwa seemed inexplicable. The morning after the night he had spent with the gypsy he found that the girl had become cold and distant. Time passes and the author explains that she had grown sick of Ilaiwa's reliable goodness and of the predictability of this new way of life. The reader has already been led to expect such a development from the author's previous explanation that the gypsy had not felt passion in Ilaiwa's arms, but rather relief and safety.

Through the author, the reader enters the gypsy's head. He listens to the recitation of the story of Abu Zaid and feels the heaviness of the atmosphere evoked by the tale. Although Ilaiwa also was presumably listening, the reader is unaware of him. The atmosphere now is not mundane and confused but magical: a world in which poets actually become the heroes of whom they sing; a world totally strange and alien.

Then, when the action is once again introduced, it is the narrator as usual who takes over and once more the reader is plunged into Ilaiwa's confusion. Although "A Story from Prison" seems to have been written primarily from the narrator's viewpoint, in fact first person narration constitutes only a third of the content. The remaining two-thirds enrich a simple man's story that without this second perspective would lose poignancy and structure. The transition from narrator to author is smoothly effected within the same paragraph so that total integration is achieved. For example, after the author has indulged in an extravagant description of the dog's death, the event is taken up by the narrator thus enabling the reader to feel the effect which the poisoning had on Ilaiwa. Haqqi has achieved the intimacy of a first person narrative informed by the critical account of a participating outsider: the observer observed. In this way Haqqi has eluded a danger of the first person narrative pointed out by Barthes:

> When a narrator recounts what has happened to him, the *I* who recounts is no longer the same *I* as the one who is recounted. In other words . . . the *I* of discourse can no longer be a place where a previously stored-up person is innocently restored.[54]

Finally, observer and observed converge in the emergence of a third element: a change in the narrator's perception of time. When Ilaiwa began his story, he was reliving his past; details were important, and explanations lengthy. But as the narrative proceeded, the narrator sensed his companion's lack of interest, and the story began to lose its sparkle and vivacity; he was remembering with difficulty and the reader can sense a certain boredom in the narration, a heaviness that the excitement of the story had momentarily allayed. The narrator has ceased to live the story; he is merely relating and the pace of the story ends as it began—slow, deliberate, and heavy.

It is interesting to note that although the three stories of the *Blood and Mud* collection are set in the same environment with the same people sketched into the background, yet each story is quite different—a difference that is enhanced by the varying distances of the author from the action. In "The Postman" the action is told from the vantage point of the participating outsider. "A Story from Prison" is told as a "yarn,"[55] and "Abu Fuda" is witness to the complete separation of author from action; not once is the reader vouchsafed a glance into the workings of the hero's mind.

Imagery

> I believe that appropriate imagery is a noble instrument on which artistic style depends. The writer's philosophy is revealed in the aggregation of diverse elements into a meaningful unity. This is the writer's method of making a rapprochement between the material and non-material spheres. It is a measure of the incisiveness of his vision into the universe.[56]

Haqqi writes of the odes of the *jahiliya* and early Islam which were full of similes: after the first word there was usually a *ka*, *kaanna*, or *kaannama*. According to Haqqi, this was because the nomads were so accustomed to looking at the open spaces with the eyes of falcons, that all was described pictorially and in terms of other physical phenomena observed.[57] Imagery is not only an expedient, but is the yardstick of a writer's spiritual and cultural richness. In a world where language rarely renders precisely the exact shade of feeling, the image helps to define that which must remain indefinite and imprecise.[58] The image is the color-scale that contains all tints and shades. Imagery is not merely a simple comparison but a complex structure which infuses the material at hand with new life. And it is this life that is the aim of the best literature.

As can be seen from Table 1,[59] over a third of Haqqi's imagery is drawn from nature[60]—39.2% of a total of 418 images collected from the following works: "The Vacant Bed," "The Mosque Mat," "The Perfume Bottle," "We Were Three Orphans," *Leave it to God, A Tear Then a Smile, Come to the Concert, People in the Shade, Dawn of the Egyptian Story,* and *An Anthem to Simplicity.* Table 2 shows that more than half of the images drawn from nature are vehicled by animals—23.4% of the total imagery. Finally, Table 3 shows the heavy preponderance of wild animals (hawks, wolves, snakes, etc.) over tame (cats, chickens, etc.), mythical (Circe's pigs, griffins, etc.), and unspecified animals. These statistics cast an interesting light on Haqqi's animals. Instead of drawing his imagery from the tame world of domesticated animals, Haqqi prefers wild animals which never appear as direct objects of discourse. It is they who provide color and specificity, for instance, in the vivid comparison between the last two surviving Melvevi mosques in Istanbul and the severed tail of a gecko.[61] A rich man who had been prevailed upon to give a guinea to a poor relative felt as though a mountain were weighing down on his chest: he imagined a large army to be attacking him, tearing off his flesh, drinking his blood, eating his liver and bowels and crunching his bones. The army then turned into a fierce predator whose voracity knew no limit. The image finally fuses with reality: the man is described as actually feeling the pain.[62] In "We Were Three Orphans," animal images aptly illustrate the evil effect which social intercourse has. Upon his parents' death a young man is left with the responsibility of caring for his two sisters. The three of them live in harmony until they meet and become involved with their neighbors. Suddenly the brother feels threatened by his sisters; their eyes have become those of owls, their teeth those of mice. They were as obstinate as bulls, impetuous as billy goats. The neighbors, for their part, have become scorpions.[63]

It is curious that of the twenty images used to describe eyes in the selected works sixteen are vehicled by animals: hawks, falcons, and eagles—all wild birds. The look is direct perception, in itself innocent and "untamed." A man is described as seeming to merge into the universe through his look, and then as enfolding creation in the mighty embrace of an eagle. Notice the wild look which allows the shift from absorption into the universe to reincarnation in the eagle: the two images melt into one when the first subject is absorbed into the incarnation of the second as a legendary eagle.[64]

> With most people I feel that in their heads, behind their eyes there is a screen against which images are projected and then reflected back. But these heads (of peasants) do not have such

screens, because they are in touch with the secrets of the universe. Images pass through their eyes and drop into infinity, never to return—such are the eyes of animals, dreaming artists and some madmen.[64]

Through this image Haqqi conveys succinctly the significance of both the peasant and the artist in his world view. Each is inherently innocent and in direct touch with nature by means of this clear look that culture cannot sully. The moment of perception is a pure merging of observer and object observed. The look is the instrument of fusion. Although both the fellah and the artist are rooted in nature, the peasant, like the animal, is the passive receptor[66] and the artist is the active agent. By means of this living contact with the primitive in himself,[67] the artist can bypass his mortal self to achieve a measure of divinity through his creation. But before this catalytic process can take place the artist's vision is that of the peasant, the animal and the madman.[68] This look is not merely innocent; it is also piercing, since it contains no filter. Flaubert is described as soaring up to the peaks whence he looks down on creation with the eye of the eagle. His vision encompasses great distances but also the worm in the heart of the apple. Such a look does indeed hold the secrets of the universe.[69] Here Haqqi has given his metaphor a third dimension which grants it a life of its own. Not only is Flaubert able to view great distances; he has also acquired extraordinary acuity of vision. It is precisely by means of this extended image that Haqqi achieves full impact.

It is particularly in his later work, *An Anthem to Simplicity*, that the reader can sense the throb of a second life beating throughout.[70] This collection of critical essays is alive and teeming with images. As his concept of the artist and of art has evolved, so has his need for a language that will adequately express this new perception. In the title essay this richness can be clearly seen and appreciated:

Recently I read a short story . . . of the contemporary type. From the first line I felt as though I were being sentenced for life to hard labor at the prison of Turra. Not only did I have to cut up the gravel but I had to chew it. The words were searching, not my eyes. It was a fruit whose peel was a thousand tough layers thick. A hammer and much brain and arm power were required to remove each layer. Metaphors and similes were stolen by cunning, and the thief—in contrast with his contemporaries—is skilled in all the special activity of thieves: opening safes, climbing up water pipes, snatching chickens, removing laundry from the line before it is dry, taking brass cooking pots with the foul left-overs still inside, pickpocketing wallets and Parker pens, stealing televisions and radios and chandeliers by lowering them out of windows on the end of a rope . . . As for the words, they are a collection of opponents bound together. Each expression groans under the heavy load, fettered together by the toughest of ropes. Each meaning shrieks out for freedom and release from the role imposed on it by force. Philosophers act like clowns and clowns like philosophers. This is a writer who digs a well looking for water to quench his thirst. The gradual descent into the bowels of the earth has acquired a magic of its own; and suddenly he forgets the water and is captivated by the digging alone. His one and only concern is to plunge in . . . Instead of shouting out to us as he is diving down gradually: "I've got good news for you. I'm approaching the water!," his cry is: "Patience! After the deep there is more deep. Look at the beauty of the inmost of the inmost."

And yet I felt that I had to read it again, because it presents a challenge. And this is the response to a challenge. The next time he was trying to tell me a story as we were walking together. No sooner had he said something than he stopped me short, holding me by the arm and poking his finger into my shoulder, digging his elbow into my stomach and dragging me along by the scruff of the neck, saying: "Watch carefully. Open your eyes and ears. Take note of this word, compare it with the one preceding, prepare yourself for the one that follows. Beware of ignoring the unseen thread which comes out of it to toss about in the air for four pages, only to fall on to a word which is still unknown to you. But when you pass it, you will realize that it is connected with the word that had (originally) stopped us."

And so on relentlessly for every word. The stroll had become a series of stops. I was not walking at his pace nor he at mine. A situation that Pavlov should have investigated while research-ing into diseases of the nervous system, and conditioned and unconditioned reflexes in a man whom this psychologist has turned into soulless substance . . . Really he (the contemporary writer) deserves to have a corner in one of our museums reserved for him, on condition that he be encased from head to toe in armor like a knight of old with the visor down. In his hand a huge drill as a relic of a terrifying project to reach the heart of the earth. Standing on a pedestal of raw granite, his thick teeth glinting and shining like the tip of a needle.[71]

In a frenzy of images thrust one on top of the other the reader is made vividly aware of the dilemma of contemporary literature. Just as these images run together helter-skelter, so do the unlikely ideas that the modern writer juxtaposes. The difference is that Haqqi's images are held together by a thematic unity—the difficulty of reading contemporary liter-ature. The writer seems to condemn the reader to hard labor, and then it is the words which have become prisoners . . . then obstacles lying in wait for a password to evoke them. They are not part of a cohesive expression. Each word is condemned to solitude, hoping but failing to be the integral, inalienable part of a greater meaning. Haqqi is jostled by the author who rushes ahead leaving his companion behind. Finally, the writer—as had been the case with the reader—becomes part of the "word" tenor. Like his words, he is unreachable; he should be put on display in a museum in a suit of armor with his visor down. He is impenetrable; all the reader can glimpse is the glint of his teeth. So far removed is he from the common touch that he seems to be on a pedestal of granite. Writer, reader and text have merged through the imagery; there is a precisely defined absence of control.

On another occasion, language in one "who is panting his way through life" is compared to chewing dried-up sugar cane. In the hands of such a one the precious booty slips away like water through a sieve. Such a man is weighed down by his heavy armor. Although he came to be a hero on earth, his life passes like that of an animal without once stepping on to the battlefield. Battles may, and indeed do, end, but not because someone has won. Instead, they end because the combatants have to learn to live together; they have no strength to continue the fight. The image hurtles on: man witnesses life as though judgment had already been passed and there was no point continuing the fight. The cup out of which the fighter drinks is bitter, containing nothing but rancid dregs. Here we see a list of images, each one apparently inspiring the next by remote association, with little cohesion. Although this would normally constitute a fault, here it serves Haqqi's purpose since it illustrates precisely the imprecision of language in contemporary fiction.[72]

Ideally, the artist is not the confused individual so graphically described above. The artist is a visible branch and his roots reach down to make contact with primitive man. He is a mother embracing her baby in an ecstatic joy that has obliterated all memory of the birth pangs. He is the one whose bucket will never come up empty out of the well of life; his pen is the trumpet on the Day of Judgment. He is the sponge of the essence of all that he hears and sees, the camera without a cover over the lens. His stories are like bullets shot from the heart. He is the passage-way of the Arab house, leading the guest into an unexpected courtyard. He draws aside the veils of fog to disclose the perfect picture that the soul had only dimly guessed at.[73]

On occasion Haqqi may pack a story with so many images that it seems to swell and become turgid, the juices of this second subliminal life seeping out from all conceivable angles, as in "The Vacant Bed":

> On entering Raihan Street from Imamain Square, the left hand
> of the passerby will soon touch a small shop that he may have
> overlooked as he was passing by a row of poor shops . . . And
> this shop and its neighbors are lost behind a shabby veil of
> darkness woven by a spider which died long ago. Thereafter
> security, contentment, lethargy and frozen time have nested
> there.[74]

After the macabre introduction of *raihan* (basil)[75] and Imamain[76] in the first line, the atmosphere has been established. The street is indeed dead, buried under a veil of darkness woven by a spider so long ago that even time had come to a standstill and had nested there. The latter part of the image takes the story into another realm, not the real world of men but a timeless sphere where objects are not so much seen as felt and where the impalpable—abstract concepts of security, contentment, lethargy and time—acquire substance as the physical beings who inhabit this dark timelessness. And the shop is out of place, a mistake; and there follow three metaphors: it is a tumor on a smooth cheek, a prostitute among free women, and a leper in the harem of an Eastern prince. It is the contrast presented within each metaphor that prepares the reader for what is to come—this shop is an undertaker's parlor. These images have assured the author of his reader's understanding. Having established the atmosphere, the author can now project the story. The mood generated by the inauspicious presence of the undertaker pervades all and, as at the beginning, the impalpable acquires substance in the picture of the pickled aubergine above a vegetable shop—its seeds pour out as though the eggplant were giving birth to decomposed intestines through its torn flesh. Unperturbed, Haqqi proceeds to describe the customers with their mouths watering at this delicious sight, almost like vultures or hyenas. These images are later rendered concrete by the action.

Once or twice a month a car would stop outside the house opposite the undertaker's parlor and disgorge its occupant. The car is likened to a noble horse giving birth to death. Its strange occupant—"the dead embryo"—is the hero's uncle who is periodically let out from the insane asylum accompanied by a male nurse. He is compared to a corpse, and this image anticipates the end when the necrophiliac nephew takes over the hospital bed that his uncle had occupied. The hero is then introduced in an atmosphere charged with all the weight of macabre anticipation. His numerous failures in life culminate in the desire for a totally innocent wife whom he can shape, so that through her he may exert his will completely. This hope is foiled when he marries a young divorcee from Upper Egypt. Her modest looks and downcast eyes at their introductory meeting had belied the violence of her desires, which go from the bestial to the demonic. The image is pursued in the description of the young man whose spirit had been sucked out of him (understand: by the devil); he had become a corpse activated by a coiled spring. It was as though gangrene had eaten the flesh beneath the skin. Blood no longer flowed in his veins, but colocynth. When his wife left him after two nights, he turned to prostitutes in search of a passive partner, but all to no avail. Each relationship seemed to demand something spiritual of him, something he would not, could not, give. He then became interested in the undertaker's boy and accompanied him on all his outings to wash corpses. The climax—which the reader has been led to expect from the outset because of the nature of the imagery—comes when the boy tells the young man of an Upper Egyptian bride who had died on the night before her wedding:

Two ghosts slipped out into the heart of the darkness. One wild predator devouring everything, the other with his crushed, decayed soul abandoned by God's grace.[77]

The hero's craving for total surrender by the object of his desire had made him seek sexual satisfaction with a corpse.[78] The next day his family was informed that the uncle's bed in the hospital had been vacated—for his nephew, the reader presumes.

But the second life that Haqqi evokes is not always fierce or macabre; it is at times also mysterious, mystical. The following description introduces the reader to Haqqi's images for music:

> If ever there were a moment of purity, then this is it. The soul is ecstatic, free of cares, the brow is radiant, the eyes shining, the heart purified.[79]

Purity, ecstasy, peace, radiance, purification—all common terms used for the mystical experience. Music is the release mechanism from this world into another dimension:

> The entire (concert) hall seemed to be cut off from the earth and each individual in it seemed to be cut off from his life.[80]

It should also be pointed out that *infisal* (detachment) is generally accepted as a prerequisite of the mystical experience: separation from life being also separation from death and its terror, since within the very definition of life is the fear of its ending. Separation from life, therefore, signals the timelessness of the mystical moment. This becomes even clearer in the following extension of the image:

> (the experience) flung him into an absence that was in fact a greater presence. His insight sharpened and his feelings did not deceive him.[81]

Here is the moment of true understanding to which all mystics allude. It is in this mood of timelessness that Haqqi describes Wagner's music as sweeping the listener to the edge of an ocean where thunderous waves roll in, each different, each ephemeral and yet each containing a whole life.[82]

Whether macabre or mystical or natural, and whatever the ultimate purpose of the image may be for Haqqi in any particular context, the structure must be so sound, so rich, that it hints at something beyond itself without, however, losing its penumbral quality.

The Colloquial—A Literary Tool

The members of the Modern School may well have been united in their aim of creating a national literature, but they were certainly not united in their approach. And this was particularly true with respect to language. Should the colloquial be used in the dialogue or could the classical cope with the realism required by this new literature?[83] Indeed this was the single, greatest problem in "realistic" literature. It was not only the problem of how to write this spoken language; it was also a problem of when to use it.[84] Although Isa Ubaid had used colloquial for the dialogue to introduce vitality into the text, Haqqi accused him of failing in the successful, overall implementation of the colloquial. The reason for the failure Haqqi attributed to Ubaid's over-concentration on the form of the colloquial, which led him to pay insufficient attention to the context.[85] Another problem of the colloquial was whether it should be used for the internal monologue; for instance, in plays.[86] Such were the problems recurringly faced by the nationalists in the 1920s as they tried to create original and individual literature that went beyond the limitations of a classical heritage and borrowed genres.

It seems that it was politicians like Abdallah Nadim who first made current the introduction of the colloquial into written works, since its directness and naturalness broke down barriers which the classical had imposed between the speaker and all but the educated minority of his audience.[87] Among the first fiction writers of the twentieth century who used the colloquial, Haqqi cites Mahmud Tahir Haqqi (his uncle), Lashin, Muhammad Taimur and Haikal, although he does accuse Taimur of translating classical thoughts into colloquial written dialogue (for instance, in the play *Tabib al-markaz*).[88]

Although Haqqi was an avid supporter of the classical, he readily recognized that the judicious use of the colloquial had become indispensable to literature, particularly a committed literature. But it was necessary, he thought, to draw up a list of rules for the inclusion of the colloquial into literature. First, the vernacular should be used when the classical cannot provide the exact meaning and allusion sought in a particular word; it is not to be regarded as an easy way out for the author or for the reader.[90] Second, the form of the colloquial word should be close to the classical. Third, the colloquial word or phrase should be introduced into the sentence exactly as it might be used by the people, not subjecting it to rules of grammar (dual, broken or sound plurals, etc.). Fourth, colloquial conventions should not be followed (e.g., prefixing *ba* to an imperfect verb or suffixing *shin* to a verb to indicate the negative). Finally, and most importantly, the colloquial expression should have as much, if not more, merit or weight (*shahna*) as a possible classical equivalent.[91] It should illustrate by its use the good taste, wit and originality of the speaker, and by extension of all users of the colloquial. As Vial has said, this last rule would seem to justify inconsistencies in the other rules and their applications.[92] The question then arises: what is the norm for good taste? Indeed, Haqqi's discussion of the cunning of the colloquial would seem to contradict this thesis. Haqqi has said that the colloquial has many words and expressions for rancor and the taking of revenge, whereas it has only one expression for forgiveness: *al-musamih karim*.[93] Taking revenge is like a fetus growing in a womb, or like a chicken brooding on its eggs—nothing will divert its attention until the eggs have hatched. When he goes to work in the morning, the man seeking vengeance must not leave his rancor (*daghina*) behind, but must hide it where no one would dream of looking—under his tooth. Rancor has become like chewing tobacco: the mouth waters, the spit is swallowed with pleasure, but the lips are not once licked. Nothing shows, because the pleasure at the thought of revenge is totally private. It can even be hidden in the pocket. If this man should meet his victim in the street and his plan has not yet come to full fruition, he will greet him warmly, smiling the while, for there is still much time. Haqqi's explanation is that the colloquial does not "beat about the bush" in its attempt to express what is good, but becomes highly devious and ingenious when expressing the unpleasant![94]

Haqqi does not use the colloquial for all his dialogue, but rather introduces it as a tool to help him achieve an atmosphere. In "The Saint's Lamp," when Ismail returned from England and was waiting outside his parents' house, Fatima calls out *"min?"*[95] This simple colloquial word is interjected at a most significant moment, for it is to the Egyptian abroad that the colloquial has such a magic ring.[96] Later, when Ismail realized that Fatima had been treated with the saint's oil throughout his absence, he lost control, and shouted angrily at his mother in the colloquial; but then when he began to talk of his scientific plans, he reverted to the classical. The break occurs in the very same sentence:

أهي دي أم هاشم بتاعتكم هي اللي ح تجيب للبنت العمى// سترون كيف أداويها فتنال على يدي أنا الشفاء الذي لم تجده عند الست أم هاشم.

His mother's colloquial reply is an attempt to sooth Ismail, and finally his father intervenes with the distance, restraint, and sadness of the classical. When Ismail broke the lamp, Shaikh Dirdiri intervened at the point that the congregation attacked Ismail and explained in the colloquial that Ismail was of the neighborhood. It is important to establish a totally local atmosphere at this juncture. When Ismail entered the Zainab mosque during Ramadan, he was coming humbly and the words which he respectfully directed to Shaikh Dirdiri were in the classical. The shaikh's reply, however, was in the colloquial, as though he was breaking the distance and restraint imposed by the classical and was warmly accepting Ismail back into the fold in the language of his past.[97]

In "A Strange Creature" the colloquial is again used as a tool to create the required atmosphere. Mimi's mother, even when talking to her son, does not employ the colloquial. And yet, when Mimi offered his uncle the sweet, he said: *"di alshanik."*[98] The simplicity of this colloquial phrase contrasts well with the formality previously established by details such as the mother's language to her son.

The colloquial is not limited to the dialogue by any means. It may be introduced into the narrative, a few apposite colloquial words, and a different atmosphere is evoked. In "The First Lesson" the words "south" and "north" are rendered throughout by *qibli* and *bahri*. Extensive use is made of words such as *ballas* and *halla* which are visually evocative, establishing a purely Egyptian *rif* atmosphere. Also evocative is Haqqi's discussion of foods such as *masli* and *fisikh* (small salted fish); or of clothes such as the *lubda* (felt skull cap) and *zabut* (low-necked woollen garment worn by peasants), or of vendors' cries such as *quta* (tomatoes) and *faraula* (strawberries).

Haqqi uses many colloquial words and phrases in the bulk of his text where there is no simple classical equivalent that would render exactly the required meaning,[99] e.g., *shamlul* (lively), *taslaqa* (to budge), *farfasha* (luxury), *ummal ad-darisa* (railroad section gang) and *khusa* (plaitwork of palm leaves used to line a fez).

Haqqi has warned that to use the colloquial successfully requires great skill. The classical must not be thereby debased, and the distance between these two languages must be maintained without artifice or constraint. A dangerous merging of the classical into the colloquial may be seen in Jahin's quatrains, but in this case it was a sign of the writer's skill: Haqqi claims not to have realized at first that the quatrains were written in colloquial.[100] Here again the reader may notice how Haqqi relies on consensus for his judgment.[101] Whereas in other less-known and less-acclaimed writers this constitutes a serious fault, Jahin's literary production is unquestionably of considerable merit and therefore this fault has become a virtue; it is not in danger of rendering his language "unstable."[102]

Tarib

Having established a truly Egyptian atmosphere, Haqqi sometimes introduces a word which may either render simply and precisely an idea that would be too complicated to express in Arabic,[103] or it may be introduced to shock the reader. In *Leave It to God,* Haqqi describes the revolution that occurred in the life of a rich peasant when he was visited by an inspector from the Ministry of the Interior. He was warned beforehand that such a person must be correctly entertained with the proper *brutukul* and *itikit.* What was most important was that the proper alcoholic beverages be served: *abiritif* of Italian *firmut* and *sinzanu,* followed by vintage French red wine and then German Rhine wines, then French *shambaniya,* and with coffee *kuniyak* and *likur.* This is the *hai laif* which is so alien to a Muslim peasant. The detailed list of specific drinks, that conjures up images of sophisticated European society, even sounds odd to the western reader. Here is a peasant who had been a pious Muslim, never allowing a day to elapse without performing the dawn prayer in the mosque, and then with the visit of the inspector western ideas entered his home, disrupting his accustomed way of life. He died an alcoholic.[104] This disruption is rendered phonetically by the introduction into a purely Arabic text of the foreign names and types of alcohol.

There are occasions when Haqqi will show that although the foreign word is the best in a particular situation, this does not mean that a classical or colloquial equivalent does not exist. This may be seen in the first essay of *People in the Shade,* "Kumbars." Although the word that he usually uses for "chorus member" is *kumbars,* from the French *comparse,* meaning a mute character at the theater, in the last paragraph he uses *sanida* and *batana* (p. 12), thereby clarifying his use of *kumbars.* Whereas in the past the chorus, *sanida* or *batana,* had been a motley crowd of individuals, the *kumbars* is an anonymous part of a uniform whole: he is *of* the west. His use of the English word *kurus* serves the same function as the French *kumbars.*[105]

*   *   *   *   *

Thought, claims Haqqi, is not the realm of the unknown or the ineffable; thought is the realm of the explicit. Expression may indeed be complex and laborious,[106] but ultimately no thought can escape the net of language:

> Language is the refuge of beauty, of all meanings; whenever a
> man calls on language it thinks and speaks for him, melting into
> a melody.

It is a melody that cannot be heard but to which the soul responds, a melody that arises out of an inner stream which then turns into a mighty river polishing stones on the way.[107]

But how is it that words can become music, that concrete can become fluid? The art lies in the total mastery of language, in the appreciation of the word and the subtleties it holds. There will be no literature until words cease to be limited to their literal meanings and are given symbolic ones.[108] Arabic, asserts Haqqi sentimentally, has an advantage over other languages in that each word contains within itself a wealth of definitions; one word alone may provide the exact shade of meaning required by its careful selection and positioning.[109] This is the advantage of words above colors and tunes: the word brings with it a world of connotations and associations which can only be realized by a complex juxtaposition of individual colors or notes. Once it has been attached to a particular word image, the recorded word may assume a new shade of meaning having no connection with the root definition that had inspired it.[110] Thought may exceed the capacity of a particular writer, but it is not beyond the capacity of language:[111]

> Language is a thread that cannot be grasped or defined. It must
> be held from its beginning and followed through until the
> searcher finds and understands what is being revealed. Like an
> iceberg . . . only a very small part above the surface can be seen,
> and this is carried and moved by what is below.[112]

Chapter Nine

THE STYLIST AS STORY-TELLER

The basis of all literature, says Haqqi, should be a kind of dossier which the writer compiles from his observations so that characters appear to be solid, rounded figures, and not merely products of the writer's imagination. In his *Dawn of the Egyptian Story,* Haqqi quotes Isa Ubaid: fiction had failed in Egypt because writers had strayed too far from fact and had allowed themselves to sink into the world of their imaginations.[1] The problem with such criticism is that, carried to an extreme, it would seem to bless the purely photographic approach where everything is recorded but never analyzed.[2] For Haqqi, realistic literature has to be more than a mere recording of facts with a moral message—if it deserves the appellation of literature.[3] Indeed, he censures blatant moralizing and complacent preaching.[4] Haqqi is concerned not to provide a solution for social problems, but instead to ask questions and make his reader aware.[5] Rather than copy reality faithfully, literature should *appear* to do so. When the work of art is completed, the artist should feel satisfied that he has banished the principle of illusion (*wahm*) from the reader's mind: "Reality is a lie in an artistic work if it does not serve the purpose of the whole."[6] Although Haqqi does not abjure the reformist orientation of the Modern School, he does disagree as to the literary form that a cry for reform and social awareness should take:[7] he is calling on the artist to limit himself to illustration and not to judgment, because "Fiction is not a moral case."[8]

In "The Spiral Staircase" Haqqi relates the story of a poor laundry boy who is bitten by a dog when he goes to the front, instead of the back, door of a customer's flat. Vividly and sympathetically Farghali is described, and the reader is forced to smile at the picture of this little boy in a huge sweater with his white skull-cap resting on his ears. The reader is taken through the boy's anxieties, as he works out the ethics of asking the woman for the money he had lost due to the bite. His shock at the end when he is turned away by the cook is the only comment Haqqi is willing to make. The story itself has been carefully structured around the event, which starkly contrasts Farghali and Nafisa; the distance between them has been highlighted by the temporary rapprochement between the two poles. Haqqi has the ability to make his reader experience the protagonist's dilemma, arousing sympathy through identification with the wronged individual. There are no sermon-like warnings, no blatant morals to be drawn; all we have is a sad story that has moved us.

In "The First Lesson," Haqqi begins his study of a railway station in Lower Egypt with a simple description. The platform bordered by maize stalks and passing buffaloes contains no inherent threat or sense of doom. This is not the pervasive greyness, heaviness and ominousness of Gerhardt Hauptmann's *Bahnwaerter Thiel.* Nature is presented with such warmth and life that the reader is made to perceive it as separate from man and his ephemerality. And then, against this static background of the infinity of nature, Haqqi introduces the action. Drama suddenly pervades the whole of the story, even encompassing nature—the day of the accident it was raining and the sky was heavy with dark clouds. And yet, despite the horror of the accident, the reader perceives it as part of a static situation in which death is an eternally recurring phenomenon, part of an infinite cycle. What is interesting to notice is how Haqqi prepares his reader for the action. In a short, descriptive passage he introduces a sense of foreboding:

> At that time the boy was seven years old and the man was in his fifties. One by one the boy's adult teeth were growing in, and one by one the man's teeth were falling out. The boy knew nothing of life other than this station platform, the man had known both its sweetness and its bitterness . . . Their hearts were learning the meaning of true friendship. For the one, unfortunately, this came too late. For the other, unfortunately also, it came too early.[9]

The contrast between the two has been brought out in such a fashion that it has become a factor linking them to one another. But it is in the last line that the hint of the dramatic climax comes. How can love come too early? Yusuf's affection for the man who was killed by the train (the symbol of the government, of modernization) was destined to turn his innocence into bitterness, the condition Amm Khalil had been in when they had met. A cycle has been completed too quickly, and this is the heart of the drama: the tragedy of the child grown old before its time.

The accident itself is graphically described from the moment when Amm Khalil's foot slips between the platform and the train, to the moment when his mutilated body rolls to within a few yards of his fragrant hut. And of this horrific scene not a single detail has escaped the boy. For fourteen breathless lines Amm Khalil's body is being torn to shreds, and then, as suddenly as it began, the incident is over; the language returns to its previous measured pace with Form I verbs predominating: "When Yusuf's train came (*jaa*) his father pushed (*dafaa*) him on roughly, because he didn't want (*kana yawadd*) to go (*yadhhab*) to school that day."[10] No emotion, just a benumbed statement of fact. It is the simplicity that is so moving. After such a nightmare what language is adequate to describe the emotions of the witness? It is in what is *not* said that the measure of the reaction lies.[11] His confusion in class is again mute. His eyes follow the teacher as the latter moves among the rows of desks, supervising an essay on "The Advantages of the Railway"—what irony! Yusuf's glance became confused. Suddenly he felt alienated from them all. He was as blank and empty as the sheet of paper in front of him on the desk.[12] The reader experiences not so much shock at the horror of the accident as sadness and pity. The reader was with the hero at the crucial moment. Violence has been superficially imposed on a calm background. By going beyond the severed head to the ironic classroom situation, Haqqi has placed the event in a universalistic context. At a particular level, it was but one of many accidents that took place when the train was first introduced into the Egyptian countryside.[13] At a universal level, it has become part of the natural cycle, throwing the boy into adulthood. It is the intrusion of violence which supplies the turning-point in the character's life.

"A Strange Creature" is another example of an effectively structured story. This again deals with the affection that has grown up between an older man and a boy—here a bachelor uncle and his nephew, Mimi. After the initial mistrust of the boy had been somewhat allayed, he started to play with his uncle, dragging the newspaper from him. One day instead of tugging at the paper, he unexpectedly put his arm around the man's shoulders and, thrusting his little fist under his uncle's nose, offered him a sticky sesame sweet. Some time later Mimi was feverish and spent a turbulent night during which his uncle was wracked with anxiety. His only comfort was the taste of sesame. Although quite some time had elapsed between the truce and the fever incident, Haqqi writes the two events in quick succession to emphasize the importance of their association in the bachelor's extreme reaction. It is the repetition of the taste of the sesame on the uncle's lips which gives the story its poignance.

In some instances, whatever message Haqqi may wish to convey is obscured by the story itself. Transparence vanishes, and the reader is caught up in the protagonist's fate, not what he is supposed to represent. In "Abu Fuda," after fifteen years' hard work at the prison of Turra, Jasir is returning to the only home that he knows—that of his cousin, Ismail, and his northern wife, Narjis. Having set the scene, Haqqi immediately warns the reader that something is about to happen, and this he does by making Ismail protest in dismay at the prospect of Jasir's arrival—hardly the sentiment that the reader is expecting from a cousin! And then, as though to sooth the reader, Haqqi concludes the first section with a brief, but vivid, description of a sunset, the time when all have returned home with their livestock to rest their exhausted limbs. In the lethargy of such an atmosphere calamities seem very distant. And yet, the very next section begins with a renewed emphasis on the future drama:

the saying goes that there will never be peace as long as there are two men and one woman under the same roof. It may here be objected that Haqqi has overplayed his hand, that surely one warning should be sufficient to prepare the reader. But something more is at stake in this second comment. It serves to diminish the particular quality of the story and to render it universally applicable; i.e., it does not matter that it was Jasir with his prison record and proverbial toughness who is the hero and that Narjis was a "free" woman, for the nature of the *situation* was such that it would allow of no other development. Having more or less set the conditions for a situational, rather than a character, drama, Haqqi then uses the rest of the story to develop the characters so that the logical inevitability of the situation becomes obscured behind psychological drives. Jasir's fifteen years had convinced him that all that mattered was freedom, and so he spent his first few days wandering around the fields, or sitting in Khalil's shop. It was here that rumors of Narjis' dissoluteness first encouraged him to try his luck with his host's, his cousin's, wife.

Ismail had been in the army and had traveled to Damascus and Cairo; he was too worldly a man to be satisfied with a wife from his village. After meeting Narjis, while still in the army, he decided to court her, luring her with expensive gifts which very soon drained him of all his money. Finally he took this "sophisticated" wife back to the Banu Shuqair. Inevitably, she fell prey to boredom and frustration. The village allowed no scope for the excitement that she craved, and so she betook herself to the local market town, whence wild stories filtered back to the village. And of all the villagers it was Ismail who knew, or wished to know, nothing. And then came Jasir. The struggle was mild, and victory almost immediate. And yet, despite the inevitability of this development, Haqqi turns this banality into a significant turning point. It is from the moment that darkness falls on the bedroom that the reader senses that Jasir is changing. He has determined to win Narjis for himself by whatever means, fair or foul. Whereas the murder fifteen years before had been committed in a moment of passion, this crime was being coldly and deliberately calculated. His love of freedom had evaporated in the face of his greater need to possess this woman. At the moment when Jasir finally takes Narjis, Haqqi writes that Jasir's steps were small, as though something hidden were tying his feet together—is this a reference to his loss of freedom in pursuit of his desire to possess Narjis? This carefully chosen image anticipates the end when Jasir is described as walking as though his feet were bound together by a short chain. Evil had entered him, evil on whose behalf he was ready to do anything. The next day, contrary to habit, he awoke at dawn and set off full of energy, as though the last fifteen years had not been. And as Jasir stands there contemplating the Nile, Haqqi introduces a vivid, passionate image of the river's flooding, symbolic of the turmoil in Jasir's mind. On his way back to the village, he comes across the employer of the Abu Fuda quarries, and his plan starts to take shape. He gets himself inscribed on the payroll and very soon is promoted to the position of a highly respected foreman. He convinces Ismail, who has failed in his attempts to till the land, to come and work at the mine. Gradually he wins his cousin's confidence until he has him working with explosives. Ismail, who used to be terrified of explosions in the belly of the mountain, is suddenly quite happy "to suspend himself between heaven and the Nile," and he starts to work with dynamite. Having aroused the necessary trust, Jasir's next step is easy; he comes back to the mine at night, severs Ismail's rope, and then cunningly rejoins the two ends. The next day he arrives at the ferry to hear of Ismail's fatal accident. It is at this juncture that the reader can appreciate Haqqi's economy of expression. A vivid atmosphere is evoked merely by commenting on the silence—no hammering, no detonations, just the silence of death. The climax is reported, the description has preceded the event: the reader is merely presented with the way Jasir had imagined that the accident would take place.[14] The accident is lost between Jasir's fantasies and fears; there was a chasm in him, a chasm into which his soul looked and could find nothing but fear and terror staring back. The passage of time after the funeral is concisely rendered by Haqqi's description of Jasir's growing fatness in the comfort of matrimonial bliss with Narjis. His crime, however, was not to remain unavenged: while planting some dynamite, the mechanism is unexpectedly detonated and Jasir is blinded.[15] The last image of Jasir is of an obese man with a scarred face and slits for eyes. He shuffles along supported by his stick. His feet appear as though bound by the prison chain. His moment of freedom had been an illusion.

Although this story covers a long period, concentration is in fact focused on Jasir's plot: its immediate motivation and its execution. The reader has been with Jasir throughout the crucial period of his change. In "A Story from Prison," by contrast, the crucial period of change is glossed over. Haqqi does not indulge in false sensationalism, the disturbing violence of a Mahmud Taimur, but rather mutes the tone of climaxes. Events speak to the reader in such a way that he is swept along by the mood to experience the pathos of the protagonist's predicament. There is no central event; it is a study of how a woman can gradually change a man's basic nature. But this is the work of time, and Haqqi does not create the illusion of passing time. The reader is surprised to hear of the gypsy's boredom with a way of life that had apparently begun the day before—and yet, days of unchanging routine must have preceded this feeling. When Ilaiwa was lured up to the gypsies, only to have his flock stolen and so be forced to join their band and become a gypsy, Haqqi is silent. Surely this is the crux of the story, and should not be glossed over. However, if this is read as a "yarn,"[16] as a series of events, or a process, happening to the narrator, then the erratic structure becomes a virtue, reflecting as it does the highly subjective quality of this story-telling.

Sometimes it seems that Haqqi is sketching the rough draft of a story, the details of which the reader is left to provide. In "Reasons Differ" Haqqi tells the reader immediately that he enjoys stories about misers, and this one is no more than the description of a miserly woman straight out of Jahiz' *Book of Misers*. With obvious enjoyment he details Sitt Zulaika's behavior. No call for amazement that she should prefer the narrator's house: did he not, unlike his neighbors, have a radio? Every evening was spent visiting so as to cut down on lighting expenses. She chain-smoked cigarettes which she rolled herself, thereby saving the expense of matches—"the match saddened her, since the moment of its use was to her the moment of its ending."[17] She used to take all the narrator's old newspapers, for which she seemed to have endless uses. It is only in her statement at the end of the first part that the reader feels Haqqi is attempting to structure a story: "These papers can also be used for something else."[18] This anticipates the end when, after her death, all her money was found wrapped in these old newspapers and hidden in the ceiling. As a story, "Reasons Differ" is weak. Haqqi does not develop any personal characteristic of Sitt Zulaikha, and show it to be totally flawed. The reader has been aware throughout of the threat to her life by her envious relatives, and her murder comes as no surprise; it is just the kind of thing that could happen to such a person. But "Reasons Differ" is a highly entertaining account of the anxieties, dangers, cunning and petty satisfactions of miserliness. The final twist is a wry comment on such behavior.[19] Lashin's story "Hello" in *It Is Said That . . .* can be drawn upon for comparison: a young man married a girl for the money she expected to inherit from her father. Finally, in desperation at the longevity of the old man, he divorced her. That very same day he received a telephone call in his office informing him of his father-in-law's demise.

"Mother of Miracles" is another such sketch. Haqqi is painting on the canvas of Ibrahim's life, filling in some gaps and leaving many empty. He is telling us of Ibrahim's ups and downs, focusing on two events that were partly instrumental in his downfall: the arrival of Badr with her children, and then of the diligent incense vendor in his green turban. These events are not developed in such a way that they become crucial to Ibrahim's life. Rather, they are introduced by way of example: of such a type were the misfortunes that Ibrahim encountered. There is no clear structure to the story, other than that it reflects Ibrahim's decline, seeming to peter out to nothing in the end. The structure itself, therefore, is a vital element, reflecting as it does the shape and intensity of Ibrahim's life. After reading one of these sketched stories, the reader feels as though he knows not only the hero but also the whole group of people of whom the hero is merely a prototype. Although the hero may be vividly portrayed as a character in his own right, with time it is the universality of his condition which asserts itself, and what is then remembered is his *situation*. There are no piquant conversations that make the reader feel that he has zoomed in briefly to the heart of another person's life.

It is interesting to compare Haqqi's earliest works with his later production to see to what extent time has shaped his story telling. An obvious example is of "Filla, Mishmish, Lulu," written in 1926, and "Antar and Juliet," published in 1961. The first story takes place in one building, and the characters are two cats and a dog as well as their respective masters and mistresses. On the first floor is an aristocratic Turkish lady, Sirandil Hanim, whose great comfort in her loneliness is her cat, Filla. On the second floor lived Abu Saud and his family. These people were working class Egyptians and their eldest son Aziz owned a dirty tom-cat called Mishmish. Finally, on the top floor lived a middle-class Greek couple with their dog, Lulu. Each household is described in detail, and the whole is brought together by a thinly disguised pretext: the two cats fight over a kitten and Lulu intervenes ineffectually. Description takes up four-fifths of the narrative; the event scarcely occupies a fifth. "Antar and Juliet," although comparable in many ways with this early story, has expanded the social message to create a plot with several layers of inter-pretation. It is no longer a question of animals woodenly representing different sectors of society. Here what matters is the fate of two dogs who have assumed the status of protagonists, each endowed with its own personality and individual way of life. The fact that Antar is finally denied his liberty represents more a personal tragedy (for him as well as for his mistress, Sitt Kaukab) than it does an indictment of a society that suppresses freedom and applauds suppression.[20]

Another comparison that may be drawn is between "Abd at-Tawwab Effendi the Jailer," written in 1927, and "The Vacant Bed," written in 1961. The early story concentrates on the satisfaction that a man finds in locking up a woman and exerting his will over her. Not out of generosity or love, but out of a desire to extort gratitude, he brings home oranges and tangerines for them to eat together. His relationship with his successive wives is presented entirely from his point of view; Haqqi thereby avoids the problem of dealing with the wives and their reactions. This early story seems to be a sketch for "The Vacant Bed." Haqqi has here gone beyond caricature to delineate in frightening detail a reaction, the effect that such a reaction has, and how this effect in turn brings out the true nature of the man. "The Vacant Bed" depicts not a static weakness, a condition that is merely fed by circumstances, but a violent, disturbing exposure of such a weakness worked out to the extreme. There is a desperateness in this story as the young man struggles to have his way, and with each defeat he is brought closer to the greatest struggle of all—the struggle with heredity, with madness. And although the end is not a surprise, prepared as it has been by the imagery and the morbid characterization of the young man, it is nonetheless a shock.

In the early stories the style is stilted; the reader is not allowed to forget that the author is trying to tell him something. The story telling, if there is any, is contrived, as though Haqqi felt that descriptions were not enough and that he should add an element of intrigue. "Dimitri's Cafe" (1926) is the photographic presentation of a cafe in Mahmudiya. Haqqi had understood Realism at that time as being a "recording":

> This story gave me an artistic lesson that was to help me throughout my life. I had recorded reality as it is ... Description pure and simple ... Later I steered clear of this approach, realizing that Realist literature is more than literal portrayal.[21]

For Sharuni the turning point in Haqqi's literary career came with the publication of "Irony or the Man with the Black Face" (1926),[22] which goes beyond pure description to combine elements of the short story and the article. However, one might also pinpoint a break (a breakthrough?) in the 1930s with the publication in journals of his *saidiyat*. Here Haqqi is no longer concerned with the presentation of facts for their own sakes but seems to be more interested in the perception of these facts. With this change in *perspective* has come a change in emphasis; details are no longer gratuitously introduced but are there to perform a function. Haqqi's emphasis on the act of writing as being the formulation of a perception guarantees a measure of detachment from the object so that it is the relationship of the subject of the statement with its object that becomes paramount.[23] The story is not merely history of the author (though it might be)[24] and it is not merely history of a narrator,[25] nor is it merely history of the protagonist;[26] the story is a construction that encompasses and goes beyond author, narrator and protagonist. It is a network woven by their relationships with one another. It is not image of the world, it is part of the world.

CONCLUSION

This has been a study of a writer who rose to prominence before the literature, of which he was one of the leading and earliest exponents, had come of age. Although most of Haqqi's collected works were published in the 1950s and 1960s, they were often written much earlier and virtually into an institutional vacuum, that was mitigated by the presence of a few others who also were writing to give the new world facing them a meaning. The early part of this century was a time of questioning old assumptions but also a time of hope, and it was writers like Haqqi, Lashin, Mahmud Taimur and other members of the Modern School who dared to face the doubt and hack away at its rotten foundations. Whatever the literary achievement, and time has condemned much of what was written during this period to a possibly unfair oblivion, the indignation and the courage to express it were there. Haqqi may be regarded as one of the pioneers of a literature that stuttered into existence about seventy years ago. He may certainly be regarded as central in charting its course, and at times as instrumental in accelerating the rate of its progress. His loyal and committed concern for over half a century has earned him the love and admiration of all with whom he has come into contact. And yet, he has admitted disappointment: he knows that love and admiration are not alone true acclaim. He has complained that when asked to cite Egypt's leading writers of this century, no one will mention Yahya Haqqi. They will list Taha Husain, Taufiq al-Hakim, Najib Mahfuz, and then perhaps . . . and even then?![1]

But even if Haqqi was not destined for such greatness, yet has his contribution been considerable, and noted. There is no work of criticism on modern Arabic literature that can afford to omit mention of his seminal *Dawn of the Egyptian Story*. There is no work on the confrontation of tradition and modernization that can afford to omit Ismail's story with its insistent optimism.[2] And the numerous tales of social cripples are a constant reminder, long after the reading is done, that the faceless ones that populate our underworlds live and hurt in a stifled silence.

But in a world that is dominated by a single crisis, the Palestinian, that has come to symbolize the crisis of the modern Arab facing a brave, bewildering new world, it is strange that Haqqi has said so little. It would seem that his focus is always Egypt, and his commitment is to man. And yet, despite this at once narrow and universal nature of his writing, every word he pens is necessarily political. As Deleuze and Guattari have observed, in a society that does not boast a wide array of talents there is no room for the individual enunciation, the work of a master, that stands out above the collective enunciation. In such a society the word of the writer is a communal action in a collective enterprise that may be referred to as "minor" literature.[3]

Maybe Haqqi did not live at the right time? Perhaps he should have lived and written at a time when the individual had the freedom and the context to express himself and not others; where success was not measured according to some indicator of political applicability and ingenuity, but rather according to his own criteria: that when the work is read again generations later, it will strike a chord.[4]

That Haqqi has given the color and taste of his age and his people through essays, sketches and short stories cannot be denied. And yet, he never embarked on a *magnum opus* that could be drawn upon as a concrete guide, or as a social panorama; and those with whom he compares himself have done just that. Taha Husain, whom Haqqi rarely mentions by name but whose presence looms large, wrote novels and books on Islam, on Arabic literature, on great Arab thinkers, on Egypt in tension with the modern world. He was, throughout his life, highly visible in the public realm through his university and government posts. He has been acclaimed not only in Egypt but also elsewhere. Taufiq al-Hakim, to whom Haqqi does make several references, was the first accomplished playwright in the Arab world. He shaped the dramatic form, with which Arabic literature was at first so uncomfortable, into a tool that could communicate widely and effectively, while retaining its authenticity as a work of art. Similarly, the last of Haqqi's *bêtes noirs,* Najib Mahfuz, is the doyen of the novel in the entire Arabic-speaking world.

Taha Husain, Taufiq al-Hakim, and Najib Mahfuz all pioneered projects to shake society, make it look at itself and think . . . They looked beyond the individual to encompass the whole while drawing attention to themselves as observers. Haqqi never raised his head that high. He kept his feet on the ground and his eyes darting around among the crowd. Only there did he feel comfortable. Every foray into the heart of town from his apartment in Heliopolis was an adventure that had to be lived to the hilt, and then . . . perhaps . . . penned. In this fullness of life there was little room for theories and models, and also little inclination to laud his own role as an individual observer. Even though he lived through one of the most traumatic periods that the Middle East has witnessed since the rise of Islam, Haqqi consistently retained a distance that allowed him to remain close to his people.

But who are Haqqi's people? The Egyptians certainly, but not all Egyptians; only those who belong to the spirit of the nebulous entity that

Egypt is. Egypt: a principle existing outside time, beyond the reach of a corrupting modern society. Through his word Haqqi resolves the contradictions of individual identities, so that Egyptianness is perceived as a line of continuity, an eternal consciousness of which each Egyptian must perceive himself to be a part, and which he thus perpetuates.[5] Through his art Haqqi expresses this perception, a formulation that goes beyond him to inform others, so that they may in turn perceive him on the line as Egyptian. This is perhaps how literature as a collective enunciation drowns subjectivity while retaining the individual intention.

Each literary work, whether it be an essay, a short story, a sketch, a piece of literary criticism, attempts to formulate a perception; each serves as a window on to one man's view of the world and his position in that world. For within the collective enterprise that literature is, even when subjectivity is suppressed or disappears, an individual intention still transpires, the need of some *one* to speak to his people, and on their behalf.

But whatever his intention, Haqqi throughout is evolving as an *adib*. Interspersed among anecdotes and humorous descriptions appears the teacher.[6] He discusses faults at home, and introduces the reader to what is good in the west so that the Egyptians may come to some informed understanding of what the future could hold for them. It is perhaps in the concept of *adab*[7] that the unifying factor of Haqqi's words may be found. For Haqqi is not merely a fiction writer or literary critic;[8] he is also an eminent *adib* tirelessly dipping the bucket of his own imagination into the well of life to illumine a wide panoply of diverse topics that appeal to him. What is paramount is Haqqi's concern to effect maximum impact with a vivid image, a well-turned phrase or a colloquial word interjected opportunely into a purely colloquial passage.[9]

How easy it would be to attempt a judgment of Haqqi, to assess the faults and highlight the qualities of his work, comparing him with other writers. Yet, I have resisted the judgmental approach, in the hope that I might bypass sympathy and antipathy as well as objectivity in order to sustain the empathy necessary to connect with Haqqi.[10] Neither praise nor appraisal, this study will have succeeded if it delineates for the reader the profile of a twentieth century Egyptian *adib*, Yahya Haqqi.

Appendix One

NEW COLLECTIONS

Fuad Dawwara has organized over 1000 of Haqqi's articles in some 15 journals and newspapers published between 1925 and 1970 into 12 books which will appear in the following order of publication:

Safha min tarikh Misr: Egyptian history in general, from Tutankhamun to Jabarti and to Abdallah an-Nadim.

Min faid al-karim: Religious matters from the Prophet's *Sira* to festivities connected with Ramadan and Shaban.

Madrasat al-masra: The theater and the people whom Haqqi has known in the theater, such as Salah ad-Din Kamil and Husain Riyad.

Humum thaqafiya: Covering all sorts of cultural problems; e.g., illiteracy.

Al-farash ash-shahir: This is a collection of all the early short stories inclu- ding many others that were published in newspapers after 1927 and not yet included in collections. In addition to the earliest stories (cf. p. 148, n. 23), there are: "The Guarded Treasure" (1934); "The Soldier" (1934); "Oblivion" (1961); "A Poor Woman" (1961); "The Vacant Bed" (1961); "As Though" (1967-1968); "The Fruit of Disappointed Love" (1962).

Turab al-miri: These are articles criticizing the government; e.g., bribes.

Ishq al-kalimat: Literary criticism, but dealing more particularly with the younger generation and the problems they find publishing their works. There are also articles on the problems of language and printing; e.g., use of unified script.

Min bab al-ashm: These are articles that have been collected from *At-Taawun,* where he contributed articles under this title. They are mainly concerned with criticism of superstitions.

Fi as-sinima: Films, both Egyptian and foreign. There are a number of articles on French and Soviet festivals in Cairo—there were a considerable number of Soviet film festivals during Nasser's era.

Hadha ash-shir: Dealing with poets such as Mutanabbi, Shauqi, and Ghalib.

Fi mihrab al-fann: musiqa, tashkil, imara: Music, the plastic arts and architecture. There are articles on the opera, as also on the Beatles, and he writes of the visit by a Turkish dance group in 1969.

Kunasat ad-dukkan (Shop Sweepings): As the title suggests, this is a miscellany: articles include memories of his childhood and of his time in Jeddah. There is also an article criticizing the medical system!

Appendix Two

TRANSLATIONS

Haqqi has done a number of translations which he considers to be an important part of his literary production. He has often emphasized the importance of translations in achieving precision in one's own language.[1] Translation is also important for progress: it is only with a clear understanding of the principles underlying the dynamics of another civilization that a young nation may evolve. In fact, Haqqi has quoted Tahtawi as an ideal example of the value of translations. When Tahtawi was sent out to the west, neither he nor the people sending him had felt threatened by this new civilization that had so much to teach them. They had been eager to translate into Arabic as much as possible, so that they could then incorporate into their own culture what they found of value in the west.[2] The works that he has translated are: Jules Romains, *Duktur Knuk* (1960);[3] Maurice Maeterlinck, *Al-usfur al-azraq* (1966);[4] Desmond Stewart, *Al-Qahira* (1965);[5] Edith Saunders, *Al-ab ad-dalil* (1970);[6] Mihail Sadoveanu, *Ad-Balata* (1972);[7] Stefan Zweig, *Laib ash-shatranj* (1973);[8] Thomas Mann, *Tunyu Krujir* (1973).[9]

Appendix Three

INTRODUCTIONS TO WORKS
OF OTHER WRITERS

Many young writers have turned to Haqqi for encouragement, if not for direct inspiration. The extent of the debt of the young generation to Haqqi may be measured by the number of introductions that he has written to their books. The following are some of the books that he has introduced:

Jean Girodoux, *Electra,* trans. Muhammad Ghalab (1960).

Muhammad Shalan, *Hikayat min shairina* (1960).

Abd al-Munim Shalabi, *Mana al-ibtisama* (1960).

Muhammad Salim, *Ustadh fi al-hara* (1960).

Ish wa milh (collection of short stories by five young writers, ed. Muhammad Salim, int. 1960).

Ahmad Lutfi, *As-sabr tayyib* (1962).

Muhammad Kamal ad-Din Ali Yusuf, *Al-adab wa al-mujtama* (1962).

Mahmud Tahir Lashin, *Sukhriyat an-nay* (2nd ed. 1964).

Hasan Dhulfiqar Sabr, *Ya nafs la turai* (1968).

John Edison, *Al-musamir (The Entertainer),* trans. Muhammad Taufiq Mustafa (1969).

Ismail Wali ad-Din, *Hammam al-malatili* (1970).

NOTES

Introduction

[1] See below Chapter One. Another example is Haqqi's view of government/ *fellah* relations which then connects with his own problem as an individual/ functionary, and these two lines can be seen to connect at any point with his problem of identity as an Egyptian of non-Arab origin (see above Chapter Three).

[2] See Chapter Five, where descriptions of middle-aged women contain reflections linking power relations in the familial context to sexual anxieties, culminating in legal political statements.

[3] In his autobiography Barthes wrote on the fly cover: "Tout ceci doit être considéré comme dit par un personnage de roman." R. Barthes, *Roland Barthes* (Paris, 1975); cf. Tzvetan Todorov, *Les Genres du Discours* (Paris, 1978), p. 16; Claudio Guillén, *Literature as System* (Princeton, 1971), pp. 107-134; Maxine Haig Kingston's autobiography, *The Woman Warrior* (New York, 1975).

[4] Rashad Rushdi has denied "The Saint's Lamp" the status of fiction; for him Haqqi's works are merely contemplations and analytical descriptions (Yusuf ash-Sharuni, *Sabun shama fi hayat Yahya Haqqi* [Cairo, 1975], p. 14).

[5] Muhammad Abdullah ash-Shafaqi, "Dama fa ibtisama," in *Al-Katib al-Arabi,* March 1966.

[6] Yusuf ash-Sharuni, pp. 13-16.

[7] Abbas Khidr, *Al-Qissa al-qasira fi Misr mundhu nashatiha hatta 1930* (Cairo, 1966), p. 253.

[8] Abbas Khidr, p. 258.

[9] Mustafa Ibrahim Husain, *Yahya Haqqi mubdian wa naqidan* (Cairo, 1970), pp. 75, 81. He has called "The Postman," usually regarded as a short story, a novel (pp. 77-80); and *Leave it to God,* Haqqi's self-avowed autobiography, has been called a novel by Raymond Francis, *Aspects de la littérature arabe contemporaine* (Cairo, 1960), p. 222. Sayyid Hamid an-Nassaj has claimed that Haqqi's works after Rome (1934-1939) are not short stories, but novels (*riwayas*), *Tatawwur fann al-qissa al-qasira fi Misr 1910-1933* (Cairo, 1968), p. 280.

[10] "Mais ne craignons pas let redites: la matière est la même, les lumières sont neuves," J.P. Sartre, *L'Idiot de la Famille* (Paris, 1971), Vol. 1, p. 51.

[11] "En ajoutant son langage à celui de l'auteur et ses symboles à ceux de l'oeuvre, le critique ne 'déforme' pas l'objet pour s'exprimer en lui, il n'en fait pas le prédicat de sa propre personne; il reproduit une fois de plus, comme un signe décroché et varié, le signe des oeuvres elles-mêmes, dont le message infiniment

ressassè, n'est pas telle 'subjectivitè,' mais la confusion mème du sujet et du langage, en sorte que la critique et l'oeuvre disent toujours: je suis littèrature," Roland Barthes, *Critique et Vèritè* (Paris, 1966), p. 71.

[12] Although it was a charity school the boys that attended belonged to the more privileged classes of the district; Mustafa Kamil had been a pupil.

[13] Samir Wahby, "A Critical Evaluation of the Writings of Yahya Haqqi," unpubl. M.A. thesis, A.U.C., Cairo, 1965, p. 12.

[14] *Qindil*, p. 24.

[15] "Taufiq al-Hakim between Hope and Fear," in *Al-Hadith*, Feb. 1934.

[16] *Khalliha*, p. 44. The division between *Ahli* and Mixed (foreign) courts continued until 1949 (see above, pp. 46-47).

[17] *Khalliha*, p. 60.

[18] Government service at that time was highly regarded, and the following proverb was coined: "If you miss government service, then wallow in its dust," cf. *Khalliha*, p. 43.

[19] *Khalliha*, p. 152. Compare with Taufiq al-Hakim, *Yaumiyat naib fi al-aryaf* (Cairo, 1938) where a peasant is fined for washing his clothes in the river, the only source of running water in the village. (p. 39)

[20] See Chapter Two.

[21] The school comprised Ahmad Khairi Said, Mahmud Tahir Lashin, Hasan Mahmud, Husain Fauzi, Mahmud Azmi, Ibrahim al-Misri, and Habib Zahlawi.

[22] See pp. 130-131.

[23] "Filla, Mishmish, Lulu" (July 15, 1926); "Death and Contemplation" (July 22, 1926); "Irony, or the Man with the Black Face" (August 19, 1926); "Muhammad Bey Visits his Country Estate" (October 28, 1926); all in *Al-Fajr*. "A Robber's Life" (December 10, 1926) and "Dimitri's Cafe" (December 22, 1926), in *As-Siyasa al-Usbuiya*.

[24] *Fajr*, p. 88. The article was signed "Labib." Haqqi now regrets that he signed so much of his earlier work with pseudonyms. He feels that many of his articles have been lost (Interview with Haqqi, Cairo, March 27, 1979).

[25] Egyptian television, *Najmat al-Mufaddal*, November 24, 1963.

[26] This is a collection of stories written between 1939 and 1940.

[27] *Qindil*, pp. 40-47.

[28] Interview with Noha Suudi, Cairo, April 4, 1979.

[29] See conclusion for elaboration of Haqqi's place among contemporary Egyptian writers, including Taha Husain, Mahfuz, and al-Hakim.

[30] *Ya Lail*, p. 12.

[31] *Ibid.*, p. 125.

[32] The *tahtib* is danced by men only. There are no set steps and what is important is the use of the stick (*hatab*). The purpose of the dance is a display of virility (*murua*).

[33] See *Al-Masa*, October 25, 1965 and February 2, 1970.

[34] *Haqiba*, p. 83.

[35] Interview with Mahmud Hadari, director of the Cinema Club, April 2, 1979. He said that many young directors had begun their work under Haqqi's tutelage.

[36] Interview with Yahya Haqqi, Cairo, March 27, 1979.

[37] Fuad Dawwara, his assistant in *Al-Majalla*, has collected Haqqi's articles

written over 50 years and scattered throughout journals and papers. See Appendix I: New Works.

³⁸Haqqi expressed sorrow that people have said to him: "I *saw* you on TV" and not "I *heard* what you said"—he was referring to the television interview organized by Faruq Shusha on the occasion of his 74th birthday.

³⁹See Appendix III: Introductions Written for Young Writers.

Chapter One

¹*Itr,* p. 10.

²"It is possible even for Islam in certain manifestations to displace in men's loyalty the very God to whom it witnesses, if it becomes, thereby an end in and unto itself." K. Cragg, introduction to M.K. Hussein, *City of Wrong* (tr. K. Cragg) (Amsterdam, 1959), p. xviii.

³The hero of Najib Mahfuz's *Trilogy* (1956-1957).

⁴*Haqiba,* p. 101.

⁵Cantwell Smith discusses the use of the terms *islam* and *iman* over the centuries, and he shows how *islam* has come to dominate. Whereas "in the Quran the ratio between the two is five to one in favour of *iman*. In Arabic book-titles until the end of the nineteenth century *islam* slightly outnumbers 'faith' in a ratio of three to two. In modern times this ratio jumps to thirteen to one." (p. 105)

⁶*Itr,* pp. 8-9

⁷Mirza Asad Allah Khan Ghalib (1797-1869). In a letter to Murshi Hargapah Tafta: "I hold all human beings, Muslim, Hindu or Christian, dear to me, and regard them as my brothers." (See A. Bausani, *Encyclopaedia of Islam,* new edition [Leiden-London, 1965].)

⁸"Ghalib's prayers were not kneelings and protestations . . . but the intimate conversation of one friend to another, joined to one another by intimacy, rebuke and even coquetry." *Unshuda,* p. 165. Haqqi repeats several times: "He was upright before his Lord." *Ibid.,* pp. 162-166.

⁹*Dama,* p. 27.

¹⁰*Fikra,* p. 53.

¹¹By liberating Islam of one national affiliation he could then use it to support another (*Dama,* p. 39).

¹²*Dama,* p. 54. See also *Haqiba,* p. 102; *At-Taawun,* May 23, 196.

¹³An interesting demonstration of Haqqi's attitude to Israel can be seen in the articles and editorials he published in *Al-Majalla.* The tone in which his political articles are written seem to be eloquent of his true feelings. In July 1967 the reader is first made truly aware of the extent of Haqqi's bitterness and cynicism. He uses the usual July format to celebrate the Revolution: he praises achievements such as the Dam, a thriving agricultural economy, progress in the theater and the popular arts, the entry of Egypt into the world literary arena with the English translation of Taufiq al-Hakim's *The Tree Climber.* And then suddenly he interrupts himself to embark on a bitter diatribe against the United States who had at first, through President Wilson, tempted Egypt to open herself to American cultural activity and had then perfidiously planted Israel into the heart of the Arab world to sow the seeds of anger and hatred. By August all veiled references to the evil that Israel and her collaborators represent have been cast aside. He feels

himself to be surrounded by enemies, and Zionism, which has created these enemies, is compared to a cancer; a cancer that is growing among the Arab nations, awakening feelings that had been dead since the Crusades. The dream of a merging of religions and races in universal cooperation had been shattered. Israel had stemmed the tide of evolution, and had introduced suspicion and generalized mistrust: "This was my own spiritual dilemma: I had become a fanatic." *Dama*, p. 55.

[14] Hitler had claimed that "Nazism was the religion which would free mankind, raising from off its shoulders its burden and loosening its shackles." *Itr*, p. 12.

[15] Sri Sarvepalli Radhakrishnan, "The World's Unborn Soul," an inaugural lecture delivered before the University of Oxford (Oxford, 1936), p. 10.

[16] *Dama*, p. 17.

[17] The Egyptian Jews who had until the 1940s lived in peace and harmony with their neighbors suddenly ceased to be Egyptians first and foremost: they were Jews and, as such, alien (*Itr*, p. 199).

[18] For another Arab's view of Israel's role in the arrest of evolution with specific reference to the Arab world: "Le fait nu, impossible, à nier, est qu'Israël, par son existence seule, a bloqué les arabes et a été une des causes déterminates dans le processus de continuelle traditionalisation. Toute pensée libérale, laïcisante, progressiste, apparut comme une ruse de la propagande sioniste et impérialiste." Abdallah Laroui, *La Crise des Intellectuels Arabes: Traditionalisme ou Historicisme?* (Paris, 1974), p. 212.

[19] *Dama*, p. 25.

[20] *Ibid.*, p. 62. "At that time Azhar, unlike today when it has become isolated from Cairo, was the city's throbbing heart. Only here did revolutions break out, their war cries resounding from its minarets. The people of Cairo used to keep a close eye on Azhar and its activities." Haqqi, "The Humorous Aspects of Egyptian Society in Jabarti's Day," in *Al-Balagh*, Apr. 1, 1930.

[21] *Dama*, p. 32.

[22] *Ibid.*, p. 57.

[23] *Ibid.*, p. 33.

[24] *Ibid.*, p. 41.

[25] Haqqi writes of the *imam* of a mosque in Istanbul who had harangued his congregation on the evils of dirt that could only be truly cleansed with rose water that he sold them (*Dama*, p. 23). Another *imam* in Manfalut had memorized the 52 *khutbas* for each week of the year, including the thanksgiving for the flooding of the Nile. When one year the Nile caused widespread destruction, the *imam* did not change the text of the speech. (*Khalliha*, p. 18.)

[26] *Dama*, p. 39.

[27] "His spirit moaned and squirmed under the blows of her chisel . . ." *Qindil*, p. 88.

[28] This tolerance for spiritual paths may be noted in Lashin's *Eve Without Adam* (Cairo, 1934). Although Eve felt that she had been used by her grandmother and Hajj Imam when they claimed to have cured her with charms and talismans, she was perfectly well aware that unless she had something to offer in their stead she should not shake their beliefs. What was important was to have a belief. (p. 48)

[29] Wine is also mentioned twice in connection with dervishes: they claim to

spend their entire lives in the mosque (Islam) whereas in fact they are always in the wineshop (Sufism). See *Dama*, pp. 21, 104.

[30] *Ibid.*, p. 14.

[31] *Ibid.*, pp. 13-14.

[32] *Dama*, p. 12.

[33] See above, n. 7.

[34] "Sufi teaching has it that union (*wusul*) cannot always be achieved by prolonged, devoted effort, but rather is a gift from God." *Khutuwat*, p. 90.

[35] Interview, Mar. 22, 1979; cf. "The Prophet's Maulid," in *Dama*, pp. 56-60.

[36] "Our instincts and our nature are the image of the animal's instincts and nature, is this good or bad?" *Umm*, p. 56.

[37] *Dama*, p. 48.

[38] J.M. Masson, "Psychology of the Ascetic," in *The Journal of Asian Studies*, Vol. xxxv, 4, August, 1976, p. 616; cf. *Dama*, p. 79 and *Qindil*, p. 102.

[39] *Antar*, p. 44 (my italics). Since the narrator had already hinted at the desirability of killing this "monster," the reader is tempted to believe that the accident was primarily the narrator's fault. It is interesting to note that Haqqi writes of "wiping away" sin (not finding redemption), a truly Islamic view of sin. What is additionally noteworthy is that it is the narrator who seems to take upon himself the responsibility for wiping away this particular sin by allowing the child to slip out of his arms from the balcony.

[40] Cf. "Khalid Muhammad Khalid drew once more the familiar distinction between true and false religion, between what was essential and what was not. But in his hands true religion virtually lost its meaning and became no more than a 'source of strength, fraternity, equality,' a spiritual attitude rather than a creed. Moreover, he drew the distinction more sharply, even crudely, than earlier thinkers would have done, religion which interfered in the secular realm was false, it was the tool of 'priesthood' in its attempts to gain power and keep the people poor and ignorant." A. Hourani, *Arabic Thought in the Liberal Age 1798-1939* (London, 1970), p. 353.

[41] *Dama*, p. 48.

[42] Haqqi recounts the story told by cave drawers of primitive man's capture of his second mate. After catching her, he dragged her back to his cave where he was met by his first spouse who was much troubled by this new turn in events. She spent an anguished night wondering how she could repay her husband for his disloyalty. Finally she lit on a plan. By dawn she had managed to consume the leg of a bull that her husband had wrenched out of the mouth of a lion. When her husband awoke she told him that during his sleep his new wife had devoured the meat. The lie was soon discovered, and to allay his anger the scheming lady announced that her belly had swollen with his child. The husband's only option now was to play her game: he told her that she was the most beautiful creature in the world. The artist, says Haqqi, is this woman's son. (*Fikra*, pp. 63-65.)

[43] Cf. the Italian artist, Boldini, who despite his fame remained in the village school scorning the limelight of Rome; his prime concerns were privacy and integrity. (*Fikra*, pp. 181-182.)

[44] Muhammad al-Muwailhi, *Hadith Isa ibn Hisham au fatra min az-zaman* (Cairo, 1964), p. 131.

[45] *Dama,* pp. 12, 107, cf. p. 80.

[46] *Ibid.,* p. 141.

[47] *Ibid.,* p. 80.

[48] *Nas,* p. 112.

[49] *Fikra,* p. 65; cf. *Dama,* p. 80.

[50] *Fikra,* p. 66.

[51] *Dama,* p. 103.

[52] *Ibid.,* p. 51.

[53] "A language filled with light that poured from between his pearly teeth," *ibid.,* p. 58.

[54] Before reading this ode, which has assumed the characteristics of a talisman, the reader must perform ablutions, face the *qibla,* and articulate carefully (*ibid.,* p. 90).

[55] Haqqi is one of the few critics to question its literary value; he told me of Shauqi's *muarada,* written in the same meter and style as the *Burda,* but which he considers to be much better. (Interview, Cairo, Mar. 30, 1979.)

[56] *Dama,* p. 60.

[57] *Ibid.,* pp. 106-107.

[58] *Ibid.,* p. 90.

[59] *Ibid.,* p. 121.

[60] My italics.

[61] *Itr,* p. 76.

[62] *Unshuda,* p. 105. "Man searches out others so that he may there see his own face." *Nas,* p. 121.

[63] *Taala,* p. 52.

[64] *Antar,* p. 4: "It is more difficult to know oneself than to know another," and "It is from this other that he is suddenly made aware of his own old age." *Nas,* p. 109.

[65] Haqqi has said that he had unconsciously chosen a photographer, and on reflection had realized the appositeness of his choice when he remembered the Quranic verse: "We form you in the womb" (the actual quotations is: "He is the one who forms you in the womb" from Al Umran, 3). The first time the narrator met Fahmi was in the dark room, or, as Haqqi put it, in the womb. After this meeting the "development" of the "photograph" would show who was the positive and who was the negative. (Interview, Cairo, Mar. 24, 1979.)

[66] *Umm,* p. 22.

[67] "My inclination for mysticism did not arise out of its theoretical logic alone but out of the behavior of masters. Man before his path (*madhhab*)." (*Dama,* p. 12.) Haqqi has said that he never found his *qutb,* although he searched for many years. An interesting comment he made in this connection was that a *qutb* cannot hold a religious position, because in the religious group he would lose the spiritual innocence characteristic of the *qutb.* At one time he was told of a Turk he should visit in Istanbul—a possible *qutb.* Although his trip was fruitless, he did have an interesting experience on the way. One day he entered a lift and felt a powerful attraction for one of the men in the elevator. The man turned out to be Paul Strand, an American photographer (see n. 65). Although they corresponded briefly nothing came of the relationship. Haqqi feels that this might have been the longed-for *qutb.* (Interview, Cairo, Mar. 20, 1979.)

[68] *Haqiba*, pp. 73-81.

[69] *Dama*, p. 16.

[70] *Ibid.*, p. 46.

[71] *Ibid.*, p. 55.

[72] *Ibid.*, p. 46; cf. p. 14.

[73] *Nas*, p 116.

[74] *Khutuwat*, p. 99.

[75] *Dama*, p. 16.

[76] Khalid Muhammad Khalid, *Min huna nabda* (Cairo, 1950), p. 43.

[77] *Dama*, p. 53.

[78] Cf. "This is the case with good writers, they are always dreaming, and their dreams often reach a dazzling, amazing level." Taha Husain, *Naqd wa islah* (Beirut, 1960), p. 152.

[79] *Itr*, p. 38.

[80] *Dama*, pp. 52-53.

[81] *Ibid.*, p. 49.

[82] *Khutuwat*, p. 82.

[83] *Ibid.*, p. 88.

[84] *Ibid.*, p. 90.

[85] *Dama*, p. 45.

[86] *Ibid.*, p. 46.

[87] According to Levi-Strauss, food is divisible into a Nature/Culture antithesis. At the former end are the raw foods, at the latter end are the roasted meats.

[88] See above, p. 61.

[89] *Fajr*, p. 160.

[90] *Dama*, p. 47.

[91] "We seem to walk along a narrow path between two abysses. Although we appear to live securely . . . yet it is with the constant, secret dread of slipping." *Fikra*, p. 164. Cf. Nietzsche: "Der Mensch is ein Seil, geknüpft zwischen Tier und Übermensch—ein Seil über einem Abgrunde. Ein gefährliches Hinüber, ein gefährliches Zurückblicken, ein gefährliches Schaudern und Stehenbleiben." Nietzsche, *Also Sprach Zarathustra* (Paris, 1969), Vol. I, p. 62.

[92] *Dama*, p. 51.

[93] *Taala*, p. 62.

[94] *Dama*, p. 109. See also *Sahh*, p. 122.

[95] *Fikra*, pp. 155-156; *Fajr*, p. 35.

[96] *Ibid.*, p. 49.

[97] *Ibid.*, p. 12.

[98] *Ibid.*, p. 33.

[99] "The poet's proximity to God, and his enjoyment of His light have come next only to those of the prophets, but above those of any great man or reformer in the world. For a great man . . . is made . . . by the combined efforts of the home, the school, historical events, opportunities, time and environment. But the poet is the sheer creation of God." Badawi al-Jabal quoted in Salma Khadra Jayyusi, *Trends and Movements in Modern Arabic Poetry* (Leiden, 1977), p. 213.

[100] In the Sultan Hasan Mosque the arch surrounding the *qibla* seemed to have been created "by the compasses which placed the stars in the heavens, but

this time the hand of a human being had held them." *Dama,* p. 32; cf. *Unshuda,* p. 142, where art is described as raising man to divine transcendence.

[101]"For having fathomed all that primitive man knew of purity and the joy of the first encounter, and the happiness of virgin love, he has also inherited that respect for the terrifying, mysterious unknown and the roar of nature with its earthquakes and volcanoes." *Itr,* p. 188.

[102]*Dama,* p. 12; *Itr,* p. 24. Haqqi says that Taufiq al-Hakim saw that all is emanation from God and therefore all is divine (Taufiq al-Hakim, "Between Fear and Hope," in *Al-Hadith,* Feb. 1934), and at the moment of creating he seems to have freed himself of time and place (*Fajr,* p. 117); cf. description of Tolstoy at the moment of writing (*Khutuwat,* p. 79).

[103]*Dama,* p. 103. "Light as symbolically viewed as white, descends from the sun and symbolises Unity. As it is through white that color is made manifest so though black it remains hidden, 'hidden by its very brightness.' Black is a 'bright light in a dark day,' as only through this luminous black can one find the hidden aspects of the Divine." N. Ardalan and L. Bakhtiar, *The Sense of Unity* (Chicago, 1974), p. 48.

[104]*Fikra,* p. 182.

[105]"I do not believe that inspiration can last for any length of time if the artist does not communicate and does not establish that spiritual response that is the support and aim of all artistic production." *Sahh,* p. 72.

[106]*Fikra,* pp. 184-185. "Flaubert put his finger on the secret that makes a work of art eternal: floating above the lines and the pages there is a special atmosphere which affects your being, your hearing and your sight—you feel as though you were living in it." *Unshuda,* p. 71.

[107]*Ibid.,* p. 131.

[108]*Ibid.,* p. 132.

[109]"The truth is that the only field I know that approaches fiction is the field of mystical experience (*tadhawwuq*), but in reverse. The reader finds and perceives himself when he is observing the protagonist. As for the mystic, when he looks at his innermost self his 'I' appears to him, but as though through a window looking out on to a void stretching into infinity, so that before long the weak 'I' that he had known is replaced by the Almighty 'One.' " *Majalla,* June, 1970.

[110]*Itr,* p. 17.

[111]*Unshuda,* p. 58; cf. *ibid.,* pp. 138, 143.

[112]Haqqi has attributed Iqbal's rejection of atheism to his readings of Wordsworth, whose works Haqqi has compared to those of Ibn Arabi. ("Maa an-nas," in *Al-Masa,* July 21, 1969.)

[113]*Qindil,* p. 11.

[114]*Fajr,* p. 35; see also Muhammad Jalal Kishk, *Sharaf al-mihna-qissat assihafa wa ath-thaura* (Cairo, 1961), appendix by Haqqi, p. 251. Beauty is, for Haqqi, the re-establishment of order and harmony in a troubled universe; the melting away of details to reveal the essence; childlike happiness; transcendence of daily trivia; an escape; a merging with nature; a deep sadness that empties the observer and turns him into beauty's own reflection. (*Fikra,* pp. 167-173.)

[115]"Art transcends rules and principles . . . . Indeed, it may have to break these rules and principles should they become obsolete . . . and here we find the artist not art." *Unshuda,* pp. 15, 84; cf. also *Itr,* pp. 19, 41. Haqqi has written of his

acquaintance with his uncle, Mahmud Tahir Haqqi, Mahfuz, and Lashin, thereby substantiating his qualification to write about them.

[116] Taufiq al-Hakim, *Fann al-adab,* p. 245.

[117] Cf. "The secret of artistic creation and of the effectiveness of art is to be found in a return to the state of *participation mystique*—to the level of experience at which it is man who lives, and not the individual, and at which the weal and woe of the single human being does not count, but only human existence." C.G. Jung, "Psychology and Literature," in *20th Century Literary Criticism,* ed. D. Lodge (London, 1972), p. 187.

[118] *Antar,* p. 6.

[119] *Itr,* pp. 187-230.

[120] *Ibid.,* p. 190.

[121] "Every contact the artist has with life is one of amazement and joy: the joy of a first discovery . . . . The artist may see an object again and again and yet each encounter is the first." (*Unshuda,* pp. 72-73.)

[122] Appendix to Kishk, p. 243; cf. *Dama,* p. 104.

[123] Haqqi's description of the *qutb* (see above, n. 67) fits with that of the members of the Malamati Sufi order: "Des saints vivent parmi les hommes, inconnus et méprisés. Personne ne les reconnaît comme tels, ils ne se révèlent qu'à des élus, destinés à mèner la mème vie qu'eux et à atteindre la mème perfection . . . non seulement le saint parfait doit mèner une vie qui ne permette pas aux autres de deviner son état, mais il se fait mème insulter, passe pour un fou . . . se considère comme le pire de tous et agit en conséquence. Ce sera le principe mème des *malamatiya* islamiques." M. Molè, *Les Mystiques Musulmans* (Paris, 1965), p. 12. In "Hadha al-ghul," in *Al-Masa,* Mar. 4, 1968, Haqqi mentions this obscure secret order: "Forgive me if I begin this article with the narration of a memory. You may well say: 'This is no sin that you should ask forgiveness, are you a Malamati Sufi, who loves to stand in the dock?' " And in "As Though," the narrator is shown to identify with the prisoner in the dock.

[124] *Al-Katib,* April, 1961, p. 160 (the Preface, although signed by Luis Awad, was in fact rewritten by Haqqi) (Interview, Cairo, Mar. 26, 1979); cf. *Qindil,* p. 192.

[125] "So that when my body is close to his, I should be drained by him. I should become him, his past would be mine, his future mine, so that this feeling of cold—the cold of fear doubtless—should contain a weird pleasure; the satisfaction of an old desire . . . to be rid of my self . . . to melt into another human being." *Al-Masa,* Dec. 25, 1967, p. 8; "so that I should merge fully into him," *ibid.;* "Because I had merged into him," *ibid.,* p. 10; "It was essential for my peace of mind that I should live the past of this young man, a hidden fate had decreed that I should be him." *Al-Masa,* Jan. 22, 1968, p. 4.

Chapter Two

[1] *Dama,* pp. 74, 104; *Antar,* p. 25; *Khalliha,* pp. 175-176.

[2] For a man like Ibrahim Abu Khalil ("Mother of Miracles"), "life is like a leaf in autumn, the wind may raise it somewhat, but even as it is rising it speaks of its predestined fall." *Umm,* p. 7.

[3] *Al-Majalla,* July 1968.

[4] The Upper Egyptians preserve the Pharaonic custom of transporting the dead from the east to the west bank of the Nile (*Dima*, p. 138); cf. also: "They are the descendants of the builders of the pyramids." (*Antar*, p. 23); "Dans les villages du Said . . . fellahs des deux confessions cultivent leurs champs côte à côte, en se référant tous à l'éternel calendrier pharaonique." Eric Rouleau, *Le Monde*, 25 November 1977. (The solar calendar is another factor of unity beyond history.)

[5] See above, p. 151, n. 42.

[6] *Fikra*, p. 64.

[7] *Umm*, pp. 107-110.

[8] *Ibid.*, pp. 16-46.

[9] *Khalliha*, p. 21. See above, p. 71.

[10] *Fikra*, pp. 99-104.

[11] *Dima*, p. 69; *Fikra*, pp. 140-141.

[12] *Antar*, p. 84; cf. p. 121.

[13] *Khalliha*, p. 178.

[14] In "Filla, Mishmish, Lulu" Haqqi uses a dog and two cats to represent the Turks, Egyptians and Greeks in Cairo in the early 1900s.

[15] *Antar*, p. 115. Cf. the narrator in "The Turtle Flies," who had "wanted to leave the ranks of the workers who are paid daily, to become part of the class of effendis who earn a monthly salary." *Qindil*, p. 136. (But to no avail! Only a woman's evil can overcome this apparently insurmountable barrier [see above, p. 77].)

[16] *Umm*, p. 34.

[17] See above, p. 71.

[18] *Umm*, pp. 34, 37.

[19] *Khalliha*, pp. 100-101.

[20] *Umm*, p. 12.

[21] Introduction, *Irony of the Flute* (Cairo, 1964). Cf. also "Izrail" where Mahmud Taimur writes of the inhumanity of the poor and oppressed to one another: a man killed his best friend, the corpse-washer, because he felt that he was bringing him bad luck.

[22] *Khalliha*, p. 128. In this connection it should be noted that in "The Perfume Bottle," Sami, who had spent some time in Upper Egypt as a prosecuting attorney, had had a passing affair with the young daughter of a rich merchant. Her interest in him was not for the man but for the function alone (*Umm*, p. 153).

[23] *Khalliha*, pp. 162, 119, 197.

[24] *Fikra*, p. 164.

[25] *Qindil*, p. 9; cf. "Talking About Oneself," in *Antar*, pp. 157-158.

[26] *Fikra*, p. 74.

[27] *Ibid.*, pp. 156-157.

[28] *Antar*, p. 173.

[29] The village was appropriately called Kaum an-Nahl, a village so old and remote that it had "escaped the Arab hurricane" (*Dima*, p. 49). The bees which had given the place its name were now in the custody of some Copts—note the double connection with the Pharaohs: untouched by the Arabs (cf. *ibid.*, p. 31).

[30] "The Upper Egyptians forgive many things, but they will never forgive one who trespasses into their house and family—that is the greatest of crimes."

Khalliha, p. 215.

[31]*Khalliha,* p. 131.

[32]Haqqi describes the fellah as seeming to endow animals with a rational consciousness: on one of his trips through the villages of Asyut he had come across a fellah with his water-buffalo. The latter was ill, and its master had determined to curtail its agonies. Haqqi describes them both looking at the knife in the fellah's hand; the buffalo appeared to be "grateful," reassuring "her" master in his grief. (*Khalliha,* p. 115; cf. *Dima,* pp. 29-30.)

[33]*Dima,* p. 37.

[34]*Khalliha,* p. 31; *Dima,* p. 30.

[35]*Ibid.,* pp. 6-7.

[36]*Khalliha,* p. 32. (Here Haqqi is talking of the small landed farmer, and not the fellah who never had or ever would own land; cf. Sharqawi, *Al-Ard.*)

[37]Any comfort is hidden from the "blue eye" of envy; envy whose power is so great that it is said to kill or destroy the coveted object (*Khalliha,* p. 156). For an interesting treatment of envy among the fellahs, see W.S. Blackman, *The Fellahin of Upper Egypt* (London, 1927), pp. 218-222.

[38]*Khalliha,* pp. 131, 151-152.

[39]*Umm,* pp. 139-146.

[40]*Khalliha,* p. 183.

[41]*Khalliha,* pp. 166-177. For a discussion of doctors' exploitation of the poor in the 1920s, see Said Abduh, "A tabib wa jarrah am jazzar wa sharrah?" in *Abu al-Haul,* January 1923; Hasan Mahmud, "Jarima," in *As-Sufur,* Cairo, 17 April 1922.

[42]*Khalliha,* pp. 209-210.

[43]*Ibid.,* pp. 136, 144.

[44]*Ibid.,* pp. 171-172; *Haqiba,* p. 84.

[45]Cf. Fathi Ghanim, *Al-Jabal,* 1959; Lashin writes of peasants who curse the day when they first heard of modern civilization (*Yuhka anna,* 1964, p. 86); cf. also Taufiq al-Hakim's peasants in *Yaumiyat naib fi al-aryaf;* although exploited and unarmed, they are cunning and united.

[46]Haqqi tells the story of two servants, a boy and a girl, employed in separate households in the same district. They fell in love, but their only opportunities to meet were when they were out shopping: "the economic status of the *hara* did not allow for more than one domestic per household" (*Nas,* p. 37). The situation was hopeless and they committed suicide—this, according to Haqqi, is true tragedy. Not the grand theater of Romeo and Juliet, but the tragedy of man struggling against forces so much greater than himself that to oppose them were folly. Dull submission, with the hope of dreaming, is as much choice as he is given (*ibid.*).

[47]*Fikra,* p. 65.

[48]"They, the Upper Egyptian fellahs, have not been spoilt or led astray by knowledge. Civilization with all its innovations has not taught them that the world contains injustice, and that one should rise above it. They are a people who live by instinct." *Haqiba,* p. 71.

Chapter Three

[1] *Qindil,* p. 113.

[2] Haqqi has compared the Nile to a wilful child which once a year rebels against his mother, Egypt, and bursts his banks. The child becomes a giant roaring his way through the valley, flooding the land as far as the eye can see. But it is only in Upper Egypt that he finds his freedom—by the time he has reached the Delta his strength has gone. The youthful giant of Upper Egypt has changed into an old, old man—thousands of years old (*Dima,* pp. 120-121). It is in this exuberance that man merges with nature; "When the Nile floods creation, he turns people, earth and animals upside down." (*Khalliha,* p. 235); cf. *Nas,* p. 144; for a fuller treatment of the role of the Nile in Egyptian literature, see Nimat Ahmad Fuad, *An-Nil fi al-adab al-misri* (Cairo, 1962).

[3] *Khalliha,* p. 159; cf. *ibid.,* p. 120.

[4] *Dima,* p. 31.

[5] *Qindil,* p. 116. See above, pp. 29-30.

[6] Cf. "Der Feldweg," trans. A. Prèau in *Questions III* (Paris, 1968), pp. 9-15.

[7] "Even though I am of recent Turkish stock I feel that I have merged into the land of Egypt and its people." *Qindil,* p. 56.

[8] *Dama,* pp. 130-131.

[9] *Fajr,* p. 26.

[10] *Dama,* p. 129. "The fellah had been outside the literary arena, as though he did not exist; he had not even risen to the rank of an enigma to baffle mankind." *Nas,* p. 50.

[11] Surely this is rhetoric rather than a claim grounded in fact.

[12] *Fajr,* p. 157.

[13] "How amazing it is that one of Turkish stock can express the conscience of the Egyptian people." *Dama,* p. 129. For a discussion of Haqqi's Turkishness, see Abd al-Aziz Muhammad az-Zaki, "Yahya Haqqi bain al-misriya wa at-turkiya" in *Alam al-Fikr,* vol. 9, no. 2, 1974.

[14] *Fajr,* p. 83; cf. also Husni Lashin (Mahmud Tahir Lashin's brother), whose library had been the inspiration for many young artists, and that, despite the fact that he was of Balkan origin (*Fajr,* p. 264).

[15] *Ibid.,* pp. 65-66.

[16] *Khutuwat,* p. 186.

[17] *Al-Majalla,* April 1970.

[18] Haqqi attended the oral of a blind Azhar student who had completed research into *Political Economics in Islam,* a controversial topic for Azhar University. Haqqi sat near the student and noticed the young man's anxiety about the fate of his sandals, which were buried under the pile of shoes that had accumulated since their arrival. At the call to prayer there was a stampede as everyone rushed off. When they had all gone, the blind student was left without his sandals, and he exclaimed: "By God, please don't take my shoes. I don't want your certificate—I can do without it." *Dama,* p. 64. This story recalls Taha Husain's loss of sandals outside his village mosque.

[19] *Ibid.,* p. 125. Muhammad as-Sadiq Husain had been a teacher in Haqqi's Walidat Abbas al-Awwal primary school, and he had been connected with the establishment of teacher training courses in Egypt.

[20] *Khalliha*, pp. 44-81.

[21] *Sahh*, pp. 56-62.

[22] *Khalliha*, pp. 8, 41.

[23] *Ibid.*, pp. 51-55.

[24] *Qindil*, pp. 108, 112.

[25] *Fikra*, pp. 31-44; *Antar*, p. 68.

[26] *Khalliha*, pp. 153-155.

[27] *Dama*, pp. 69-74.

[28] Taufiq al-Hakim, *Yaumiyat naib fi al-aryaf*, p. 90.

[29] *Khalliha*, p. 22.

[30] Haqqi's use of images in connection with trains is eloquent of his condemnation of this symbol of modern civilization. When he first mentions the train in *Good Morning!*, he compares it to a "thread passing through a huge patchwork" (p. 7); later, however, when it is no longer idle speculation but a fact, it is described as a "snake passing through the green diked fields of Upper Egypt" (p. 80). When writing of the Square in "The Saint's Lamp," Haqqi is depicting an era when the electric tram made its first incursion. To the crowd of peasant pilgrims to the shrine of Umm Hashim (Zainab), it was a monster mercilessly running down a victim a day (*Qindil*, p. 68). And in "The First Lesson," the station is described as watching the rails fearfully, like a cat retreating before a snake (*Umm*, p. 119).

[31] "I took the ticket and studied the name of our village on it, and I smiled in surprise and joy." *Sahh*, p. 99.

[32] The inhabitants are often referred to as *ashira* (clan, tribe) or *usra* (family). The tavern-keeper's wife, a Cairene, did not mix with the women and was therefore hated for she had refused to become part of the family (*Sahh*, p. 18). "The villagers were known for their innocence and for their trust in the creator of the universe, the provider of sustenance" (*ibid.*, p. 8), and, "We would rather die than leave our village" (*ibid.*, p. 38).

[33] *Ibid.*, p. 80.

[34] *Ibid.*, p. 139; cf. p. 93.

[35] Haqqi describes the station-sweep who complained about the unfairness of his lot compared with equivalent workers elsewhere. He assailed the narrator with a shower of questions and complaints when he discovered that the latter had just returned from abroad. When the narrator pointed out the actual improvement in the sweep's life, the latter was annoyed that the narrator was denying him the right to complain. The fireman was another: there were four men to do the job of twenty! The houses by the railway tracks kept burning down, because of sparks from passing trains, and the firemen were expected to reconstruct the rubble (*ibid.*, p. 104).

[36] *Sahh*, pp. 121-123. It is interesting to compare Haqqi's attitude to that of Lutfi as-Sayyid: "We lack independence of spirit, the real freedom, and lacking that we are not in the fullest sense human. But if we examine all these weaknesses and others like them, we see that they all spring from one root: a wrong attitude toward authority. We expect too much from the government. We rely on it to do for us all we should do ourselves, we have surrendered to it our rights and duties. But we do not trust or love it; we fear and distrust it, try to avoid its attention, think of it as alien and hostile." And why did the Egyptians have the wrong attitude?

"The answer is that we have always had the wrong sort of government. Our government has always been despotic, and despotism has bred in us the vices of servitude. We are easy-going and tolerant because we are impotent." Lutfi as-Sayyid quoted in Hourani, pp. 175-176.

[37]*Sahh,* p. 109.

[38]*Ibid.,* pp. 109, 115, 139.

[39]*Ibid.,* p. 83.

[40]"The village was a single family known for its laziness" (p. 11), but now all this had changed. The cripple's husband, the only villager whom the *umda* had been forced to register as unemployed (p. 64), was the one in whose mouth Haqqi put the following words: "I used to play, the time has come for me to buckle down to some serious work like everyone else" (p. 134).

[41]*Ibid.,* p. 42.

[42]*Ibid.,* p. 148.

[43]*Ibid.,* p. 138. See above, p. 22.

[44]*Sahh,* p. 89. "The regime accepts the cultural value of religion and its significance as the moral basis of society. The regime, however, is definitely committed to a secular concept of national identity, loyalty and legitimacy. It must, nevertheless, use religion (refer to it) in order to retain contact with the masses, until the desired standards of education and economic improvement are attained." Ihsan Abd al-Qaddus in P.J. Vatikiotis, *The Egyptian Army in Politics* (Bloomington, Indiana, 1961), p. 241.

[45]*Sahh,* p. 106; cf. "Nature has died all around us and we are buried under piles of books." *Khalliha,* p. 41.

[46]*Dima,* p. 5.

[47]In 1925 when Haqqi graduated the law schools were still under French jurisdiction (*Khalliha,* p. 25). To succeed, the resourceful Egyptian had to lose his national identity, if indeed such existed at these political, social and economic levels, to assume an international one. Haqqi has satirized the Egyptians who were so used to changing regimes that they were quick to change their clothes, habits and language to suit changed circumstances: "What is more ironic than a man—previously a staunch supporter of the French praising their customs and copying them in every conceivable way (even learning their language)—clearing the path for the new Turkish ruler—his only insult being: 'Get out of the way, Frenchman, unbeliever!' " *Al-Balagh,* April 1, 1930.

[48]*Sahh,* pp. 55-56. "How noble it is to die for truth and honour, how sad to die as a despicable plaything in the hands of sly politicians." *Dama,* p. 83. Note the similarity in vocabulary—the sly government, the toy people.

[49]By saying that he is a *poor* man of Turkish stock, he has freed himself from the ranks of the ruling Turkish aristocracy in Egypt: see *Qindil,* p. 28.

[50]By freeing Islam from the Arab affiliation (cf. above, p. 14), he has rejected religion as a means of national identification.

Chapter Four

[1]"Dans le domaine rural, l'organisation des coopératives ne doit pas être intreprétée autrement: il ne s'agit pas d'une forme inspirée du socialisme moderne, mais seulement d'une résurrection de l'étatisme pharaonique." Hassan Riad,

L'Egypte Nassérienne (Paris, 1964), p. 231.

²"The West represents the primacy of the human being and his integration at the same time into the 'organic' state . . . loyalty to persons was opposed by loyalty to an impersonal whole, to institutions." G.E. von Grunebaum, *Modern Islam, The Search for Cultural Identity* (New York, 1964), p. 176. For an exhaustive treatment of identity in the modern era, see E. Mayo, *The Human Problems of an Industrial Civilization,* Cambridge, Massachusetts, 1933.

³See above, p. 22.

⁴*Khalliha,* p. 7. (See above, p. 84, n. 52.)

⁵*Qindil,* p. 87.

⁶*Haqiba,* pp. 5-10, 64. ("For the European the world is a cosmos where each person corresponds intimately to the function he performs, for the Argentine [Egyptian?] it is a chaos." J.L. Borges, *Other Inquisitions, 1937-1952,* trans. R.L.C. Simms [Texas, 1964], p. 34.)

⁷*Antar,* pp. 153-155.

⁸*Dama,* pp. 65-68; see also *Nas,* p. 77, for the failure to establish a lotteries committee.

⁹". . . députés ou délegués, qui parlent *pour* les autres c'est-à-dire en leur faveur mais aussi *à leur place,* ils sont portés à tromper, le plus souvent de bonne foi, aussi bien ceux dont ils parlent que ceux à qui ils parlent; quant à ceux d'entre eux qui sont issus des classes dominées, transfuges ou parvenus, ils ne peuvent parler que parce qu'ils ont abandonné la place sans parole de ceux dont ils portent la parole en se mettant à leur place en parole, et ils sont enclins à livrer, en échange de la reconnaissance (au double sens du terme), le capital d'information qu'ils ont emporté ave eux." P. Bourdieu, *Esquisse d'une théorie de la pratique* (Geneva, 1972), p. 158.

¹⁰*Haqiba,* pp. 6, 46, 80.

¹¹*Ibid.,* p. 67. "Shall we all be like them, acting the part of a chorus in a theater where heros are hidden forces which neither ear nor eye can detect?" *Nas,* p. 7. "A strange feeling overwhelmed the people around me. It was as though these huge mountains of goods were puppets, easily seen and understood, reliable, and yet they had strings attached, hidden strings in hidden hands . . . which manipulate them. Whose hands are they? In the past they were . . . the factory owners and bank managers . . . But today production has become highly complex, and the new manipulators are scientists, administrators and technicians . . . Control is entrusted to an electronic brain." *Haqiba,* pp. 54-55.

¹²*Ibid.,* pp. 12, 55.

¹³*Dama,* p. 80; *Haqiba,* p. 80.

¹⁴*Khutuwat,* p. 75; cf. Muwailhi: "You may have recorded your history for 7000 years, but we have recorded ours for hundreds of thousands of years." (p. 300)

¹⁵See above, p. 14.

¹⁶*Haqiba,* p. 73.

¹⁷*Ibid.,* pp. 32, 89, 67-68. Compare Taha Husain and Ahmad Fathi Zaghlul in the following passages: ". . . our real national duty . . . is to spend all we have and more, in the way of strength and effort, time and money, to make Egyptians feel, individually and collectively, that God has created them for glory not ignominy . . . and to remove from their hearts the hideous and criminal illusion that

they are created from some other clay than Europeans, formed in some other way and endowed with an intelligence other than theirs." Taha Husain in Hourani, *op. cit.,* pp. 329-330. Ahmad Fathi Zaghlul, in the preface to his translation of E.R. Demolins' *Sirr taqaddum al-inkiliz as-saksuniyin,* 1899, complained that the Egyptians did not believe in themselves, and were unaware of their rights as individuals and as a nation, which explains why they had made no effort to improve their condition.

[18]*Haqiba,* p. 73.

[19]"Perhaps the greatest reason for the west to commit crimes against us are European translations of the *1001 Nights.* From the moment they were first translated, these people have had an unchanging and distorted picture of oriental civilization." *Ibid.,* p. 85; cf. *Fikra,* p. 58.

[20]*Haqiba,* p. 86.

[21]*Fikra,* p. 58.

[22]*Nas,* p. 20; cf. *Dama,* p. 124, where Haqqi again refers to the children of slaves (*aulad jawari*).

[23]See above, pp. 83-84.

[24]*Haqiba,* p. 67; he also denounces the Ku Klux Klan (*Khutuwat,* p. 73). Muwailhi bemoans the fact that what had originally been intended to improve civilization was then turned into tools for destruction (Muwailhi, p. 299; see also Taufiq al-Hakim, *Fann al-adab,* p. 116).

[25]"Of our world and (yet) cut off from it; not subject to its time; not definitely existing; and although it has one form yet does it seem as changing as a wave in the sea." *Ibid.,* p. 30; cf. pp. 26, 29, 33, 35.

[26]*Haqiba,* pp. 80-81, 74, 92. Cf. Shihata Ubaid's preface to *Dars mulim* (1922), where he compares the occidental with the oriental. To his grief he is compelled to acknowledge that the westerner is at all times seeking to increase his knowledge, while the Egyptian is intent only on entertainment and escape (p. ii).

[27]*Qindil,* p. 89. "Le renouvellement s'accomplira non par le jeu des influences, ou par l'automatisme de l'emprunt ou par la contagion des idées et des moeurs, mais par une double, remise en cause: de l'autre et de soi." Jacques Berque, *Egypte,* p. 217.

[28]When about to leave Manfalut, Haqqi makes the following remark: "I am leaving a society where woman lives behind the veil for a society where woman is queen." *Khalliha,* p. 238.

[29]*Haqiba,* pp. 38-39, 45.

[30]See Chapter Five.

[31]*Fajr,* pp. 34-37; *Khutuwat,* p. 204. See also above, pp. 132-133.

Chapter Five

[1]The Quran tells women to lower their gaze and to draw the veil over their bosoms (*Sura Nisa,* 24.31). Charis Waddy in *Women in Muslim History* (London, 1980) traces the history of the adoption of the veil: "The move to Baghdad marked an increase in the influence of Persian custom which had grave consequences for women. The Persians, like the Byzantines, and earlier the Assyrians, were accustomed to protecting their women by the wearing of a veil" (pp. 41-42) and "The Ottoman period brought the segregation of women to its

height. Gradually, the curtain that ensured the privacy of the Prophet's home hardened into what for many were prison walls. The covering pulled across the face to ensure respect became an impenetrable veil." (p. 123)

[2]"One notable feature of women's advance in the Muslim World has been the number of far-sighted men who have worked for a greater freedom for women," Waddy, p. 139. The struggle never became sexist but was always political: a struggle for enlightenment against backwardness; for progress against reaction. The politicization of domesticity is characteristic of a society at a turning point of national self-awareness. This creation of the Patriotic Mother is often supported by men because it relegates women to the home. By acknowledging their role as educators of a new generation, women have been put on the social map in such a way as to distance them from the political map.

[3]"Woman is truly hidden, and Egyptian literature should illustrate the effect of this absence on society and its morals." *Khutuwat,* p. 61.

[4]"For the Arab man, women exist in various personifications: virgin girl, wife, mother. There is no room for the woman friend or lover . . . There is no love, only sexuality . . . Marriage is a sexual pleasure on the one hand and a means of procreating on the other; the image of the wife is thus identified with that of the mother." A. Khalili, quoted in Magida Salman, "Arab Women," in *Khamsin,* 6, 1978, p. 26.

[5]*Fikra,* p. 7.

[6]*Nas,* p. 48.

[7]*Qindil,* p. 148.

[8]Appendix to Kishk, p. 243.

[9]See above, p. 27.

[10]"She is an animal who will only submit to absolute control, she can only be taken by force, like her 'foremothers' who lived in the forest." *Umm,* p. 77.

[11]*Qindil,* p. 91. Naim Atiya suggests that Mary awakens Ismail's will, *Yahya Haqqi wa alamuh al qasasi.* (Cairo, 1978), pp. 13, 101.

[12]Cf. the prostitute begging Umm Hashim for salvation and intercession (*Qindil,* p. 80). A poor peasant married a prostitute in a distant village and decided to take his bride home. On the return journey their taxi crashed into some water and they were drowned. She was found in her "savior's" embrace. It seems that for her soul to be saved, her body had first to be saved so that the final absolute loss of the body, now purged, could free a purified soul. (*Khalliha,* pp. 220-222.)

[13]Her body has become merchandise. Haqqi writes that at the turn of the century Egypt was importing everything, even prostitutes. Cromer prided himself on forbidding the import of English prostitutes! (*Khalliha,* p. 57.)

[14]See above, pp. 31-34.

[15]*Khalliha,* pp. 216-218, 172; *Dama,* p. 22.

[16]*Khalliha,* p. 21.

[17]*Fikra,* pp. 127-138. Cf. "This father had to kill his daughter for public opinion had put the knife in his hand." (*Khalliha,* p. 171.)

[18]*Khalliha,* pp. 175-176, 208-209.

[19]*Ibid.,* p. 214.

[20]It is interesting to note the similarity in description between the idealized peasant woman and Salima. "My heart inclines to them wrapped as they are in

their *milayas* . . . slender and upright." (*Antar,* p. 38.) Although most peasant women are not veiled, Haqqi describes them as veiled. When I questioned him about this poetic license, referring in particular to "The Postman," he said that that was how he saw them. (Interview, March 2, 1979.)

²¹*Antar,* p. 10.

²²"A Robber's Life," in *As-Siyasa,* 10 December 1926. "The Postman" is an example of what happens to the girl in the country when "She thinks lightly of her chastity," and steps out from behind the veil of uniformity.

²³*Umm,* p. 158.

²⁴See above, pp. 33-34.

²⁵*Dama,* p. 60.

²⁶"Women are made happy because of an upsurge of maternalism when they comfort their weeping husbands." (*Sahh,* p. 19) Cf. "Maulid without Chickpeas," where Haqqi writes of the beautiful Inayat who had married an effete young man, much to her friends' surprise. Haqqi writes that she had chosen him specifically so that she might satisfy her maternal instinct. (*Antar,* p. 73.) Another such example is the crusty matchmaker who married her client after he had stirred her maternal instinct. (*Umm,* p. 50.)

²⁷*Fikra,* p. 8.

²⁸*Ibid.,* pp. 165-166.

²⁹F. Hauswirth, *Purdah: The Status of Indian Women.* (London, 1932), p. 110.

³⁰*Fikra,* p. 10.

³¹*Haqiba,* pp. 21-22; cf. *Antar,* pp. 167, 142.

³²*Fikra,* pp. 14-15.

³³*Dama,* pp. 75-79.

³⁴Compare with the following description: "Most of them . . . were women with heavy celluloid legs, like those of a billiard table. Legs that had been poured into stockings which had been transformed into sacks." (*Antar,* p. 164.)

³⁵*Khalliha,* pp. 6, 134. "I did not enjoy the freedom which other children do when I was a child." "Irony, or the Man with the Black Face," in *Al-Fajr,* 6 September 1926, and "Our mother was particularly strict with Yahya." (Interview with Musa Haqqi, Cairo, 28 March, 1979.)

³⁶Did she suppress her sexuality, or had the child on reaching puberty suddenly discovered what had been there all along? It would seem that the narrator is blaming his mother for his own inability to deal with a rite of passage. What is strange is that the narrator could not bypass this stage, remaining fixed in his trauma.

³⁷"As Though," in *Al-Masa,* 25 December 1967 and 22 January 1968.

³⁸"(The woman's own sexual impulsivity if) unleashed, it can disrupt the recreated harmony, it can revive . . . the first intimations of isolated, non-omnipotent selfhood; it can reactivate . . . the malaise that originated in the nursling's discovery of the mother's separate, uncontrollable subjective existence." D. Dinnerstein, p. 61.

³⁹See Haqqi's synopsis of Lashin's "Fate"—"The tragedy of a young man who discovers that his mother had given him the best education with money that she had 'earned' at the expense of her chastity." (*Fajr,* p. 89.) Cf. above, pp. 106-107.

⁴⁰*Dama,* p. 79.

[41] The girls in Zainab square pull their *milayas* close to their bodies, so that the men come to rub up against them like dogs, says Haqqi. (*Qindil,* p. 102.)

[42] "He wanted to catch her with some horrific, rich man with money drooling out of his pockets just as the saliva was drooling out of his drunken mouth." (*Umm,* p. 161.)

[43] *Umm,* pp. 63-64.

[44] *Antar,* p. 44.

[45] It is interesting that Haqqi should have referred to cave drawings for a biblical view of woman as original sinner. In Islam Adam and Eve share equally the responsibility for their sin; see A. Yusuf Ali, *The Holy Quran, Translation and Commentary.* (Beirut, 1965), p. 344, n. 1006.

[46] See above, p. 151, n. 42.

[47] The fellah; see Chapter 2.

[48] Survival—the gypsy regarded as member of a wolf pack (see above, p. 156, n. 15).

[49] *Dima,* p. 126.

[50] Sharuni, *op. cit.,* p. 16.

[51] Mustafa Ibrahim Husain, *op. cit.,* p. 67.

[52] Naim Atiya, *op. cit.,* pp. 33-63; cf. Samir Wahby, "Critical Evaluation," p. 54.

[53] Ghali Shukri, *Azmat al-jins fi al-qissa al-arabiya,* (Beirut, 1962), pp. 127-140.

[54] "The strength of my love will teach you how to believe first in your humanness, after which your belief in God will be sound." (*Qindil,* p. 177.)

[55] "How glad women are, how their greedy eyes gleam with the pleasure of conquest when a man has been reduced to their level." (*Antar,* p. 141.)

[56] *Umm,* p. 131.

[57] *Sahh,* p. 27; cf. "A Story About a Petition," where Lawahiz, a dancer, seduces a man, and then runs off with his chauffeur. (*Umm,* pp. 100-103.)

[58] *Sahh,* p. 136.

[59] *Al-Katib,* April 1961.

Chapter Six

[1] Aqqad and Mazini used to mock Egyptians who wrote of nightingales in poetry despite the fact that there are no nightingales in Egypt; they also censured the idealization of spring—Egypt's most unpleasant season (*Khutuwat,* p. 227).

[2] *Khutuwat,* p. 10. Without the critic there is a grave danger that communication will be lost; the critic forms a vital link. (*Itr,* pp. 26-30.)

[3] *Khutuwat,* p. 65.

[4] *Fajr,* p. 7; *Kaukab ash-Sharq,* February 1927; *Khutuwat,* p. 11.

[5] *Khutuwat,* p. 14.

[6] *Ihsan Hanim* was the first collection of short stories to be published, 1921.

[7] *Khutuwat,* pp. 15, 287, 299.

[8] *Kaukab ash-Sharq,* February 1927.

[9] *Khutuwat,* p. 110.

[10] *Fajr,* pp. 130, 131.

[11] *Ibid.,* pp. 124-125, 127.

[12] *Khutuwat,* pp. 119, 203.

[13] Shakespeare, Thackeray, Morrison, Carlisle, Scott, Stevenson, Dickens, Corneille, Molière, La Fontaine, Balzac, Hugo, Dumas, Flaubert, Maupassant, Verlaine, Rimbaud, Baudelaire, Goethe, Pirandello, Boccaccio, Dante, Oscar Wilde, Poe, Mark Twain (*Fajr,* p. 81).

[14] Gogol, Pushkin, Tolstoy, Turgenev, Dostoevsky, Artzybashev (*ibid.,* pp. 81-82).

[15] *Qindil,* p. 37. Tolstoy and Dostoevsky "had their missions which, in their different ways were aspects of the feeling that Russia had an untainted Messianic role to play in the World; both had their religion and indeed in Dostoevky's journalism the idea of mission was politically imperial." V.S. Pritchett, *The Gentle Barbarian* (London, 1977), p. 155.

[16] *Qindil,* p. 37. Muhammad Taimur also admitted to borrowing from Maupassant when writing: "Lord, for whom did you create this paradise" in *What The Eyes See;* Lashin acknowledged his debt to Chekhov when writing "The Explosion" in *Irony of the Flute* (introduction). At that time some wrote collections entitled *Borrowed Stories* (*Qisas muqtabasa*), *Khutuwat,* p. 15.

[17] *Khutuwat,* pp. 275, 280.

[18] *Fajr,* p. 82. For a comparison of Lashin with the best European short story writers, see *ibid.,* p. 83.

[19] *Khutuwat,* pp. 260, 125. Muhammad Taimur wrote a series of articles in *Minbar* against Rihani and all "low" comedians and ham actors, because they degraded drama—this criticism despite his own *Abd as-Sattar Effendi* (1918).

[20] *Fajr,* pp. 60, 49.

[21] *Ibid.,* pp. 28-29, 44.

[22] *Ibid.,* p. 60.

[23] *Ibid.,* p. 117.

[24] *Ibid.,* pp. 21, 22.

[25] *Fajr,* pp. 61-62. "The short story appeared to be an attempt by the authors to enter the national political field, and so it began to reflect precisely the post-revolutionary society." Sayyid Hamid an-Nassaj, *Tatawwur fann al-qissa al-qasira fi Misr, 1910-1930* (Cairo, 1968), p. 388.

[26] *Fajr,* pp. 149, 62, 200, 98; *Khutuwat,* p. 111. "The Egyptian author should now . . . describe complex, mysterious, hidden emotions or he should present us with examples of emotionally charged situations, by means of which he could clearly demonstrate the good and the evil in the world, the beautiful and the ugly. He should show that man's soul is so complex that one emotion is not seen to be separable from another. He should describe the lowest levels of humanity, as also the highest, to show that man can be either an angel or a devil." *Fajr,* p. 215.

[27] *Khutuwat,* pp. 200, 245. Such an idealistic aproach to literature in Egypt was beset by problems; Lashin, for example, would only write when his stories met with acclaim. (Introduction to *Irony of the Flute,* 1964.)

[28] *Fajr,* p. 62; *Khutuwat,* p. 226.

[29] *Fajr,* p. 128.

[30] *Ibid.,* pp. 130-131.

[31] "I beg the present generation not to be put off by its naïveté, but to handle it

with the care and respect that they would display when coming across an old box which their grandmother had left behind, and when the box was opened her perfume is smelled and glimpses of her world are caught." *Fajr,* p. 164.

[32]*Ibid.,* p. 124.

[33]*Ibid.,* pp. 198, 241, 105.

[34]"Increase in observation is a positive sign, since it indicates that the nation is generally progressing." Abd ar-Rahman ar-Rafii, *Thaurat sanat 1919* (Cairo, 1946), vol. ii, p. 193.

[35]*Khutuwat,* p. 80.

[36]Haqqi deplores the tendency of the young to write directly political literature, in which political pamphlets and government communiqués may be included in full. He claims not to read contemporary Russian literature because it is mostly propaganda. (*Unshuda,* pp. 114-118.)

[37]*Khutuwat,* p. 91.

[38]*Ibid.,* pp. 110-111, 211. This was how Haqqi felt that the songwriter, Rami, had been annihilated in Umm Kulthum (*ibid.,* p. 40). He criticizes the use of rhymed prose (*saj*) (*Fajr,* pp. 22-23).

[39]*Ibid.,* p. 210.

[40]Haikal asserted that had he not loved Egypt he would not have written a word (*Fajr,* p. 43)—when in Paris he would close his curtains, and in the darkened room he would imagine Egypt. Haqqi claims that Muhammad Taimur's inclination to literature arose out of his love for Egypt (*ibid.,* p. 65). Cf. Introduction, *Irony of the Flute* (1964).

[41]*Fajr,* p. 201.

[42]*Khutuwat,* p. 8; *Itr,* pp. 31-37.

[43]"I was happy to add some comments which were destined to be of benefit to the writer, and to give him an unbiased idea of what an easy-going, modest reader thinks." *Khutuwat,* p. 60.

[44]*Khutuwat,* p. 100. The same kind of apology is found in *Haqiba* where he constantly reiterates the fact that his trip to France had been short, as though to excuse himself for his numerous generalizations, e.g., p. 53.

[45]*Khutuwat,* pp. 165-166.

[46]*Ibid.,* p. 181.

[47]*Fajr,* p. 220.

[48]*Itr,* p. 133.

[49]*Fajr,* p. 154.

[50]E.g., Lashin's "Noah's Journal" in *Al-Balagh,* April 15, 1930. He does, however, justify the use of the ancient theme of Cleopatra since it served an apologetic role: if Cleopatra's reputation can be salvaged, Egyptians can once again feel honor and pride in themselves and in their past. (*Khutuwat,* p. 57.)

[51]*Fajr,* p. 121.

[52]*Khutuwat,* p. 46.

[53]*Kaukab ash-Sharq,* February 1927.

[54]*Unshuda,* p. 51.

[55]*Fajr,* pp. 129-130. He even suggest that Hakim should have had one of his protagonists die for his country.

[56]"Taufiq al-Hakim between Hope and Fear."

[57]*Khutuwat,* pp. 294-295.

[58]*Fajr,* p. 200. At the end of "The Turtle Flies" Haqqi has added his "intention": the importance of the hero is that he was an early example of a working-class man trying to become a bourgeois. (*Qindil,* p. 138.)

[59]*Khutuwat,* p. 17.

[60]*Itr,* p. 158.

[61]*Ibid.,* pp. 65, 185.

[62]*Fajr,* pp. 41, 88, 146; Introduction, *Irony of the Flute* (1964); *Itr,* p. 106; cf. *ibid.,* p. 111.

[63]*Khutuwat,* p. 227.

[64]*Itr,* pp. 84-122. See above, p. 124.

[65]*Khutuwat,* p. 76.

[66]*Khutuwat,* p. 69.

[67]"Taufiq al-Hakim between Hope and Fear."

[68]*Ibid.* He also compared himself very unfavorably with the Greek, Kosti Sajaradas. (*Khutuwat,* p. 183; *Khalliha,* p. 220.)

[69]"The first we heard of Isa Ubaid was what Yahya Haqqi had written in his book *Fajr* which was published in 1960. Before this he was almost completely unknown in the literary field." Abbas Khidr, Introduction to *Ihsan Hanim* (1964).

[70]*Fajr,* p. 76. This magazine was run by Ahmad Khairi Said and seems to have been a forerunner of *Al-Fajr* (1924-1925).

[71]*Fajr,* pp. 88-97.

[72]In his recent book on the Arabic novel Roger Allen mentions the undeserved neglect that *Eve Without Adam* has suffered. (R. Allen, *The Arabic Novel: An Historical and Critical Introduction* [New York, 1982], pp. 41-42.)

[73]*Itr,* pp. 161-186; Interview, Cairo, March 30, 1979.

[74]*Itr,* on the cover.

[75]*Ibid.,* pp. 64, 69, 70-74. See above, p. 20.

Chapter Seven

[1]Cf. Luis Awad, "Fann al-ibtisam," in *Al-Ahram,* July 6, 1962; Charles Vial, "Yahya Haqqi Humoriste," in *Annales Islamologiques* (Cairo, 1972), p. 353.

[2]Haqqi has enumerated bitterness as being among the vices that he would like to eliminate (*Nas,* p. 95).

[3]*Dama,* pp. 35-39.

[4]In *Antar,* Haqqi writes of a man who had no title or function and, for lack of greater inspiration, wrote under his name on the calling card "*Subscriber to Le Courrier de Tripoli*" (p. 173).

[5]*Dama,* p. 36.

[6]*Taala,* p. 31.

[7]*Umm,,* p. 142.

[8]*Ibid.,* p. 147.

[9]*Dama,* pp. 27-30.

[10]*Fikra,* pp. 109-111.

[11]*Ibid.,* pp. 16-23.

[12]*Khalliha,* pp. 51-55; see above, pp. 47-48.

[13]*Khalliha,* pp. 82-85.

[14]When Sami hears of the loose life that Susu, the beautiful barmaid, was leading, he was furious and visualized himself coming in on a lewd scene where he would just look at her patronizingly, so that she would know that he did not care. (*Umm,* p. 161.)

[15]One of the great advantages of returning to Cairo was that "he could wear his silk shirts again." (*Ibid.,* p. 155.)

[16]He laughs at his short stature a number of times, e.g. *Fikra,* pp. 15, 87; *Dama,* pp. 68, 101.

[17]*Khalliha,* p. 166. See above, p. 40.

[18]*Ibid.,* p. 210. See above, p. 40.

[19]*Dama,* p. 23. See above, p. 150, n. 25.

[20]*Fikra,* pp. 25-30.

[21]*Fikra,* pp. 7-15.

[22]Luis Awad, "Fann al-ibtisam."

[23]*Dama,* pp. 75-79.

[24]*Umm,* p. 168.

[25]*Unshuda,* p. 63.

[26]*Khutuwat,* p. 19.

[27]*Khalliha,* p. 161.

[28]*Umm,* p. 136.

[29]*Khalliha,* p. 98.

[30]*Umm,* p. 121.

[31]In this connection remember Haqqi's description of the plight of the Sao Paulo reader of *Muqtataf.* Having sent his question to the magazine—"How many hairs grow on a head?"—he was probably rushing around excitedly, as though he were carrying an important secret (*Antar,* p. 172). Again, this sketch reveals Haqqi's sympathy for the need of a pathetic, disoriented man to belong (see above, p. 36).

[32]The nose, that part of the body that symbolizes haughtiness, is the last to decompose (*Sahh,* p. 119).

[33]*Taala,* p. 10.

[34]*Antar,* p. 159.

[35]*Fikra,* p. 14.

[36]*Antar,* p. 161.

[37]*Ibid.,* p. 165.

[38]*Fikra,* p. 25.

[39]*Ibid.,* pp. 109-110.

[40]*Taala,* pp. 41-42.

[41]*Umm,* p. 72.

[42]*Antar,* p. 163.

[43]*Khalliha,* p. 81. See above, p. 47.

[44]*Ibid.,* p. 153.

[45]*Ibid.,* p. 178.

[46]*Antar,* pp. 79-80.

[47] See above, p. 69.

[48] "Salah (Jahin) contemplates the universe and man with a deep sadness, which he not only feels within himself but which he also sees in the eyes of others." (*Itr,* p. 65.)

[49] Mustafa Ibrahim Husain has commented on Haqqi's tragic view of life: "It is a tragic sense of humor in that it reveals the tragedy in such a way that it arouses a smile torn by sadness, and not raucous laughter as is usually the case with humor." *Yahya Haqqi mubdian wa naqidan* (Cairo, 1970), p. 58.

Chapter Eight

[1] Cf. *Fajr,* p. 188 and *Khutuwat,* p. 245, for a discussion of Muhammad Dib's *Fi al-maqha* which Haqqi praises for its ability to raise the reader above the local aspect of the story to its universal significance, thus lending poignancy to the particular tragedy.

[2] *Unshuda,* pp. 24, 61.

[3] *Nas,* p. 46.

[4] The same flurry of impressions may be noted in the scene of Ismail's departure for Europe: "Farewells of the family, wailing and weeping, the station, the train, then the harbor with all its activity, and the mysterious ship and its whistle." *Qindil,* p. 81.

[5] *Umm,* p. 120.

[6] *Ibid.,* pp. 104-110.

[7] These binary epithets may be noted in much of contemporary Egyptian literature.

[8] He praises Ihsan Abd al-Qaddus for his precision; if anything were to be changed, the structure would go. *Khutuwat,* p. 172.

[9] *Itr,* p. 8.

[10] *Nas,* p. 30.

[11] *Itr,* pp. 63-64.

[12] *Unshuda,* pp. 58-59; cf. *Qindil,* p. 45, and *Khutuwat,* pp. 219-220. When describing the kind of people who buy and sell lottery tickets, Haqqi describes their movements as a "creeping" or "infiltration," for such are the shadows that people our underworld. *Nas,* p. 82.

[13] *Nas,* p. 94. For a similar use of Form V verbs, see Mazini, *Aud ala bad* (1943) for the description of the uncle after he had been stung by the ants (p. 70):

واشتهيت أن أراه وهو ينطّ، ويتلوّى، ويتعوّج، ويتحرّق ويشتم.

[14] H. Loucel, "Signification du nombre et de la fréquence des racines quadreconsonantiques dans 'Ana ahya' de Layla Baalbaki," *Studia Islamica,* XXXI, 1972, pp. 121-167.

[15] *Khalliha,* p. 142.

[16] It is interesting to note that even the Quran has only 47 different quadriliterals of which 31 are repeats: Jahiz in *Kitab at-tarbi wa at-tadwir* has only 9 different quadriliterals of which 2 are repeats (cf., Loucel, p. 122), whereas in *Dama* alone I found 79 quadriliterals of which only 11 are repeats.

[17] Loucel, *op. cit.,* p. 125.

[18]*Nas*, p. 97. Haqqi has, however, expressed repugnance at the use of *saj* (cf. *Khutuwat*, p. 226), as a result of which he had on occasion to use artifice to avoid it! E.g., in the first line of "The Vacant Bed," he wrote:

الداخل في شارع الريحان من ناحية ميدان الامامين.

instead of:

الداخل في شارع الامامين من ناحية ميدان الريحان.

(Interview, Cairo, 29 March 1979.)

[19]*Qindil*, p. 80.

[20]*Itr*, p. 194.

[21]For a similar effect, compare:

ومضى الصبح في نوم يقظ وانقضى الضحى في يقظة نائمة.

(Lashin, *Irony of the Flute*, 1964, p. 25.)

[22]Haqqi himself quotes "The Protest" as an example: "And so I used many physiological terms: the vomiting of the pregnant woman on the wedding night, the washing of the small stained towels, the smell of sweat . . ." (*Qindil*, p. 52.) Cf. his use of words like *qaml, baqq, baud,* and *burghuth* (Ahmad Abbas Salih, "Habib al-munkasirin wa al-bulaha wa al-masakin" in *Al-Jumhuriya*, 7 April 1962).

[23]*Dima*, p. 83.

[24]*Nas*, p. 9.

[25]*Unshuda*, p. 62.

[26]*Nas*, p. 33. Describing man's armor in the battle of life: *muthaqqal bi ad-duru* and *mudajjaj bi as-silah* (*Itr*, p. 7).

[27]*Nas*, p. 100.

[28]For a discussion of precision in Haqqi's style, see Mustafa Abd as-Latif as-Sihrati, "Yahya Haqqi al-insan al-fannan," *Shahr*, May 1961; Samir Wahby, "Al-bia wa tathiruha ala intaj Yahya Haqqi," *Al-Katib*, February 1965; and Sabry Hafez, "Nas fi az-zill wa qadiyat an-nathr al-arabi," *Al-Adab*, September 1971.

[29]*Khutuwat*, pp. 235-236.

[30]*Unshuda*, p. 68. Haqqi has, however, expressed his horror on hearing of Flaubert's reaction when a friend wrote to him about his wife's terminal illness. Flaubert had replied: "How lucky you are to be able to watch such a tragedy at close hand!" How callous is man, laments Haqqi, that he can allow his human passions to sink to such a low ebb in his pursuit of art—art is important, but nothing is as important as man! (Interview, Cairo, 3 April 1979.)

[31]*Qindil*, pp. 45-46; *Khutuwat*, p. 48.

[32]*Itr*, p. 89. He criticizes Mustafa Mahhud for introducing characters without due justification or explanation (*Khutuwat*, p. 293).

[33]*Khalliha*, p. 184.

[34]*Umm*, p. 119.

[35]*Taala*, pp. 7-8.

[36]*Dima*, p. 83.

[37]*Unshuda*, pp. 62-66. "Literature disapproves of ease in production, as it does of ease in consumption," Taha Husain, *Khisam wa naqd*, p. 33. See above, p. 163.

[38]"His hand fell on a wave of wool which the sun had kindled." *Dima,* p. 86.

[39]*Ibid.,* p. 84.

[40]*Ibid.,* p. 103.

[41]*Ibid.,* p. 86. As Ismail walked through the square, his ears picked out certain sounds:

ضحكات غصّة واخرى غليظة «حشّاشي».

(*Qindil,* p. 68.)

[42]*Dima,* pp. 94-96.

[43]*Qindil,* p. 52.

[44]*Antar,* p. 77.

[45]*Haqiba,* pp. 37-38.

[46]*Khalliha,* pp. 10-19.

[47]*Unshuda,* p. 63.

[48]*Nas,* pp. 9-12.

[49]See above, p. 14.

[50]See above, pp. 29, 35.

[51]*Sahh,* pp. 78, 94.

[52]See above, p. 21.

[53]In "The First Lesson," the station platform was always described as short but when it is used to describe the limits of Yusuf's world it becomes long: "Only a step away, (beyond) the threshold, was the freedom of the long platform." *Umm,* p. 122.

[54]R. Barthes, "To Write: An Intransitive Verb?" in R. and F. deGeorge (eds.), *The Structuralists from Marx to Levi-Strauss* (New York, 1972), p. 162.

[55]See below, p. 176, n. 16.

[56]*Khutuwat,* pp. 277-278; cf. *ibid.,* p. 187.

[57]*Unshuda,* p. 49.

[58]". . . comparing similar qualities in two sensations, he (the writer) makes their essential nature stand out clearly by joining them in a metaphor, in order to remove from them the contingencies of time, and links them together with the indescribable bond of an allegiance of words . . . The literature that is satisfied merely to 'describe things' . . . sharply cuts off all communication of our present self with the past, the essence of which the objects preserve, and with the future, in which they stimulate us to enjoy the past again," M. Proust, *The Past Recaptured,* trans. F.A. Blossom (New York, 1932), p. 218.

[59]Table One: Images in General

	Numbers	%
Nature	164	39.23
Other	254	60.77
Total	418	100.00

Table Two: Nature Images

	Numbers	%
Fauna	98	59.75
Elements	43	26.22
Flora	23	14.03
Total	164	100.00

Table Three: Animal Images

	Numbers	%
Wild	56	57.14
Tame	24	24.49
Mythical	3	3.06
Unspecified	15	15.31
Total	98	100.00

[60]"We may notice how imagery unites man, animal and nature, thus illustrating Haqqi's perception of the unity of creation." Mustafa Ibrahim Husain, p. 98.

[61]*Dama,* p. 16.

[62]*Nas,* p. 88.

[63]*Qindil,* p. 145.

[64]*Nas,* p. 118.

[65]*Sahh,* p. 68.

[66]See above, p. 38.

[67]See above, pp. 20-21.

[68]Not to be able to see in this way is a form of blindness:

فلا بصر مع فقد البصيرة.

(*Qindil,* p. 72.)

[69]*Unshuda,* p. 70.

[70]See also *Khutuwat,* pp. 237-249 for his articles written after 1959. The first twenty articles are written in a straightforward manner. Haqqi is not trying to create an effect; what is important is clarity so that he may be sure of communicating. In the first twenty pages there is only one image, and, at that, a dry one: i.e., his treatment of literary criticism is like a merchant's inventory.

[71]*Unshuda,* pp. 62-64.

[72]*Itr,* pp. 7-8.

[73]*Ibid.,* p. 188; *Unshuda,* p. 81; *Dama,* p. 5; *Unshuda,* p. 80; *ibid.,* p. 93; *Khutuwat,* p. 147; *ibid.,* p. 246; *Itr,* p. 112.

[74]*Al-Katib,* April 1961, p. 161.

[75]Outside the Qarafa, the city of the dead in Cairo, basil wrapped in palm leaves (*khus*) is sold to those who come to visit the dead. The basil is then placed on the tomb, a Pharaonic custom still practiced today. Cf. "They do not set aside a day to go and visit the cemetery, neither Thursday nor the forty days (of mourning) . . . they do not (use) palm leaves nor basil." *Dama,* p. 24.

[76]Imamain refers to the cemeteries in the Qarafa: Imam al-Laith and Imam ash-Shafii (Interview, Cairo, 23 March 1979).

[77]*Al-Katib,* April 1961, p. 175.

[78]The fact that the corpse was of an Upper Egyptian bride is significant: this time he was assured of surrender by an Upper Egyptian girl, unlike on his wedding night.

[79]*Taala,* p. 7.

[80]*Ibid.,* p. 28.

[81]*Ibid.,* p. 30.

[82]*Ibid.,* p. 32. Cf. "The atmosphere weighed down on the *rababa* as it whined on monotonously. The whole world had stopped still, the *rababa* was somewhere else." *Dima,* p. 98.

[83] Haqqi has said that by employing words used by Mutanabbi and Shauqi, the young writers would become part of a heritage, part of something greater than their individual selves (*Itr*, p. 33).

[84] See Charles Vial, "Contributions à l'étude du roman et de la nouvelle en Egypte, dès origines à 1960" in *Revue de l'Occident Musulman et de la Méditerranée*, 1967, pp. 113-174. Lashin went through three stages in his use of the colloquial: (1) all dialogue was in the classical; (2) colloquial used both in dialogue and in narrative, and written as spoken; and (3) return to the classical (cf. *Eve Without Adam;* Nassaj, *Tatawwur fann al-qissa al-qasira fi Misr*, pp. 215-217). According to Haqqi, Lashin was the first to try and deal with the problem of the rendition of the *qaf*. In *Irony of the Flute*, he had used the *hamza;* though, as may be seen from the following example, there was some inconsistency:

أسيب بنت زي دي تطلع فين دلوقت في البرد اللي يئسف المسمار.

(p. 22; cf. *dilwaqt.*)

[85] *Fajr*, p. 143.

[86] Cf. *Al-Hilal*, LVII, 7 July 1949, pp. 110-117, for a discussion by Haikal, Aqqad, Taufiq al-Hakim and Mahmud Taimur on the use of the colloquial. They agreed on the use of colloquial in plays, and the use of classical for universal themes.

[87] *Itr*, p. 125. Nadim's *At-tankit wa at-tabkit* is written in a language that is as close to the colloquial as classical syntax will allow—"(les partisans d'Orabi) font de lui leur indispensable adaptateur. Quand un discours a été prononcé en langue classique, il se lève, transpose en truculent dialect les pompes conventionelles du propos. Alors seulement le discours devient révolutionnaire," Berque, *L'Egypte*, p. 115.

[88] *Khutuwat*, p. 12. Taimur's play, *Usfur fi al-qafs*, was written in the classical and then translated into the colloquial. His brother, Mahmud, wrote *Al-makhba raqm 13* (1949) in the colloquial and the classical: one version for the stage, the other for reading; Taufiq al-Hakim wrote his play *As-Safaqa* (1956) in such a way that it could be read in the classical or the colloquial. After panning Muhammad Abu Tayila's *Sirr al-mara al-majhula* (1955), Haqqi does, however, praise his use of the colloquial (*Khutuwat*, p. 135).

[89] *Qindil*, p. 45; cf. *Khutuwat*, p. 200.

[90] *Antar*, p. 9. In his introduction to *An Anthem to Simplicity*, Haqqi writes that when he had been asked to contribute to the magazine *At-Taawun*, he had been told that the readership consisted primarily of peasants who were members of agricultural unions. Although he had at first been tempted to write his articles entirely in the colloquial, he eventually decided that respect for his fellow countrymen precluded such an approach to any form of writing; a writer must never feel that he is dropping to his readers' level (p. 7). Cf. Taha Husain, *Khisam wa naqd*, where he writes of the negative response of readers to newspapers written in the colloquial (p. 181).

[91] Haqqi feels that the colloquial has a certain music and wildness, and that someone like Jahin makes it sound like a sonata played on a Stradivarius (*Itr*, pp. 79-80).

[92] C. Vial, "Les idées de Yahya Haqqi sur la langue" in *Revue de l'Occident Musulman et de la Méditerranée*, 1973, p. 414. Haqqi has, on occasion, used the prefix *ba*, e.g. *biqulu* (*Antar*, p. 97) and *biyakil* (*ibid.*). He has also used

the suffix *shin*, e.g. *ma yakunsh* (*ibid.*, p. 123); *ma kadabsh* (*ibid.*, p. 122) and *ma tazalsh* (*ibid.*, p. 123). Sometimes he will change a *hamza* into a *ya*, e.g. *zaba'in* is written *zabayin* (*Unshuda*, p. 17); *jara'ir* is written *jarayir* (*Haqiba*, p. 49); *jana'ini* is written *janayini* (*Umm*, p. 57). The *tha* is sometimes changed into a *ta*, e.g. *kurath* is written *kurat* (*Nas*, p. 60); *thalith* is written *talit* (*Fikra*, p. 24).

[93] Words that can have both good and bad meanings in the classical are only understood in their negative sense in the colloquial. (*Nas*, p. 123.)

[94] *Ibid.*

[95] *Qindil*, p. 94.

[96] *Antar*, p. 10; see above, p. 72.

[97] *Qindil*, pp. 99-118. Another example of the intermixture of the classical and colloquial languages in same speech can be seen in "Reasons Differ" (*Umm*, p. 73).

[98] *Nas*, pp. 92-94.

[99] Luis Awad has said that even had Haqqi found such an equivalent, it would probably be unfamiliar to the average reader, and therefore the writer would no longer be illustrating life convincingly (*Al-Ahram*, 6 July 1962). Ni mat Ahmad Fuad has said that Haqqi does not care whether he uses a classical or colloquial word as long as it is in its right place (*Qimam adabiya* [Cairo, 1966], p. 341). Abd al-Hamid Ibrahim has said that Haqqi knows exactly when and where to put a colloquial phrase ("Yahya Haqqi wa faid al-karim," in *Az-Zuhur*, April 1973).

[100] *Itr*, pp. 77-81.

[101] See above, p. 16.

[102] *Fajr*, p. 163.

[103] Changed circumstances (new governmental systems, independence, employment of women, growing literacy and increased intellectual contact with the outside world) require a new literary expression. New material problems had given rise to concepts which were alien and therefore inexpressible, unless terms were borrowed from elsewhere—a practice which Haqqi endorses if the meaning is thereby fully rendered (*Khutuwat*, pp. 177, 228).

[104] *Khalliha*, pp. 224-225.

[105] *Dama*, p. 100.

[106] This is labor that the reader must not be allowed to suspect; see *Antar*, p. 7; *Qindil*, p. 12; and *Unshuda*, p. 13.

[107] *Unshuda*, p. 123; cf. *Antar*, p. 6.

[108] *Khutuwat*, p. 227. "Car si les mots n'avaient qu'un sens, celui du dictionnaire, si une seconde langue ne venait troubler et libérer 'les certitudes du langue,' il n'y aurait pas de littérature." Roland Barthes, *Critique et Vérité*, p. 52.

[109] *Unshuda*, p. 79; cf. *Qindil*, p. 45; *Al-Majalla*, August 1966.

[110] *Unshuda*, p. 94.

[111] *Qindil*, p. 16.

[112] *Unshuda*, p. 36.

Chapter Nine

[1]*Fajr,* p. 103.

[2]"Ils affirment un art, et une critique socialistes qui tentent de fonder l'optimisme révolutionnaire sur l'appréhension des réalités." V. Monteil, *Anthologie Bilingue de la littérature arabe contemporaine* (Beirut, 1959), p. xxvi.

[3]*Fajr,* p. 253.

[4]"(Lashin's) stories are not free from Friday sermons and a moral tone, and warnings and guidance . . . and because of this warning note the stories feel somewhat contrived." *Ibid.,* p. 86.

[5]"It is not I but the people, as always, who will judge." *Umm,* p. 5; cf. *Fajr,* p. 104.

[6]*Kishk,* pp. 239-240. "Le discours littéraire à pour fonction de constituer un spectacle, il n'a donc pas besoin, pour exister, d'être vrai ou cru tel; on ne le jugera point à son adéquation à une quelconque vérité mais à sa structuration interne, c'est-à-dire peut-être, en restreignant le sens de l'expression, à sa vraisemblance." Daniel Reig, "Le Discours Littéraire Contemporain," in Colloquium A.A.E.I., *Discours, écriture et société dans le monde islamique contemporain* (Paris, February 1977), p. 2.

[7]*Fajr,* pp. 62, 198. "No great work of art ever reveals all its secrets—the imagination is left to complete what has merely been suggested." *Taala,* pp. 45-46.

[8]*Itr,* p. 23; cf. the title of his autobiography, *Leave it to God.*

[9]*Umm,* p. 122-123.

[10]*Ibid.,* p. 127.

[11]"O horror, horror, horror! Tongue nor heart/ Cannot conceive nor name thee." Shakespeare, *Macbeth,* Act 2, scene iii.

[12]*Umm,* p. 128.

[13]Cf. Taha Husain, *Al-muadhdhabun fi al-ard.* He describes a peasant boy bringing flowers to a rich boy in the hope of being offered food in return. His hopes are dashed and the whole incident ends tragically when the little boy is run over by a train at a level crossing—"Un de ces sinistres passages à niveau de la campagne égyptienne." (Berque, *L'Egypte,* p. 683); see above, pp. 50-51.

[14]"When the body would fall on them (the rocks), they would seize it, tearing its limbs apart and smashing its head to pieces." *Dima,* p. 136.

[15]*Ibid.,* p. 141.

[16]"An elaborated anecdote or series of anecdotes, the yarn is narrated in colloquial and the casual tones appropriate to a raconteur working in oral tradition. The word derives from sailors' slang in which rope-making became a metaphor for story-spinning, and 'yarn' still usually implies the atmosphere for the foc's'le (or bar-room, campfire, club-house or the like)." Ian Reid, *The Short Story* (London, 1977), p. 33.

[17]*Umm,* p. 68.

[18]*Ibid.,* p. 69.

[19]Compare with the final twist in "A Matchmaker's Bankruptcy," where the matchmaker asks her bridegroom for the fee for providing him with herself! (*Umm,* p. 53.)

[20]See above, pp. 31-32.

[21] *Qindil,* p. 38.

[22] Cf. Yusuf ash-Sharuni, p. 16

[23] The narrator's horror and loathing of the mongol child, Susu, entails the narrator's perception of the child as well as the author's formulation of such a perception. This also holds good for the protagonist's repugnance for and loathing of sexuality in women, as illustrated in "The Vacant Bed."

[24] Haqqi's account of his period spent among the Upper Egyptian peasants was written from a perspective of thirty years, and this explains his ability to conjure up impressions and moods rather than mere visual representations and events. *Leave it to God* makes no attempt to present objectively the lives of the peasants or to analyze their customs and behavior; it is a series of observations made by an outsider who has never claimed to be anything but an outsider. And such observations are woven into stories—"true" stories as opposed to "imagined" stories. A glance at "The Perfume Bottle" reveals at once that Sami's story is in part autobiography, even including Sami's literary interests. (*Umm,* p. 155.)

[25] The narrator as observer, as in "Mother of Miracles," or as perturbed protagonist in "Susu."

[26] An experiment into the process of degradation in a man, as in "The Vacant Bed."

Conclusion

[1] Interview, March 20, 1979.

[2] How different is "The Saint's Lamp" from Abd al-Hakim Qasim's *Ayyam al-insan as-saba* (Cairo, 1969), where the climax, the verbalization of this confrontation, marks the beginning of an irreversible decline (pp. 171-173).

[3] G. Deleuze and F. Guattari, *Kafka: Pour une littérature mineure* (Paris, 1975), p. 31.

[4] See above, p. 166, n. 31.

[5] "The key to this line of continuum remains with the masses who have permeated and inspired the souls, spirits, muscles and imagination of the elites, leading artists, musicians, singers, poets, dancers and dramatists." Halim El-Dabh, "The State of the Arts in Egypt Today" in *Middle East Journal,* Vol. 35, 1, 1981, p. 24.

[6] In *An Anthem to Simplicity* Haqqi's criticisms of faults in contemporary Egyptian literature are harsh; the period of tolerance for a young, developing literature has passed.

[7] "On peut classer sous l'appellation d'*adab* tout un ensemble d'oeuvres qui ont pour but d'enseigner à l'honnète homme, un code de bienséance, la notion des devoirs, de la morale usuelle, en rapport avec sa position dans la société." J. Sauvaget, *Introduction à l'Histoire de l'Orient Musulman,* ed. C. Cahen (Paris, 1961), p. 52.

[8] Haqqi has claimed that many Egyptians do not regard him as a literary critic because he has not used jargon; i.e., he does not fit linguistically. But for Haqqi "literary criticism—like any other genre—is literature that cannot be subjected to a technical language. Jargon imprisons a piece of writing in a historical, institutionalized moment, so that however many writers there are they will all be marked by the same cachet." (Interview, Cairo, 25 March 1979.)

[9]"I would accept that the whole of my fiction should be ignored, but it will sadden me extremely if my interest in style is ignored." Haqqi is quoted by Naim Atiya in Ali Bakr Jad, "The Novel of Literary Merit in Egypt 1912-1971. A Literary Study with Some Emphasis on Technique," unpublished D. Phil. thesis, Oxford, 1974, p. 378.

[10]". . . *empathie,* seule attitude requise pour comprendre," says Sartre in *L'Idiot de la Famille,* p. 8.

Appendix Two

[1]E.g., *Khutuwat,* p. 231.

[2]*Kutub li al-mujtama,* April 1960, pp. 7-11.

[3]*Knock, ou, le Triomphe de la Médicine,* 1923.

[4]*L'Oiseau Bleu,* 1909.

[5]*Cairo,* 1965.

[6]*The Prodigal Father,* 1951.

[7]Presumably this was translated from *The Hatchet,* which is an English translation of the Romanian original (*Balatagul,* 1961, U.N.E.S.C.O. collection of representative works, European series, London, 1965).

[8]*Schachnovelle,* 1944.

[9]*Tonio Kroeger,* 1903.

BIBLIOGRAPHY

The Corpus

"A Robber's Life," in *As-Siyasa al-Usbuiya* (10 Dec. 1926).

"Abd at-Tawwab Effendi—The Jailer," in *As-Siyasa al-Usbuiya* (18 Feb. 1927).

Antar wa Juliat, Cairo, 1960.

"As Though," in *Al-Masa* (25 Dec. 1967 and 22 Jan. 1968).

Dama fa ibtisama, Cairo, 1965.

Dima wa tin, Cairo, 1955.

Fajr al-qissa al-misriya, Cairo, 1975.

Al-farash ash-shaghir, see Appendix One.

Fi mihrab al-fann, see Appendix One.

Fi as-sinima, see Appendix One.

"Filla, Mishmish, Lulu," in *Al-Fajr* (22 July 1926).

"Hadha al-ghul," in *Al-Masa* (4 March 1968).

Hadha ash-shir, see Appendix One.

Haqiba fi yad musafir, Cairo, 1969.

"Humorous Aspects of Egyptian Society in Jabarti's Day," in *Al-Balagh* (1 April 1930).

Humum thaqafiya, see Appendix One.

Irony of the Flute (Sukhriyat an-nay), Introduction, Cairo, 1964.

Ishq al-kalimat, see Appendix One.

Itr al-ahbab, Cairo, 1971.

Khalliha ala Allah, Cairo, n.d. (Dar al-Katib al-Arabi li at-tibaa wa an-nashr, Cairo).

Khutuwat fi an-naqd, Cairo, n.d. (Maktabat Dar al-Uruba, Cairo).

Kishk, Muhammad Jalal, *Sharaf al-mihna qissat as-sihafa wa ath-thaura,* Cairo, 1961, Appendix by Haqqi.

Kunasat ad-dukkan, see Appendix One.

"Maa an-nas," in *Al-Masa* (21 July 1969).

Madrasat al-masrah, see Appendix One.

Majalla, Cairo, May 1962-Oct. 1970.

Min bab al-ashm, see Appendix One.

Min faid al-karim, see Appendix One.

Nas fi az-zill, Cairo, 1971.

Qindil Umm Hashim, Cairo, 1975.

Safha min tarikh Misr, see Appendix One.

Sahh an-naum, Cairo, 1976.

"Sukhriyat an-nay," in *Kaukab ash-Sharq* (Feb. 1927).

Taala mai ila al-kunsir, Cairo, n.d. (Dar al-Katib al-Arabi li at-tibaa wa an-nashr, Cairo).

"Taufiq al-Hakim Between Fear and Hope," in *Al-Hadith* (Feb. 1934).

"The Vacant Bed" ("Al-Farash ash-shaghir"), in *Al-Katib* (April 1961).

Turab al-miri, see Appendix One.

Umm al-Awajiz, Cairo, 1955.

Unshuda li al-basata, Cairo, 1972.

Ya Lail ya Ain, Cairo, 1972.

"Yuhka anna," in *Al-Balagh* (15 April 1930).

List of Cited Works

Abbott, J.H., *In the Belly of the Beast, Letters from Prison,* New York, 1981.

Abduh, Said, "A tabib wa jarrah am jazzar wa sharrah," in *Abu al-Haul* (Jan. 1923).

Aflaq, M., *Choice of Texts from the Baath Party Founder's Thought,* Arab Socialist Party, 1977.

Ali, A. Yusuf, *The Holy Quran Text, Translation and Commentary,* Beirut, 1965.

Allen, Roger, *The Arabic Novel. An Historical and Critical Introduction,* New York, 1982.

Ardalan, N. and L. Bakhtiar, *The Sense of Unity,* Chicago, 1974.

Atiya, Naim, *Yahya Haqqi wa alamuhu al-qasasi,* Cairo, 1978.

Awad, Luis, "Fann al-itbisam," in *Al-Ahram* (6 July 1962).

Bahjat, Ahmad, "Yahya Haqqi wa al-jaiza," in *Al-Ahram* (July 1969).

Barthes, Roland, "Criticism as Language," in D. Lodge, *20th Century Literary Criticism,* London, 1972.

_____, *Critique et Vérité,* Paris, 1966.

_____, "Drame, Poème, Roman," in *Théorie d'Ensemble,* Paris, 1968.

_____, *Roland Barthes,* Paris, 1975.

_____, "To Write: An Intransitive Verb?" in *The Structuralists from Marx to Levi-Strauss,* ed. R. and F. deGeorge, New York, 1972.

Bergson, Henri L., *Laughter: An Essay on the Meaning of the Comic,* trans. B. Cloudesley, and F. Rothwell, London, 1911.

Berque, Jacques, *L'Egypte, Impérialisme et Révolution,* Paris, 1967.

Blackman, Winifred, *The Fellahin of Upper Egypt,* London, 1927.

Borges, Jorge Luis, *Other Inquisitions, 1937-1952,* trans. R.L.C. Simms, Texas, 1964.

Bourdieu, Pierre, *Esquisse d'une théorie de la pratique,* Geneva, 1972.

Deleuze, G., and F. Guattari, *Kafka, Pour une littérature mineure,* Paris, 1975.

Demolins, E.R., *Sirr taqaddum al-inkiliz as-saksuniyin,* trans. Fathi Zaghlul, Cairo, 1899.

Dinnerstein, D., *The Mermaid and the Minotaur. Sexual Arrangements and Human Malaise,* New York, 1976.

Francis, Raymond, *Aspects de la littérature arabe contemporaine,* Cairo, 1960.

Fuad, Nimat Ahmad, *An-Nil fi al-adab al-misri,* Cairo, 1962.

_____, *Qimam adabiya,* Cairo, 1966.

Ghanim, Fathi, *Al-Jabal,* Cairo, 1959.

Grunebaum, G.E. von, *Modern Islam. The Search for Cultural Identity,* New York, 1964.

Guillen, C., *Literature as System,* Princeton, 1971.

Hafez, Sabry, "Nas fi az-zill wa qadiyat an-nathr al-arabi," in *Al-Adab* (Sept. 1971).

Hakim, Taufiq al, *Fann al-adab,* Cairo, n.d.

_____, *Yaumiyat naib fi al-aryaf,* Cairo, 1938.

Hauswirth, F., *Purdah: The Status of Indian Women,* London, 1932.

Heidegger, Martin, "Der Feldweg," trans. A. Préau, *Questions III,* Paris, 1968.

Hourani, Albert H., *Arabic Thought in the Liberal Age, 1798-1939,* London, 1970.

Husain, Mustafa Ibrahim, *Yahya Haqqi mudbian wa naqidan,* Cairo, 1970.

Husain, Taha, *Khisam wa naqd,* Beirut, 1963.

_____, *Muadhdhabun fi al-ard,* Cairo, 1948.

_____, *Naqd wa islah,* Beirut, 1960.

Hussein, M.K., *City of Wrong,* trans. K. Cragg, Amsterdam, 1959.

Ibrahim, Abd al-Hamid, "Yahya Haqqi wa faid al-karim," in *az-Zuhur* (April, 1973).

Jad, Ali Bakr, "The Novel of Literary Merit in Egypt 1912-1971: A Literary Study with Some Emphasis on Technique," unpublished D. Phil. thesis, Oxford, 1974.

Jayyusi, Salma Khadra, *Trends and Movements in Modern Arabic Poetry,* Leiden, 1977.

Jomier, J., "Deux extraits des souvenirs de M. Yahya Haqqi," in *Mélanges Institut Dominicain des Etudes Orientales* (Oct. 1960).

Jung, C.G., "Psychology and Literature," in *20th Century Literary Criticism,* ed. D. Lodge, London, 1972.

Khalid, Muhammad Khalid, *Min huna nabda,* Cairo, 1950.

Khidr, Abbas, *Al-qissa al-qasira fi Misr mundhu nashatiha hatta 1930,* Cairo, 1966.

Kingston, Maxine H., *The Woman Warrior,* New York, 1975.

Kishk, Muhammad Jalal, *Sharaf al-mihna: qissat as-sihafa wa ath-thaura,* Cairo, 1961.

Laroui, Abdallah, *La Crise des Intellectuels Arabes: Traditionalisme ou historicisme?,* Paris, 1974.

Lashin, Mahmud Tahir, *Hawwa bila Adam,* Cairo, 1934.

_____, *Sukhriyat an-nay,* Cairo, 1964.

_____, *Yuhka anna,* Cairo, 1964.

Loucel, Henri, "Signification du nombre et de la fréquence des racines quadriconsonantiques dans 'Ana ahya' de Layla Baalbaki," in *Studia Islamica,* XXXV, 1972.

Mahmud, Hasan, "Jarima," in *As-Sufur* (17 April 1922).

Masson, J.M., "Psychology of the Ascetic," in *Journal of Asian Studies,* XXXV (Aug. 1976).

Mayo, E., *The Human Problems of an Industrial Civilization,* Cambridge (Massachusetts), 1933.

Mazini, Abd al-Qadir al-, *Aud ala bad,* Cairo, 1943.

Molé, M., *Les Mystiques Musulmans,* Paris, 1965.

Monteil, Vincent, *Anthologie bilingue de la littérature arabe contemporaine,* Beirut, 1959.

Muwailhi, Muhammad al-, *Hadith Isa ibn Hisham au fatra min az-zaman,* Cairo, 1964.

Nassaj, Sayyid Hamid an-, *Dalil al-qissa al-misriya al-qasira: suhuf wa majmuat, 1910-1961,* Cairo, 1968.

_____, *Tatawwur fann al-qissa al-qasira fi Misr, 1910-1933,* Cairo, 1968.

Nietzsche, Friedrich, *Also Sprach Zarathustra,* Paris, 1969.

Pritchett, V.S., *The Gentle Barbarian,* London, 1977.

Proust, Marcel, *The Past Recaptured,* trans. F.A. Blossom, New York, 1932.

Qasim, Abd al-Hakim, *Ayyam al-insan as-saba,* Cairo, 1969.

Qutb, Sayyid, *Kutub wa shakhsiyat,* Cairo, 1946.

Radhakrishnan, S.C., "The World's Unborn Soul," an inaugural lecture delivered before the University of Oxford, 1936.

Rafii, Abd ar-Rahman, *Thaurat Sanat 1919,* Cairo, 1946.

Reid, Ian, *The Short Story,* London, 1977.

Reig, Daniel, "Le discours littéraire contemporain," in *Discours, écriture et société dans le monde islamique contemporain,* Colloquium A.A.E.I., Paris, Feb. 1977.

Riad, Hassan, *L'Egypte Nassérienne,* Paris, 1964.

Salih, Abbas, "Habib al-munkasirin wa al-bulaha wa al-masakin," in *Al-Jumhuriya* (7 April 1962).

Salman, Magida, "Arab Women," in *Khamsin,* 6, 1978.

Sartre, J.P., *L'Idiot de la Famille,* Vol. I, Paris, 1971.

Sauvaget, J., *Introduction à l'Histoire de l'Orient Musulman,* ed. C. Cahen, Paris, 1961.

Shafaqi, Muhammad Abdallah ash-, "Dama fa ibtisama," in *Al-Katib al-Arabi* (March, 1966).

Sharuni, Yusuf ash, *Sabun shama fi hayat Yahya Haqqi,* Cairo, 1975.

Shukri, Ghali, *Azmat al-jins fi al-qissa al-arabiya,* Beirut, 1962.

Shusha, Faruq, "Maa al-udaba," in *Al-Adab* (July 1960).

Sihrati, Mustafa Abd al-Latif as-, "Yahya Haqqi: al-insan wa al-fannan," in *Shahr* (May, 1961).

Smith, W.C., *The Meaning and End of Religion,* New York, 1964.

Todorov, Tzvetan, *Les Genres du Discours,* Paris, 1978.

Ubaid, Isa, *Ihsan Hanim,* Cairo, 1964.

Ubaid, Shihata, *Dars mulim,* Cairo, 1922.

Vatikiotis, P.J., *The Egyptian Army in Politics,* Bloomington (Indiana), 1961.

Vial, Charles, "Contributions à l'étude du roman et de la nouvelle en Egypte, des origines à 1960," in *Revue de l'Occident Musulman et de la Mediterranée,* 1967.

_____, "Les idées de Yahya Haqqi Sur La Langue," in *Revue de l'Occident Musulman et de la Mediterranée,* 1973.

_____, "Yahya Haqqi Humoriste," in *Annales Islamologiques,* Cairo, 1972.

Waddy, C., *Women in Muslim History,* London, 1980.

Wahby, Samir, "A Critical Evaluation of the Writings of Yahya Haqqi," unpublished M.A. thesis, A.U.C., Cairo, 1965.

_____, "Al-bia wa tathiruha ala intaj Yahya Haqqi," in *Al-Katib* (Feb. 1965).

Zaki, Abd al-Aziz Muhammad az-, "Yahya Haqqi baina al-misriya wa at-turkiya," in *Alam al-fikr,* vol. 9, 2, 1974.

INDEX

Z

DATE DUE